ROLLBACK! RIGHT-WING POWER IN U.S. FOREIGN POLICY

Rollback!

Right-wing Power in U.S.
Foreign Policy

by Thomas Bodenheimer
and Robert Gould

South End Press   Boston, MA

Cover by Eric Drooker
Typesetting, design and layout by the South End Press collective
Manufactured in the U.S.A.

Library of Congress Cataloging-in-Publication Data

Bodenheimer, Thomas.
    Rollback! : right-wing power in U.S. foreign policy.
Includes bibliographies.
1. United States--Foreign relations--1981-   .
2. Conservatism--United States--History--20th century.
I. Gould, Robert, 1952-   . II. Title. III. Title:
Right-wing power in U.S. foreign policy.
E876.B631989327.7388-29479
ISBN 0-89608-346-2
ISBN 0-89608-345-4 (pbk.)

South End Press, 116 Saint Botolph St., Boston MA 02115
98 97 96 95 94 93 92 91 90 89   1 2 3 4 5 6 7 8 9

Authors' Note

Rollback should be a household word in the United States. Defined as the overthrow of foreign governments deemed unwanted by the United States, *rollback* has been a fundamental part of U.S. foreign Policy since 1947. *Rollback* is not a commonly used word because the government does not admit that rollback is a commonly used policy.

This book is not an exposé. Nor does it seek to uncover hitherto unread documents nor to interview major historical actors. Our sources are books and periodicals found in any library or bookstore, and current newspapers and journal articles. The book simply explores the policy of *rollback* as the central international goal of the U.S. right wing. It reinterprets events well known to students of postwar United States.

Unlike many volumes on foreign policy, our main actor is not the U.S. government; rather, our focus is on the social movement known as the *right wing*. Taking the right wing as our centerpiece provides a different perspective from those many works that concentrate on the actions of the government.

We are eternally grateful to Jon Frappier, Executive Director of the research group Global Options, and Mark Rabine, editor of the newsletter *ContraWatch;* they studied our manuscript word for word and actively helped us solve conceptual problems in the formulation of the book. Tony Platt and Holly Sklar also read the manuscript and sent illuminating comments. South End Press made important suggestions in its dual role as political analyst and publisher. Richard Schauffler and Elizabeth Martinez gave us sound advice from their publishing experience combined with their political insight. Franz Schurmann inspired us with his writings and supported us with his personal interest. Richard Falk provided encouragement clearly needed by two medical doctors without political science degrees writing about U.S. foreign policy. And from Tom, many thanks go to his family—his daughter Rebecca, his companion Sara and her daughter Anna—for putting up with his long hours hunched over the word processor; in addition, Rebecca and Anna assisted with the index, and Sara was invaluable in helping to solve the recurrent intellectual dilemmas and crises that spring up during the shaping of a manuscript.

Finally, we dedicate this book to those millions of people in the United States whose common sense leads them to disregard much of what they are told about foreign affairs and to support policies of sanity and peace.

Thomas Bodenheimer
Robert Gould
San Francisco, July 1988

About the Authors

Thomas Bodenheimer is a medical doctor practicing in San Francisco. He served on the governing council of the American Public Health Association. Dr. Bodenheimer has written over fifty articles on U.S. health policy, international health, and U.S. foreign policy. His interest in foreign policy derived from his seven trips to Central and South America, where it became clear that public health problems in the Third World were caused in part by policies originating in the United States.

Robert Gould is a pathologist working at the Kaiser Foundation Hospital in San Jose, California. He is co-chair of the American Public Health Association Peace Caucus and active in Physicians for Social Responsibility. Dr. Gould has studied and written about the right wing for over ten years. He has visited the Soviet Union and has developed expertise through a long history of involvement in issues relating to disarmament.

Table of Contents

Foreword   by Richard Falk   ix

Introduction   Setting the Stage:
                What Did "Contragate" Mean?   1

Chapter 1   Rollback Doctrine: 1945-1980   11

Chapter 2   How to Roll Back the "Evil Empire"   37

Chapter 3   The Global Rollback Network:
                From Chiang Kai-Shek to Oliver North   53

Chapter 4   The Reagan Doctrine: Third World Rollback   81

Chapter 5   The New Drive for Nuclear Supremacy   117

Chapter 6   Economic Decline:
                Fertile Soil for Right-wing Growth   143

Chapter 7   Ruling Elites Move to the Right   161

Chapter 8   The Breadth of Right-wing Influence:
                From Think Tanks to Democrats   179

Chapter 9   The Prospects for Future Right-wing Power   203

Chapter 10   Rollback Doctrine:
                Undermining the United States   217

Notes   239

Index   267

Foreword

Never before in history has a great imperial power been as self-deluded about its political identity as has the United States over the course of the last four decades or so. The essence of this self-delusion is the insistence of American leadership on portraying this country as playing an essentially defensive and selfless role in world affairs during a period when the reality was one of unprecedented ambition and global commitment. There is no simple explanation for this geopolitical confusion, but its persistence is dangerous and costly for others and for ourselves.

The immediate postwar effort to validate the defeat of fascism in World War II and to condemn its recourse to expansionism without risking a repetition of isolationist complacency by the United States has had a lasting impact. The Eastern Establishment in the early 1940s was preoccupied with a fear of recurrent depression and a third German bid to dominate Europe that might produce yet another world war. For this foreign policy elite, learning the lesson of the 1930s meant achieving centralized management over the capitalist world economy and avoiding, at all costs, a diplomacy of detachment or appeasement toward future expansionist challenges. Soviet ambitions and anxieties in 1945 simultaneously fed western fears and served geopolitical needs, the extension of Soviet influence over Eastern Europe being perceived as evidence of an expansionist design, and as such, a new challenge to the political democracies of the West. Such perceptions, when joined to pressures on Greece, Turkey, and Iran in the immediate postwar years, attributed directly or indirectly to the Kremlin, lent great weight to the efforts by George Kennan, Dean Acheson, and others to forge an internationalist policy that built international security around a central alliance among leading capitalist countries sharing a cultural heritage identified as Western Civilization.

Atlanticism as positive ideology served as a backdrop against which the darkening clouds of the Soviet-American rivalry swept across the geopolitical skies. The Truman Doctrine and the Marshall Plan were expressions of ascendancy for an internationalist diplomacy that has kept American troops in Europe indefinitely, long beyond plausible expectations when the fighting ended in 1945.

At the same time, both the architects of internationalism and the general public were eager to avoid World War III. War avoidance was now primarily associated with war readiness. The postwar mood was dominated by an attempt to heed the lesson of Munich, widely interpreted as the climax of "appeasement" diplomacy in which the western democracies conceded German rights to Czechoslovakia in 1938, hoping thereby to satisfy Hitler's appetite for territorial expansion. It predisposed western leadership in the 1940s and 1950s to fashion a foreign policy around the maxim, "In time of peace, prepare for war." The realists at the helm regarded those who advocated disarmament with an ambivalence that hovered between scorn and the anxiety that America could be induced by the disarmers to let its guard down once again by signing onto a charter of pious hopes. In effect, the militarist claim was that if another world war erupted it would be the fault of the peace-mongers, those who put their faith in treaties rather than weapons.

At the same time, the public held onto the vision of a better world and was worried that the weaponry in existence, and on the horizon, was a real threat to national, and even to human, survival. As well, the internationalists included in their ranks those who professed liberal ideals, including a belief in the gradual growth of international institutions and an extension of the rule of law, sources of normative authority which at the time were conveniently perceived as being consistently on our side in the great contested issues of international life. As well, the United States had taken the lead in pronouncing a moral and legal judgment upon the defeated Axis powers, especially Germany and Japan. The Nuremberg and Tokyo war crimes tribunals, although historic occasions, were then viewed by most world leaders as primarily American morality plays; in those criminal proceedings against the remnant of the German and Japanese wartime ruling elites, an emphasis was placed upon the idea that planning and initiating aggressive war was a crime of state for which political leaders would from now on be held responsible. It would be a mistake to regard this effort to condemn aggression as merely an expression of "victors' justice" or as a cynical exercise for popular consumption. It made an imprint on political consciousness that has started to influence perceptions about the limits of obedience owed to the state by citizens, as well as about the importance of subordinating foreign policy to the contraints of law.

All through the early part of the postwar period the United States government made a consistent effort to present its internationalism as essentially "defensive" in character. The stated goal was to be active within the global arena, yet adhere to the UN charter commitment that force would be only used in situations of self-defense. A major, yet controversial and ambiguous, confirmation of this orientation came in 1956 when a conservative Eisenhower/Dulles leadership sided with the anti-western government of Gamel Abdul Nasser rather than endorse aggressive use of force by Great Britain, France, and Israel in the so-called Suez Operation. Even though other factors were involved, this American willingness to subordinate geopolitics and alliance relations to legal principle represented the last gasp of a commitment to transcend power in the postwar world. A similar charter-oriented response would be virtually inconceivable today.

Soviet acquisition of nuclear weapons and long-range delivery capabilities also toned down American notions of what was possible. Since the late 1950s it has been understood by U.S. policymakers that the relevance of American nuclear superiority had to be qualified by an undeniable Soviet capability to deliver a knockout blow of its own if pushed to the wall. Supreme Soviet interests could not be altogether neglected if one pillar of policy was to avoid devastating the general welfare. Again in 1956 this attitude was displayed through the failure to do anything to protect the Hungarian uprising against Soviet intervention. Such a failure was surprising because United States propaganda efforts at the time had been provoking resistance in Eastern European countries partly through seeming promises of support for indigenous movements of resistance. But the moment of truth came as Soviet tanks rumbled through Budapest, and the response from an anti-communist administration in Washington was carefully confined to words of censure.

This complex series of factors helps us grasp our continuing condition of imperial self-delusion. Even now we explain our foreign policy as essentially defensive, relying on the rhetoric of "containment" and "deterrence" to convey an attitude toward relations with the Soviet Union and world communism. Such imagery is quite compatible with obligations under the charter of the United Nations and, more importantly, with that elementary geopolitical prudence that seeks, above all else, to avoid precipitating World War III. To keep up this defensive facade there has been pressure all along on Washington to pursue more "aggressive" projects covertly and under some kind of cover of multilateral authorization. The principled stand taken by the United States government toward the British and French in the Suez setting must be set off against earlier CIA operations to overthrow constitutional governments in Iran (1953) and Guatemala (1954). In this regard, the covert operations program of the CIA and political manipulation of regional security arrangements, especially in the western hemisphere, has been an ingredient since 1945 in Washington's search for a coherent foreign policy.

The great contribution of Thomas Bodenheimer and Robert Gould's *Rollback!* is to strip away the normative veils of illusion. Despite the strong pretense of defensiveness, the actual course of American foreign policy has been much more contradictory in practice, seeking above all else as much space as possible for capitalist expansion. This rollback undertaking is far wider than the announced commitment to stem the tide of *further* or *additional* Soviet aggressiveness. The main challenges to capitalist control in recent decades have been the largely indigenous pressures of revolutionary nationalism. The authors document with care the consistent, bipartisan pattern of U.S. anti-nationalist intervention in the Third World that has certainly had as its primary character a quality of "aggression" as this term is understood by most international lawyers and in relation to the balance of forces in the target society. This pattern of aggression has translated into massive human suffering for many non-western societies, often prolonged over a span of many years. It would be an instance of infantile leftism to believe that if the United States had decided to live with nationalism in the Third World, then all would have been smooth and easy in this period. Far from it. Turmoil and many violent encounters would still occur, but some would not and others would be resolved more rapidly, and with far less bloodshed. For instance, without a rollback commitment by U.S. policymakers, there would not in all likelihood have been a Vietnam War, nor a Cambodian debacle, nor a contra insurgency, nor atrocity-generating anti-government forces in Mozambique and Angola.

Bodenheimer and Gould enable us to understand, as well, the domestic dimension of rollback. Secrecy is the necessary basis for claiming one kind of policy while pursuing another quite contradictory line of action, but secrecy produces lies and the exclusion of Congress. In opposition, Congress seeks to recover its influence. The ebb and flow of domestic politics induces Congress to challenge Executive prerogatives in foreign policy, especially in the aftermath. Ever since Vietnam, the public and Congress have been wary about interventionary diplomacy. The War Powers Act, oversight of covert operations by the CIA, and legislative conditions on support for anti-marxist insurgencies have constrained the Executive branch. The Reagan administration could either defer to law or find a new means to pursue a back channel foreign policy that was constrained neither by overt positions nor by procedures of Congressional accountability.

Aid to the contras has provided the main testing-ground of this policy of domestic institutional forces in the 1980s. After the Boland Amendment, it became impossible for the White House to secure desired levels of legislative support for the contras' military undertaking, but core elements of the Reagan administration were determined to maintain the policy. Given the formal expression of congressional will, even intelligence agencies were reluctant to join with the White House in circumventing clearly expressed legislative intentions. Hence, a rollback enclave in the national security bureaucracy, with at least the tacit blessings of the president, proceeded to fund the contras by a series of illicit measures, including funds diverted from arms sales to Iran. Yet the practical difficulties of implementing such a policy in the face of its unpopularity and governmental opposition led supporters to rely upon the criminal underworld, cutthroat arms traders, and extreme right-wing political organizations within and beyond the borders of this country. This private network—mercenaries with extremist political identities—took shape under the aegis of William Casey and Oliver North. The whole mechanism of diversion is what North termed "a neat idea" in the course of his congressional testimony. The meaning of such an open-ended rollback constituency, especially in circumstances in which the ear of the president is receptive, involves an ominous opening to fascist politics and personalities at the highest levels of policymaking, hardly reassuring in the nuclear age.

There is another dimension here, that of the unfinished business of Vietnam diehards, those who fought in the jungles and felt betrayed by the bureaucrats. Oliver North seems spontaneously to represent this embittered constituency. His penetration of the bureaucracy gave him an opportunity to sustain the soldiers on the battlefield, this time in the jungles of Central America, but in actuality he was upholding the cause of those who were betrayed by a shift of governmental policy during the latter stages of the Vietnam War.

Rollback! documents several further, disturbing aspects of U.S. foreign policy in the Third World. First, rollback is not just a creation of right-wing politics and has been on stage or just off stage throughout the entire postwar period. It has been attractive as a foreign policy option to liberals as it has been to conservatives. Further, as the dynamics of imperial decline have unfolded, the United States has found itself under pressure again and again to reverse the tides of history, inducing recourse to covert action and, in the event of geopolitical setbacks, a backlash that deepens the vulnerability to extreme right-wing solutions. Because the Vietnam Syndrome has made the prospect of war using U.S. troops unpopular at home, foreign policymakers have been led where possible to make their military undertakings indirect and covert, an orientation that tends to generate an anti-democratic style of foreign policy. For instance, in a Pentagon report written by a blue ribbon commission of national security celebrities, released in January 1988 under the title "Discriminate Deterrence," the notion of rollback is implicitly endorsed ("The free World will not remain free if its options are only to stand still or retreat"). Further, secrecy is approvingly embraced as an instrument of foreign policy, especially in relation to the Third World ("In carefully selected situations...the United States should help anti-Communist insurgencies" and "By designating the U.S. support as a 'Special Activity' [also known as 'covert action'], the U.S. Government can maintain official silence"). The commission that issued the report, chaired by defense intellectuals Fred Charles Iklé and Albert Wohlstetter, received the unanimous endorsement of its membership that included Henry Kissinger, Zbigniew Brzezinski, and Samuel P. Huntington. As such, a central thesis of Bodenheimer and Gould's book is convincingly confirmed, namely, that selective rollback, not containment, represents the operative consensus of a bipartisan foreign policy elite even in the post-Vietnam years. Such evidence of continuity is especially distressing during this period of Gorbachev leadership of the USSR when the opportunity to put international politics and East-West relations on a far more moderate, less militarist basis now exists, but will not last indefinitely.

It would be a mistake to blame only the mainstream political parties, the militarized state, and their supporting cast of pliant intellectuals. The political culture of the United States lends itself to this kind of disguised aggressiveness. Many Americans want to nurture an image of innocence and decency, and yet most Americans want most of all to stay on top and continue to applaud clear victories in the Third World however achieved. Additionally, the rejection of the Carter presidency by the electorate was certainly based in part on a perception of a failure by that administration to do enough to resist geopolitical setbacks in the Third World. True, Americans want no more Vietnams, but even more, they want no more Iranian hostage crises. This American thirst for victory, his scorn for defeat, gives the militarist line great leverage over political debate, although its degree of dominance ebbs and flows with the nature of the issue and the public mood, the latter itself significantly shaped by a media that defers to the state on national security policy in most matters. Mainstream opposition to aiding the contras is as inhibited by the Loss-of-China-Syndrome as policy by the interveners is constrained by the Vietnam Syndrome.

What *Rollback!* does is to give us a far clearer, if more distressing, image of what U.S. foreign policy has been about in the postwar years than is conveyed by the misleading, standard operating rhetoric of containment and deterrence. Not only this, it explains that this radicalism is no rightist aberrant of the 1980s, but is an expression of social forces that have been near the center of power ever since 1945, and are so well entrenched in the national security bureaucracy as to be constants in the political setting within which foreign policy takes shape. As citizens, we are reminded once again that the formal procedures of political democracy (political parties, elections) give virtually no voice to principled criticism of interventionary diplomacy in the Third World, and obscure the more militarist nexus of the dominant mindset by cleaving to a cover story that is a mixture of propaganda and disinformation: that poor old Uncle Sam is out there in the boonies helping victims of aggression, at risk among hordes of terrorists, and that this country would never lift a finger except to act in self-defense or in the interest of its friends.

Rollback engenders an ideological mindset that is particularly destructive in its persistent attempts to fashion foreign policy responses to revolutionary nationalism. It induces a tendency to confuse nationalist passions for self-determination with geopolitical challenges. It inclines toward militarist tactics of response to challenges that are political, cultural, and religious, that is, challenges where the relations of forces ultimately are resolved by values, not weapons. Over and over again in this postwar period the nationalist side has prevailed despite its military inferiority, its constant series of battlefield defeats, and its far worse casualties. Rollback increases the pain level of nationalist victory in the Third World. As long as this rollback mindset keeps the imagination confined to an inter-imperial rivalry we should expect additional, tragic variations on this same theme.

We are confused by seemingly heavy obstacles to curative action. Given what we know, what can we do? A first step is to acquire the sort of political clarity enabled by this fine book. As John Locke advised, the main task of philosophy is to remove the rubbish from the pathway to truth. Thoughtful, caring citizens of this country will want to read this book to discover their own path to a rediscovery of an appropriate foreign policy in the years ahead.

Richard Falk
Princeton, New Jersey
July 26, 1988

Introduction

Setting the Stage: What Did "Contragate" Mean?

The inner workings of U.S. foreign policy are hidden from public view. But in 1987, the Iran-Contra (Contragate) scandal gave people of the United States a rare glimpse at the messy reality of foreign affairs, and serves to illustrate those inner workings.

The president had proclaimed Iran to be an enemy and a terrorist state; in secret he was selling Iran major shipments of weapons. In public the Reagan administration claimed to respect the 1984 Boland Amendment banning aid to the "contra" army trying to overthrow the government of Nicaragua; in fact the administration was funding the contras with money from the Iran arms sales and other sources. For almost a year, news media coverage of this scandal failed to mention that the Contragate activities were business as usual in post-World War II United States.

Given the rule of secrecy in conducting foreign affairs, why were the Iran-Contra details exposed? Why did a parade of officials and operatives show the world so much dirty laundry? We believe that Contragate was ultimately a clash between alternative presentations of the United States in the world. We call these two tendencies the *right wing* or the *Right*, and the *traditional conservative elites*. During Contragate the on-again, off-again conflict between these groupings boiled to the surface. Knowledge of Israeli and later U.S. arms sales to Iran were published by the *Washington Post, New York Times* and columnist Jack Anderson well before these sales became a national scandal. The Contragate scandal broke not because news of the Iran arms sales was entirely new, but because a significant element of the power elite was dissatisfied with Reagan's policies.[1] In order to embarrass the Right, some traditional conservatives unveiled secrets that both groups usually agree to keep under wraps.

Since World War II the traditional conservative elites, prominent in both the Democratic and Republican parties, have represented internationally-focused economic interests in the United States. Prominent members of this tendency have included presidential advisors George Kennan, Dean Acheson, Paul Nitze, Robert McNamara, Henry Kissinger, Zbigniew Brzezinski, and the Reagan administration's Secretary of State George Shultz. We will hear more about this grouping in Chapters One and Seven. Their overriding priority has been to prevent the spread of Soviet influence in the world, but within an overall atmosphere of global stability and trade. Traditional conservatives are not opposed to military force, but after Vietnam they recognized that military solutions can be counterproductive by causing economic difficulties or by alienating allies. They prefer to exercise economic or political clout, seeking to work through domestic bipartisan consensus and international alliances. They have usually been cautious about undertaking actions that might risk World War III.

The rival troupe of actors includes many who belong to a shadowy international ring of right-wing zealots, free enterprise ideologues with a sizeable streak of monetary greed. This right-wing grouping shares the traditional conservatives' view that communism is the enemy of humankind. But the Right goes much farther, vowing to remove communism from the planet and to install their particular brand of freedom. Freedom is their battle cry, a noble end justifying any means, which—as we shall show—include lying, killing, selling arms, trafficking dope, and making a tidy profit on the side. This international conglomerate includes CIA and ex-CIA operatives, representatives of the military-industrial complex, foreign governments, anti-communist ideologues in such organizations as the World Anti-Communist League, Third World death squad organizers, international narcotics and arms dealers, and counter-revolutionaries displaced from social revolutions in such places as China, Cuba, and Nicaragua. Contragate figures related to this network include Lt. Col. Oliver North, retired Maj. Gens. Richard Secord and John Singlaub, the late CIA Director William Casey and Nicaraguan contra leader Adolfo Calero. We call this grouping the *global rollback network,* described in Chapter Three.

Containment and Rollback

A distinction between traditional conservatives and the right wing involves U.S. goals concerning Soviet power. Since 1947, U.S. foreign policy has rested on a foundation generally called *containment,* whose purpose is to contain or prevent the spread of Soviet influence in the world. Containment—the policy of traditional conservative elites—is supposed to allow the coexistence of capitalism and socialism as long as socialism does not expand; behind containment lies a long-term strategy of ensnaring socialist countries into the logic of the capitalist economy. The Right has vehemently criticized containment as defensive and has pushed for global rollback, an offensive strategy of complete victory over communism—the sooner the better.

Rollback has involved the overthrow of governments that seek full independence from the economic, political, or military influence of the United States. Such governments might be socialist, radical nationalist, or simply uncooperative with U.S. business interests. The right wing has generally regarded such countries as communist or as pawns of a Soviet "evil empire." Global rollback refers to the overthrow of the entire socialist world, including the Soviet Union, and its replacement with capitalist nations. Examples of rollback are Guatemala in 1954, Cuba (attempted) in 1961, Chile in 1973, and Grenada in 1983.

Though the Right and the conservatives disagree on the goal of forcefully overthrowing the Soviet regime, the two groups have frequently cooperated in rolling back selected governments in the Third World. Thus while U.S. policy since 1947 has sought containment of the USSR, it has also operated under a bipartisan consensus of selective rollback—the ouster of particular governments deemed unfriendly toward the United States. Whereas the Right has loudly trumpeted its desire for rollback, the traditional conservatives have publicly emphasized the containment goal and have tried to keep rollback operations covert. Rollback has been decided on a case-by-case basis, measured against the traditional conservative imperative of maintaining a stable East-West relationship.

Rollback and containment are not implacably rival policies, but are two poles on a continuum of aggressiveness toward the Soviet Union and its supposed allies in the Third World. Many containment advocates, cognizant of the constraints imposed by Soviet nuclear might, opt for strategies that would gradually persuade or pressure the USSR to transform itself into a capitalist nation, a view which amounts to long-term rollback.

To clarify the complexities of the containment-rollback relationship, we will define these terms as follows: *rollback* or *global rollback* seeks the deliberate overthrow of the Soviet Union and of other nations seen as unfriendly to the United States. *Selective rollback* seeks the deliberate overthrow of particular (mainly Third World) nations, but not of the Soviet Union or the Eastern Bloc. *Containment* attempts to prevent the spread of presumed Soviet influence. Because almost all policymakers have supported some rollback operations as part of overall containment strategy, we regard *selective rollback* as an essential feature of containment.

Historically, *right-wing* means conservative or reactionary, with the term deriving from the French Revolution. In the French National Assembly of 1789, the conservative nobility sat on the president's *right* while the liberal commoners sat on the left. Analogously, we roughly define the U.S. right wing as those forces that embrace a reactionary world view, *i.e.* those wanting the world to return to the time when communism did not exist, which means global rollback.

In foreign policy, the standard liberal vs. conservative distinction is less evident than with domestic policy. "Cold War liberals" are actually foreign policy conservatives who happen to be domestic liberals. Foreign policy liberals do exist; they are less concerned with containment than with world peace and justice, and they have played a minor role in postwar U.S. policymaking. Most mainstream Democrats and Republicans fall into the traditional conservative camp, with conservative generally signifying the maintenance of the global status quo—containment including selective rollback.

Our definitions of right-wing and traditional conservatives, which we use to explain historical tendencies in U.S. foreign policy, represent polar positions on a continuum of views. In the real world, of course, individual policymakers will take stands based on a variety of influences that do not conform neatly to these ideal categories. For example, Contragate figures such as former National Security Advisor Robert McFarlane and Defense Secretary Caspar Weinberger partake of elements of both worldviews. Traditional conservative and veteran advisor Paul Nitze has shifted his position over forty years; he coalesced with the Right when fighting détente in the 1970s, but antagonized the Right when resisting global rollback in the 1980s. The two foreign policy worldviews cannot be viewed as distinct boxes; rather they are overlapping circles whose relationship shifts depending on general world conditions and specific regional issues.

The Contragate Clash

In the 1970s, the rollback Right gained enormous strength. In 1964, while achieving dominance in the Republican Party, the Right had lost the election; in 1980, it appeared to have won both the Republican Party and the election. After the defeat of Sen. Joseph McCarthy in 1954, serious public advocacy of global rollback took a nosedive; by 1980, rollback views were accepted by a portion of mainstream foreign affairs intellectuals and policymakers. In the 1950s through the 1970s global rollback was little more than an organizing slogan for the Right; by the 1980s it had a well-developed theoretical foundation and strategy for implementation. With this new position of respectability, global rollback adherents dared to do in the 1980s what they had seldom dared before: take over the foreign policy apparatus of the United States of America. They came close.

The 1980 Reagan election was the Right's best opportunity ever. But by 1984, the right wing was highly frustrated. Ronald Reagan had forsaken them. True, he had hired their heroine Jeane Kirkpatrick as UN Ambassador; but she, rather than "wishy-washy" George Shultz should have been Secretary of State. True, Reagan had expanded the military budget; but he also entered into hated arms control talks. True, he had conquered the menacing fortress of Grenada; but he was getting nowhere in Nicaragua. The problem? Liberals in the State Department. Liberals, as the right-wing magazines scoffed, whose lunches and politics were made of cucumber sandwiches. Worse yet, were liberals in Congress, and a conspiracy by which bureaucrats in State allied with congressional liberals.[2]

The solution? If you can't change the State Department, go around it. If you can't beat Congress, lie to it. The right wing had failed to control the foreign policy apparatus by the legitimate process of presidential appointments. It needed another mechanism to implement its policies: an apparatus deeply hidden from public scrutiny.

For decades the CIA has conducted covert operations that could be "plausibly denied" by the presidency. But legislation in 1974 and 1980 requiring formal presidential approval and congressional notification of covert operations made such deniability difficult. Thus under Reagan, an apparatus was established whose actions could be plausibly denied not only by the president but by the CIA as well. To staff this apparatus, right-wing ideologues inside government—led by CIA Director William Casey and National Security Council staff member Oliver North—came together with their rollback-oriented companions outside government, most prominently retired Gen. Richard Secord. This right-wing apparatus derived enormous power from its access through Oliver North to National Security Advisor Adm. John Poindexter. As one of the top foreign policy officials, Poindexter—especially with a president widely considered to be incompetent—had the power to place enormous resources of the United States government at the service of the global rollback network.

What went wrong for the right wing? First, the arms sales to Iran were a national disaster. They were a slap in the face of U.S. allies, both the moderate Arab states and Western Europe. In the public's view, they represented appeasement of international terrorism; as Secretary of State Shultz has said over and over, he who bargains for hostages today will face more kidnappings tomorrow. According to veteran conservative foreign policy expert Robert W. Tucker, "what stands out above all is the breathtaking incompetence characterizing the Iran initiative."[3]

But perhaps more important, the traditional conservatives were angry at the right-wing attempt to take over excessive portions of the foreign policy establishment. The secret apparatus itself was nothing new as we will see in Chapter Three, CIA covert operations involving private individuals and companies were part of the conservative elites' tradition. What stood out about Contragate was the loss of control by the conservative elite. For example, an ambassador received instructions from the national security advisor without the knowledge of his boss, Secretary of State Shultz, and Shultz was apparently misled and kept uninformed about key foreign policy activities. Shultz could not have been pleased to learn that the North-Secord enterprise had a code name for his State Department: wimp.

The Contragate exposé was the backlash of the conservative elite, who viewed the Right as overly reckless and assuming far too much power. Congress entered the action, angry at being fed a long string of lies. Rep. Lee Hamilton deplored the "series of lies—lies to the Iranians, lies to the Central Intelligence Agency, lies to the attorney general, lies to our friends and allies, lies to the Congress, and lies to the people of the United States." One member of the public, in a press interview, commented about Oliver North: "We expect people in Washington to lie to us. At least, he tells you when he is lying and when he isn't."[4] In spite of the popular appeal of Oliver North on the Right's behalf, much of the political establishment—Republicans, Democrats, the media, and the intellectuals—condemned the Iran-Contra undertakings.

While Ronald Reagan and his rollback henchmen drew criticism from Congress and the entire nation, the scope of the investigation remained extremely limited, with the leadership of the House and Senate committees specifically avoiding delving into the history of the CIA-linked proprietaries and public-private networks. The inquiry into the numerous allegations of contra drug-running was superficial, attributable to the involvement of the Senate panel's chief investigator, Thomas Polgar. This was not surprising given that Polgar, a 30-year CIA veteran, had been station chief in Saigon during the Vietnam War.[5] Thus the CIA's capabilities for covert and illegal interventionist operations remained protected for the future, while the "rogues" of the Right were conveniently and temporarily scapegoated.

Fifteen years earlier, Richard Nixon had tried to disrupt the foreign policy bureaucracy, and his "efforts to sweep away the old elites generated revolts powerful enough to topple" him.[6] Why, then, did Ronald Reagan personally survive? One reason was that in contrast to Watergate, the far stronger Right of the 1980s did not give in and brought its case to the public via the Contragate congressional hearings.[7] The right wing was highly effective in promoting Nicaraguan rollback during the hearings; Oliver North created the first wave of public contra sympathy since the contra war began, and contra leader Adolfo Calero compared himself to George Washington.

But Ronald Reagan survived for a more fundamental reason. On a critical Contragate policy issue, the conservative elite and the right wing were in agreement: the rollback of Nicaragua.

For the Right, Nicaragua represented the planetary battlefield between good and evil, between West and East, between capitalism and communism. If the United States could not defeat Nicaragua, how could we reverse history in our favor? Nicaragua was a key building block in a global rollback scheme that would end with the triumphant march of the U.S. Marines—led by Oliver North—through the streets of Managua and on to Red Square. Turning our backs on Nicaragua meant abandoning the entire scheme.

For the conservative elites, Nicaragua was not a moral crusade but a geopolitical national security problem: consolidating friendly neighbors on the U.S. southern flank.[8] Some conservative elites supported the contras as a method to overthrow the Nicaraguan government; others preferred economic and political destabilization without a dominant military effort. But during the entire nine months of the Contragate affair, no policymaker took the position that the United States should mind its own business and stop bothering Nicaragua.

Thus while Contragate was a clash between the two sets of foreign policy actors, there were strong elements of unity between these groups. Even more broadly than Nicaraguan policy, the conservative elite and the Right were jointly trying to rid the United States of a 15-year plague: the Vietnam Syndrome.

United States' Foreign Policy Syndromes

The conservative elite in the late 1940s and the right wing in the 1980s have always warned: "Remember Munich." Munich, Germany was the site of a disastrous 1938 meeting between Hitler, Mussolini, French Premier Daladier, and British Prime Minister Neville Chamberlain. At Munich, Chamberlain allowed Hitler to occupy a portion of Czechoslovakia and received a promise by Hitler to leave Britain alone. The result of Chamberlain's appeasement was that Hitler gobbled up Czechoslovakia, went on to Poland, Denmark, Norway, the Netherlands, Belgium, France, and then attacked Great Britain itself. Following World War II, when relations with the Soviet Union turned cold, U.S. foreign policymakers vowed never to allow another Munich; war was preferable to appeasement of the USSR. The hardline "Munich Syndrome" dominated U.S. foreign policy until the Vietnam War, after which Vietnam replaced Munich in the public's consciousness as the most serious foreign policy error. The "Vietnam Syndrome" has come to mean the unwillingness of the people to support foreign wars in which U.S. troops may be killed with no clearcut national benefit.

The right wing has taken the lead in blaming U.S. foreign policy failures—Southeast Asia, Angola, Nicaragua, and Iran—on the Vietnam Syndrome, comparing Soviet international gains with Hitler's aggressiveness. For the Right, the détente of the 1970s was the new Munich.[9] Right-wing journals are filled with articles decrying the culture of appeasement:

> Until the Soviet Union is recognized universally as the dangerous and evil empire that it is, neither the Reagan Administration nor any subsequent conservative administration will be able to achieve such worthy goals as the...rollback of international Communism....Seven years after Ronald Reagan's arrival in Washington, the United States government and its allies are still dominated by the culture of appeasement that drove Neville

Chamberlain to Munich in 1938. While President Reagan has eloquently and properly defined the struggle between the United States and the Soviet Union as one between good and evil, even he has fallen victim to this culture.[10]

The fact that the Vietnam Syndrome—still strong within the public—inhibits foreign interventions is a problem for both the Right and the traditional elites. Thus while the Right frequently accuses the conservatives of appeasement, the populist right-wing attack on appeasement helps both groups in their quest to erase the Vietnam Syndrome.

The Roots of Contragate

It is the thesis of this book that since World War II two tendencies—the Right and the traditional conservative elite—have cooperated and competed with each other in setting U.S. foreign policy. The right-wing tendency grew substantially in the late 1970s and the 1980s. By the late 1980s, the Right had begun to tread on the toes of the traditional conservatives, who moved to reassert more control. However, the Right will continue to exercise major influence on foreign policy for years to come, regardless of which political party controls Congress and the presidency.

Contragate brought to light a major force in U.S. foreign policy: the global rollback network. This book explores the history and beliefs of that network and the degree to which it has influenced U.S. policy. Where did rollback policy originate and how has it been implemented? Who makes up the global rollback network? What is the theory and the strategy underlying global rollback, and how has this strategy been incorporated into official U.S. foreign and military policy? What are the economic roots of right-wing growth in the 1980s? What is the past and current state of the love/hate relationship between the Right and the traditional conservative elites; where do they agree and where do they differ? And finally, in the current new period of reduced East-West tension, why should we worry about the foreign policy of the Right?

Rollback Doctrine: 1945-1980

Soon after World War II a shift occurred in the foreign policy of the U.S. right wing from isolationism to military interventionism. Abandoning the view that world problems are someone else's business, the Right took on a crusade to wipe communism off the face of the globe. By 1950, people who had resisted U.S. entrance into World War II were calling for U.S. military power to "liberate" China from the communists and were proposing atomic war against the Soviet Union. This was the foreign policy of global rollback.

The Origins of Rollback

In *The Logic of World Power,* an insightful study of the postwar world, Professor Franz Schurmann explains the switch from isolationism to rollback. The ideology that linked pre-war isolationism and postwar rollback was nationalism. Nationalists opposed getting involved in entangling alliances or in other people's wars, but believed in the extension of manifest destiny westward and southward. The United States expanded from thirteen colonies on the Atlantic coast across the North American continent to the Pacific. Mexico was defeated and a large portion of its territory taken. The Monroe Doctrine justified interventions in Latin America (which took place at least 55 times prior to World War II[1]) any time U.S. property was threatened. The United States went into an underdeveloped Pacific island, Hawaii, and remade it in the U.S. image. Thus it was perfectly natural to continue Westward, bringing U.S. civilization and business to the entire Pacific basin.[2] But the Chinese Revolution of 1949 got in the way, and had to be reversed. In its initial expression, rollback was a modern extension of "Go West, young man."

Schurmann viewed the nationalists as competing with the Roosevelt internationalists, who were concerned with the fate of Europe and who saw the United States as part of the world economy rather than as simply a domestic (albeit expanding) economy. The nationalists, of course, had economic reasons for their ideology. They tended to represent either domestic business whose profits did not come from international trade, or business with specific interests in the Pacific and Latin America rather than in Europe. They tended to be located more in the South and West of the country, giving them a more Pacific and Latin American outlook than the Atlantic worldview of the "Eastern Establishment" internationalists. The nationalists were protectionists while the internationalists, who tended to profit from foreign trade especially with Europe, were ardent free traders. Schurmann argues that the internationalists had reservations about getting into wars because, for business based on trade, "peace was best for profits." For the nationalists, military power was the way to expand the United States into the Pacific, and military industry became an ally of the nationalists. Since communism was the arch-enemy of private property, both the nationalists and internationalists were fiercely anti-communist.[3]

Because nationalist businesses tended to have interests in the Pacific rather than in Europe, the nationalists wanted the U.S. government to place its priority on Asia rather than on Europe. They were "Asia-firsters," (and later on with the Cuban Revolution in 1959 and the Nicaraguan Revolution in 1979, "Latin America-firsters") as opposed to the "Europe-firsters" of the internationalist Eastern Establishment. The nationalists, who also tended to be anti-New Deal in their domestic policy, strongly opposed the taxes needed to support big government; they disliked expensive foreign aid programs to shore up the European economies. Such programs as the Marshall Plan meant paying higher taxes to stimulate Atlantic trade for the benefit of the internationalists. But the nationalists had their own fiscal dilemma: the military power needed to support their expansionist aims in Asia cost money. Their solution was to oppose the expensive peacetime draft and employment of U.S. troops in foreign land wars. Instead they favored the air force and the A-bomb: a cheap and effective way to project U.S. military power.[4]

Two events had transformed the nationalists from isolationists to international rollbackers. The first was Pearl Harbor. While, as Asia-firsters, they had opposed entering the European war against Hitler, they strongly believed in fighting the Japanese. The second event was the Chinese Revolution. China made rollback doctrine a serious current in U.S. foreign policy. The China of the 1950s is linked to the Nicaragua of the 1980s—not only in rollback ideology but also by the specific people who put that ideology into practice. (See Chapter Three.)

During and after World War II, representatives of internationalist business ran the Executive Branch of government. The six "Wise Men"—Dean Acheson, Charles Bohlen, Averell Harriman, George Kennan, Robert Lovett and John J. McCloy—who led in setting the course of U.S. foreign policy from 1947 to the present—were generally Ivy League, connected to the Wall Street banking-trade establishment, and groomed in the Rockefeller-linked Council on Foreign Relations.[5] These individuals spoke for the traditional conservative elites. Between 1945 and 1947, these men became convinced that the Soviet Union was a deadly beast that must be forcibly contained in its cage. Thus the term containment.

The man who crystalized the Eastern Establishment's overriding concern with the Soviet Union was George Kennan. In his February 1946 "Long Telegram" from the U.S. Embassy in Moscow where he was *charge d'affaires,* Kennan stated: "At the bottom of Kremlin's neurotic view of world affairs is traditional and instinctive Russian sense of in-security." The Russians see the outside world as "evil, hostile and menacing." Kennan warned of the

> steady advance of uneasy Russian nationalism, a centuries-old movement in which conceptions of offense and defense are inex-tricably confused. But in the new guise of international Marxism, with its honeyed promises to a desperate and war torn outside world, it is more dangerous and insidious than ever before....In summary, we have here a political force committed fanatically to the belief that with U.S. there can be no permanent *modus viven-di.*

Even with this blast, Kennan did not call for rollback. He cautious-ly concluded: "the greatest danger that can befall us in coping with this problem of Soviet communism, is that we shall allow ourselves to be-come like those with whom we are coping."[6]

By the middle of 1947, almost the entire political spectrum ac-cepted the key premise of containment: that Soviet communism, which had already expanded into Eastern Europe, would continue to expand and become a danger to the United States. The historical analogy was Munich, where in 1938 the British had tried to stop Hitler by making concessions. Since the appeasement of Hitler led to World War II, the appeasement of Russia could only lead to World War III. For the internationalists who made postwar U.S. foreign policy, Munich "came to be not merely an analogy, but an iron law—never again."[7]

What and Where to Contain

Consensus on the details of containment was elusive. In a debate that has continued into the 1980s, disagreement raged over what needed to be contained and whether containment was sufficient. For Kennan, the primary force in Soviet expansionism was the Russian nation attempting to make itself secure and powerful. The drive for world communism was a secondary, though significant, additional factor. The beast to be contained, therefore, was Soviet Russia. Some internationalists and most nationalists had another view: the United States faced an international communist conspiracy, and Russia was only one part of that conspiracy. The drive for world domination was not traditional nation-state power politics but a fanatic ideological quest for communism. The beast to be contained was communism, not simply the Soviet Union.[8]

This debate had important foreign policy implications, as it does today. (See Chapter Two.) Kennan felt that if the United States stood up to the Russians, they would gradually moderate their goal of world domination and accept the necessity of peaceful coexistence. The right wing, believing that a fanatic ideology combined with an aggressive nation-state was the enemy, disagreed. Communism could be stopped only by eliminating it entirely. Containment was not sufficient. The goal must be total victory: rollback.

Another practical implication of this debate concerned China policy: Secretary of State Acheson felt that serious differences existed between Mao Tse-Tung and Josef Stalin, and that the United States could widen this split by influencing Mao rather than attempting to overthrow him.[9] This view rested on the Kennanesque belief that national interests rather than international communism motivated both Russia and China. The right wing still could not imagine a split between China and Russia—since they were simply two actors in a single international communist conspiracy—was incensed at attempts to influence Communist China, and demanded its rollback.

Containment advocates, then, tended to be pragmatists, looking at world balance-of-power considerations, while rollbackers were often ideologues, making the battle against communism into an absolute principle. Those favoring containment were so pragmatic that they disagreed among themselves on where to draw the line across which the Soviet Union should not be allowed to step. Dean Acheson, for example, made a January 12 1950 speech in which he left South Korea out of the list of countries that must be defended; the Right later blamed him for all the deaths of the Korean War since he had signaled the Russians that South Korea was fair game.[10] Naturally, Europe-firsters tended to draw their containment lines in Europe, United Fruit drew its line in Guatemala, sugar companies and the Mafia drew their lines in Cuba, and ITT and Kennecott Copper drew theirs in Chile. Specific policy was dictated both by strategic concerns and by narrow interests. As we shall see in Chapter Nine, this great debate continues as the foreign policy question of the 1980s and 1990s: Where to intervene?

As we noted in the Introduction, containment and rollback are two poles of an anti-Soviet continuum. On some issues the advocates of the two tendencies were in agreement; on other issues they battled. The entire constellation of disagreements—Europe-first vs. Asia-first, where to draw the line, containment/selective rollback vs. global rollback—came to a head over China and Korea.

Setting the stage for the China-Korea foreign policy battle was the promulgation of the Truman Doctrine of 1947. The first policy test for the containment advocates was Greece. Leftist insurgents were supposedly threatening the Greek regime, and the British were unable to bolster its Greek ally. In 1947, Great Britain asked the United States for help. But the congressional outcome was in doubt. The right-wing switch from isolationism to rollback was not complete, aid to Greece would be expensive and distasteful to the fiscal-minded conservatives, and besides, Greece was a Europe-first issue. The "Wise Men" told Truman he needed an "all-out" speech to win this one.[11] The result was the Truman Doctrine, which committed the United States to hold the line against communism not just in Greece, but all over the world. The tactic worked; the money was appropriated. Containment was now U.S. policy. Based on this success, the Truman administration used the anti-communist theme—the Soviet threat to Western Europe—to push through the Marshall Plan, another Europe-first scheme to salvage the war-torn European economies so that international business could trade with and invest in a recovered Western Europe.

Selling the specter of Russian expansionism recruited the right-wing nationalists to the policy of anti-communist interventionism and forever killed serious isolationism. While the nationalists were horrified at the new spending needed, and had few business interests in Europe, the warnings about an expanding Soviet Union shut them up.[12]

But a glaring contradiction emerged. If containment was now accepted policy, what was the Truman administration doing about containing communism in China? While the internationalists were worrying about Europe sliding into communism, Asia in 1947 was acutely threatened by immediate communist takeover. Truman had walked into a right-wing trap.[13] By preaching worldwide containment and practicing only European containment, the Truman administration set itself up for the first great confrontation between containment and rollback. By the time the confrontation came, China had been won by the communists and could only be salvaged through rollback.

The Great Containment-Rollback Confrontation

For the Asia-firsters, Truman's tolerance of communism in China was horrifying. The right wing made China the symbol of U.S. nationalism. "Chiang [Kai-shek] was a beleaguered fighter struggling against an international communist conspiracy directed against him not only by Moscow and its Chinese tools but by Washington, New York, and Harvard as well.... The backlash of McCarthyism indicates how violent the conflict had become."[14] The right-wing attack centered on the State Department. For the Right, the State Department was the government agency most linked to the Eastern Establishment and free-trading, Europe-oriented international business. It did not matter that State contained some of the strongest anti-communist views in government. It did not matter that it was the State Department in 1950 that dragged the Defense Department into agreeing to the vast military build-up proposed in policy document NSC-68.[15] What the Right saw in the State Department was a belief in trade, not war; a belief in profits, "and it mattered little from which side of the Iron Curtain profits came."[16] The State Department was seen as dealing with communism by entangling it in the web of world trade rather than by smashing it.

The attack got serious in February 1950, when Joseph McCarthy tied the loss of China to elite Eastern Establishment communists in the State Department:

> Six years ago...there was within the Soviet orbit 180,000,000 people.... Today, only 6 years later, there are 800,000,000 people under the absolute domination of Soviet Russia—an increase of over 400 percent.... The reason why we find ourselves in a position of impotency is not because our only powerful potential enemy has sent men to invade our shores, but because of the traitorous actions of those who have been treated so well by this Nation...those who have had all the benefits that the wealthiest nation on earth has had to offer—the finest homes, the finest college education, and the finest jobs in Government we can give.... In my opinion the State Department, which is one of the most important government departments, is thoroughly infested with Communists.[17]

McCarthy, supported by Republican Sens. Robert Taft, William Knowland, and many others, focused his fire on a group of foreign service officers in the State Department's Far Eastern Division, blaming them for the loss of China to the communists.[18] The prestigious Gen. Douglas MacArthur, Supreme Commander of the Allied Powers in Tokyo, was also vocally critical of Truman's failure to support Chiang Kai-shek. In 1950, he took a trip to visit Chiang and made unauthorized public statements backing his cause.[19] The Republican Right began to call for:

> hot war against communism wherever it reared its ugly head. That this was not just rhetoric is indicated by the word 'rollback' which they adopted as their *leitmotiv*. Rollback...was a deliberate policy of seeking to 'liberate' captive nations from communism. Chiang Kai-shek's program for rollback was the most concrete. He indicated that he would provide the ground forces (some 600,000 men) and the United States had only to provide air and naval support. When his forces landed on the China coast, uprisings would erupt throughout China and...he would quickly sweep north to Peking.[20]

In June 1950, the Korean War provided a new battleground not only for "freedom" vs. "communism" but also for containment vs. rollback. The initial goal of the Korean war was to push North Korean troops back to the pre-war border at the 38th Parallel, i.e., to contain the spread of communism in the Korean Peninsula. After U.S. troops (cleverly placed under the banner of the United Nations by Truman's

"Wise Men") under General MacArthur pushed the North Koreans back toward the 38th Parallel, the Pentagon and portions of the State Department wanted to change the goals of the war: to the defeat of North Korea and the unification of Korea under a non-communist government. On September 28, 1950, Truman approved this recommendation. The United States then helped draft the United Nations resolution of October 7 1950, calling for a unified, independent, and democratic government of Korea and for UN (read U.S.) forces to remain in Korea as long as necessary to achieve this objective.[21]

The war had changed from containment of North Korea to North Korean rollback. On October 8, "United Nations" troops crossed the 38th Parallel. But the rollback decision was a disaster. The northward drive of MacArthur brought the Chinese into the war, the U.S. forces were again forced south of the 38th Parallel, and the war was ultimately concluded with the prior division into a communist North and an anti-communist South.

MacArthur, supported by Senator Taft and the right wing, had wanted to extend the rollback policy into China; his plan was a naval blockade of China, air bombardment—possibly with atomic weapons—of Chinese industry, troop deployment points, and supply depots, followed possibly by an invasion by Chiang Kai-shek.[22] Insubordinate to his Commander-in-Chief Harry Truman, MacArthur continued to make public statements supporting the rollback of North Korea and extension of the war to China. On April 10, Truman was forced to fire him.[23] When MacArthur returned to the United States half a million people greeted him in San Francisco and equally massive welcomes took place in Washington and New York. The public outcry against Truman was huge, including the consideration of his impeachment by the Republican Right. Congressional hearings were held on the Truman-MacArthur controversy; as in the Contragate hearings of 1987, much of the questioning by Republican committee members was designed to promote a pro-rollback point of view rather than to elicit information.[24]

The presidential campaign of 1952 featured a rhetorical rollback-containment war. John Foster Dulles, campaigning for Eisenhower, blasted the "evil doctrine of containment" echoing the sentiments of the Right regarding China.[25] The 1952 Republican platform attacked the "negative, futile and immoral policy of 'containment' which abandoned countless human beings to a despotism and godless terrorism," calling instead for rollback or "liberation." On August 25, Eisenhower himself joined the call for liberation, in particular for Eastern Europe. Dulles elaborated that Voice of America broadcasts would stir up resistance, the United States would make air drops of supplies to resistance fighters, and they would fight and gain liberation. Polish-American voters defected heavily from Democratic ranks to vote for Eisenhower's rollback policy.[26] In his first public address after being chosen Secretary of State, Dulles reiterated in 1953, "To all those suffering under Communist slavery...let us say: you can count on us."[27]

The Korean War stalemate contributed to the rollback fervor. In the right-wing view, well expressed later by Gen. Nathan Twining, the continued U.S. deaths in Korea were the fault of containment. To win, the United States needed to attack China and even to bring the war to the source of the problem, the Soviet Union. If the United States limited its attacks to the borders of the Communist Bloc, we were indeed a paper tiger. Containment was a formula for peaceful coexistence, a form of appeasement rather than a plan for victory.[28] The arguments are identical to the current right-wing interpretation of the U.S defeat in Vietnam.

With the Republican victory, it appeared that global rollback would become U.S. foreign policy. After winning the election, Eisenhower set up study groups to work out U.S. politico-military strategy, resulting in the policy document NSC-162. Three alternatives were considered: 1) to continue Truman's containment doctrine, 2) to draw a line around the globe and let the Soviets know that if they crossed the line, they would be directly attacked by nuclear weapons (nuclear containment), and 3) substitution of rollback for containment, with a vigorous program of political, psychological, and economic warfare against the communist world along with paramilitary measures such as the infiltration of agents and saboteurs. The rollback option included consideration of a "preventive" nuclear strike on Russia. The outcome was a rejection of outright Soviet rollback and a continuation of containment, with possible use of the nuclear threat to deter communist aggression.[29]

In spite of the official rejection of global rollback, administration propaganda kept alive the idea of Eastern European liberation. Such propaganda petered out after the 1956 Soviet intervention in Hungary, against which the United States was helpless in the face of Soviet military power. The loud-talking but pragmatic Dulles ultimately argued that a limited intervention in Hungary would have been defeated, a full-scale intervention would have risked nuclear war with a now nuclear-capable USSR, and in either case Hungary itself would have been annihilated rather than saved.[30] The events in Hungary revealed the inability of the United States to conduct a global rollback policy.

While Soviet rollback was rejected, rollback operations in China and the Third World became official U.S. policy. The Right's rollback fever was utilized by the conservative elite to fashion the policy of selective rollback. Selective rollback was institutionalized as a covert policy residing within the Central Intelligence Agency.[31] In addition, the right wing and McCarthy had succeeded in forcing national security managers to prove constantly that they were not appeasing the communists (*i.e.* "losing" countries like China). The gravest of all political errors would be to repeat Munich. In this way, any politician or high-level appointee urging restraint in the use of U.S. power was placed on the defensive.[32] The same anti-appeasement phenomenon is very much alive in the 1980s.

Global rollback lost out. The Eastern Establishment wing of the Republican Party joined with the Democrats to support containment. Dulles, while talking rollback, proved ultimately a traditional conservative.[33] The alliance of Eisenhower with the Democrats to defeat Joseph McCarthy marked the decline of global rollback until 1980. However, a more fundamental reason than political alignments explains why global rollback was defeated as the basis of U.S. foreign policy: It was impractical.

Rollback within Containment

The containment-rollback war by no means signified that containment advocates opposed rollback in principle. As we noted in the Introduction, containment and rollback are two ends of a spectrum united in the desire to defeat the Soviet Union. Rollback advocates are impatient to speed up this process, to intensify the attack. Containment advocates have been somewhat more realistic, fearing that global rollback would likely bring on global war. To the latter, war is acceptable in the Third World, but confrontation with the Soviets would not spare the United States. Thus while the believers in containment would surely have preferred rollback, they felt they could not get away with it.

A fine line separates the ultimate goals of containment and rollback. For some, successful containment implied that the Soviet government would eventually face revolt from within or would disintegrate due to inability to expand. In this sense the ultimate goal of containment might be long-term rollback. Kennan, on the other hand, seemed to believe that if the United States were sufficiently firm, the USSR might back down and act as a responsible, non-expansionist member of the international community. Rollback was not his ultimate aim.[34]

Kennan did distinguish between containment with a long-term rollback goal and containment with a peaceful coexistence goal. In his famous "Sources of Soviet Conduct" article he stated:

> the main element of any United States policy toward the Soviet Union must be that of a long-term, patient but firm and vigilant containment of Russian expansive tendencies.... Soviet society may well contain deficiencies which will eventually weaken its own total potential.... It is entirely possible for the United States to influence by its actions the internal developments, both within Russia and throughout the international Communist movement, by which Russian policy is largely determined.... It would be an exaggeration to say that American behavior unassisted and alone could exercise a power of life and death over the Communist movement and bring about the early fall of Soviet power in Russia. But the United States has it in its power to increase enormously the strains under which Soviet policy must operate, to force upon the Kremlin a far greater degree of moderation and circumspection than it has had to observe in recent years, and in this way to promote tendencies which must eventually find their outlet in either the break-up or the gradual mellowing of Soviet power.[35]

In Kennan's language, the two containment goals are the mellowing vs. the breaking up of Soviet power. In an example of the former, Eisenhower once said that internal discontent in the USSR could turn it from military to civilian production and reduce its expansionism; hardline Dulles, on the other hand, hoped that the gap between Soviet policies and the desires of its people would become so great that the USSR would collapse.[36] These differences could have profound policy implications. In the 1970s, as Chapter Seven will show, the détente-oriented wing of the Trilateral Commission believed in the mellowing theory and felt that East-West trade was a moderating influence. In response, hardline containment advocates joined the rollback Right and ridiculed the possibility of the USSR mellowing.

Good historical evidence exists to show that many in the conservative elite expected and hoped that successful containment would lead to long-term rollback; secret (but recently declassified and published) national security documents putting forth containment policy were liberally sprinkled with rollback goals.

The National Security Council Directive of the Office of Special Projects, NSC 10/2 of June 18, 1948, established the policy for covert operations, involving "subversion against hostile states, including assistance to underground resistance movements, guerrillas and refugee liberation groups."[37]

During 1948, a general review of U.S. policy toward the Soviet Union was conducted. One of the discussion papers, NSC 7 (March 30, 1948), has a strong rollback component. It begins, "The ultimate objective of Soviet-directed world communism is the domination of the world…. The defeat of the forces of Soviet-directed world communism is vital to the security of the United States." The paper calls for "undermining the strength of the communist forces in the Soviet world," and suggests that the United States "Develop, and at the appropriate time carry out, a coordinated program to support underground resistance movements in countries behind the iron curtain, including the USSR."[38]

Another of the 1948 discussion papers, NSC 20/1 (August 18) is more moderate, calling for the neutralization rather than the elimination of Soviet power. NSC 20/1 argues that the unconditional surrender of the Soviets is not a U.S. goal. It does state, however, that an objective of the United States should be to see Eastern Europe restored to freedom and independence. The paper goes on to admit that this objective cannot be met by means short of war, and the objective of East European rollback is not advanced as short-term policy. Rather, the paper recommends placing the greatest possible strain on Soviet domination of Eastern Europe to maneuver the Russians out of their controlling position and to enable the respective governments to regain their independence of action. The crucial point is that rollback is the desired goal for Eastern Europe, but is not an immediately practical goal.

NSC 20/1 then proceeds to distinguish between peacetime, during which "It is not our peacetime aim to overthrow the Soviet Government," and wartime. In the event of war with the USSR, the U.S. maximum goal would be the disappearance of Soviet power.[39]

The final product of the 1948 policy review was NSC 20/4, approved by President Truman on November 24, 1948. NSC 20/4 reads:

> Communist ideology and Soviet behavior clearly demonstrate that the ultimate objective of the leaders of the USSR is the domination of the world.

> The objectives of the United States in light of this conclusion are:

a. To reduce the power and influence of the USSR to limits which no longer constitute a threat to the peace, national independence and stability of the world family of nations. b. To bring about a basic change in the conduct of international relations by the government in power in Russia, to conform with the purposes and principles set forth in the UN charter.... We should endeavor to achieve our general objectives by methods short of war....

Included in the methods that should be utilized to realize these objectives are "To encourage and promote the gradual retraction of undue Russian power and influence from the present perimeter areas around traditional Russian boundaries and the emergence of the satellite countries as entities independent of the USSR," and to "Place the maximum strain on the Soviet structure of power and particularly on the relationships between Moscow and the satellite countries."[40]

Thus, at least for Eastern Europe, long-range Truman administration policy aimed to roll back communism. NSC 58 (September 14, 1949) was no different: "Our over-all aim with respect to the satellite states should be the gradual reduction and eventual elimination of preponderant Soviet power from Eastern Europe without resort to war."[41]

The most significant national security document produced by the Truman administration was NSC 68, approved by Truman on September 30, 1950. Best known for its strong support of a permanent peacetime military buildup, NSC 68 also has some things to say about containment and rollback. As detailed in NSC 68, the United States has two fundamental aims in the world: to develop a healthy international community, and to contain the Soviet system.

As to the policy of 'containment,' it is one which seeks by all means short of war to (1) block further expansion of Soviet power, (2) expose the falsities of Soviet pretensions, (3) induce a retraction of the Kremlin's control and influence and (4) in general, so foster the seeds of destruction within the Soviet system that the Kremlin is brought at least to the point of modifying its behavior to conform to generally accepted international standards.[42]

There are two major conclusions to be made about rollback in NSC 68. First, point (3) implies rollback in Eastern Europe. Indeed, at a later point in NSC 68 the Eastern European rollback goals cited in NSC 20/4 are reaffirmed. Second, point (4), with its "seeds of destruction" language, signifies a tendency toward long-term rollback. Historian Gabriel Kolko concludes that "in 1950 the 'rollback' of communism was secretly adhered to in the famous National Security Council 68 policy."[43]

Global rollback clearly played a significant role in the Truman administration's foreign policy goals. The arguments against rollback were purely practical: global rollback is impossible without war. The creators of postwar policy chose containment rather than rollback only because they wished to avoid a major war. Containment could be reinterpreted as "Engage in rollback if you can get away with it, don't if you can't."

Korea provides an example of this pragmatic principle: when MacArthur's troops began to win, the United States changed its policy to rollback communism in North Korea. When the Chinese intervened, the policy switched back to containment. There was one and only one reason why Truman fired MacArthur: a fear that the General's attempted rollback of North Korea and China would bring the Soviet Union into the war, or allow the Soviets to commit aggression in other areas such as Europe.[44]

While ultimate rollback was the goal of many containment advocates, global rollback as a practical policy was abandoned due to U.S incapacity to carry it out. However, selected rollback actions directed at governments that were socialist, nationalist, or simply uncooperative with U.S. business interests, remained as a constant, generally covert, feature of U.S. foreign policy. In each case, as the remainder of this chapter demonstrates, rollback was conducted when the United States could get away with it.

U.S. Rollback Actions, 1950-1980

In August 1918, 7,000 U.S. Marines landed at Vladivostok, Russia, and remained until January 1920, as part of an Allied occupational force with the aim of rolling back the Bolshevik Revolution of 1917. In September 1918, 5,000 U.S. troops joined the Allied intervention force at Archangel. The U.S. forces suffered 500 casualties. They left in June 1919, thereby forever ending U.S. attempts at direct military rollback of the Russian Revolution.[45]

Eastern Europe

While the United States made some attempts following World War II to aid insurgents in the Ukraine and the Baltic states, the first actual rollback action—a minor one—targeted Albania. Frank Wisner, the first director of CIA covert operations, called the Albania operation "a clinical experiment to see whether larger rollback operations would be feasible elsewhere." In 1950, small groups of CIA-trained Albanians were landed in the country, were unable to find any viable resistance movements, and were generally killed or captured. The Albanians became disillusioned; as one complained, "We were used as an experiment. We were a small part of a big game, pawns that could be sacrificed." The operation was liquidated. Albania showed the CIA that Eastern European rollback was not so simple.[46] After 1953, CIA director Allen Dulles was anxious to continue operations in Eastern Europe, but a study concluded that there was little hope of success.[47] The liberation from communism rhetoric hit reality squarely in the face. Reality won.

China, 1950-1961

In China, by contrast, the CIA pursued a far-reaching covert war of rollback in association with Chiang Kai-shek. These operations resulted from the compromise made with the Asia-first right wing when overt war against China had been rejected by the Truman administration. Following the Chinese Revolution, many Nationalist soldiers fled to Burma, where the CIA trained a 10,000 soldier army that made incursions into China. For example, in April 1951, a few thousand troops, accompanied by CIA advisors and supplied by U.S. air drops, crossed the border into Yunnan province, but were driven back within a week. Another 1951 raid took the invaders sixty-five miles into China. Such harrassment continued until 1961. The reasoning behind these operations was that between 175,000 and 650,000 guerrillas were supposedly fighting inside China who would link up with the incursion teams. In fact, such guerrilla movement was minimal. The vast covert apparatus developed by CIA chief Allen Dulles involved Korea, Taiwan, Vietnam, Laos, Thailand, and Burma. By the 1950s, the rollback policies advocated by right-wing Republicans in the late 1940s had become bureaucratically entrenched in the CIA, which came to be the locus of rollback policy within the U.S. national security apparatus.[48]

A related rollback operation was underway in Tibet, where a substantial resistance developed to Chinese rule. By 1957, 80,000 Tibetans, trained and armed by the CIA, were fighting. The strategy behind the effort was that success in Tibet would stimulate similar efforts in other Chinese border regions, thus tying down the Chinese in innumerable border wars, and enabling Chiang Kai-shek to begin making raids from Taiwan. In fact, 100,000 Chinese troops were required to put down the Tibetan rebellion, which sputtered along for years even after Kennedy greatly reduced its scope.[49]

Iran, 1953

The CIA's first rollback success was achieved in Iran in 1953. Nationalist Prime Minister Mohammed Mossadegh, elected by the parliament, had nationalized the Anglo-Iranian Oil Company. The British asked for assistance and the CIA sent Middle East expert Kermit Roosevelt with a team and plenty of dollars for the purposes of bribery. In a series of machinations, the CIA overthrew nationalist Mossadegh and brought the pro-U.S. Shah into power. A key factor had been the provision of weapons, supplies, and money to Iranian army officers, winning them to the Shah's side.[50]

Guatemala, 1954

In February 1953, the government of moderate nationalist Jacobo Arbenz expropriated almost 400,000 acres of unused United Fruit Company land as part of a moderate land reform program. Compensation was offered, which United Fruit rejected. United Fruit approached the CIA to take action. The CIA trained a small army, and arranged for the CIA-run airline Civil Air Transport to conduct bombing raids flown by Chinese nationalist pilots. The main thrust of the operation was psychological warfare, organized by E. Howard Hunt, later of Watergate fame. A CIA radio station was set up to create rumors making the government and population think that a major rebellion was taking place. As a result, the small CIA army and a few bombing raids created a panic leading Arbenz to flee. Since this rollback operation, Guatemala has suffered one after another military dictatorship or military-controlled government with a high level of political repression.[51]

Belgian Congo, 1960

Patrice Lumumba was chosen prime minister of the Belgian Congo by the newly-elected parliament following independence from Belgium in June 1960. Lumumba was extremely popular, and left-leaning. CIA Director Allen Dulles authorized a fund of up to $100,000 to replace Lumumba's government with a pro-Western regime. With CIA help, Lumumba was successfully deposed, first by President Joseph Kasavubu, and later by Army strongman (cultivated by the CIA) Joseph Mobutu. The CIA, according to the 1975 U.S. Senate "Church Committee," concocted a plan to assassinate Lumumba with poison carried from the United States by CIA operative Sid Gottlieb. The poisoning plan aborted, but Lumumba was caught with the CIA's help and murdered. Former CIA operative John Stockwell has written that another CIA officer told him of driving around with Lumumba's body in the trunk of a car trying to dispose of it.[52]

Cuba, 1961-1968

On March 17, 1960, President Eisenhower approved a CIA plan to arm and train Cuban exiles to overthrow Fidel Castro. Chinese nationalist pilots recruited through CIA-run Civil Air Transport trained Cuban exile pilots. On April 17, 1961, the exiles, with the help of CIA-organized air strikes, landed a force of 1,400 men at the Bay of Pigs. Numerous logistical errors took place resulting in the exiles' rapid defeat by Castro's army. Whereas President Kennedy accepted blame, in fact there was no resistance movement in Cuba for the invaders to link up with, and the rollback operation would probably have failed in any case.

After the Bay of Pigs fiasco, the Kennedy administration redoubled its efforts to get rid of Castro with Operation Mongoose. The CIA station in Miami, directed by Theodore Shackley with close oversight by Robert Kennedy, became a $50 million per year enterprise with several thousand Cuban exile agents. During the 1960s, Cuba was subjected to countless sea and air commando raids inflicting damage on oil refineries, chemical plants, railroad bridges, sugar mills, and other targets. Several assassination attempts were made on Castro, some involving Mafia figures, utilizing techniques of shooting, bombing, and poisoning. Meanwhile the U.S. economic embargo had the aim of destabilizing Cuba economically in order to increase domestic discontent and spawn insurgent movements. One phase after another of the rollback operation failed. The net effect was that Cuba—needing economic assistance to overcome the embargo—was pushed closer and closer to the Soviet Union.[53]

Brazil, 1964

In 1960, Janio Quadros was elected president. Under pressure from the military, Quadros resigned in 1961, and Vice President Joao Goulart took over. A 1962 referendum supported Goulart's presidency by a wide margin of 4 to 1. The United States opposed Goulart because of his pro-labor and nationalist leanings; Goulart passed a law limiting the amount of profits multinationals could transmit out of Brazil. President Kennedy stated that he would not be opposed to the overthrow of Goulart.

In the 1962 congressional elections, the CIA funded about 850 anti-Goulart candidates to run for state and federal offices, spending between $12 and $20 million. The CIA carried out a constant and vicious propaganda campaign against the Goulart government, including the financing of a right-wing newspaper chain. U.S. ambassador Lincoln Gordon met frequently with Goulart's right-wing enemies, and U.S. military attaché Vernon Walters cultivated his friend Gen. Humberto Castelo Branco for a military coup. The CIA organized anti-Goulart labor unions, and many anti-Goulart military officers were trained in the United States. Major U.S. military assistance programs influenced much of the Brazilian army to oppose Goulart.

By 1964, coup plans were being made in Washington, with General Castelo Branco the chosen successor. Elaborate arrangements were designed for direct U.S. assistance if needed: air-drops of clandestine arms, U.S. emergency oil supplies, and U.S. paratroopers from bases in Panama. A U.S. Navy task force went to Brazilian waters during the coup. On March 31, 1964, the coup took place; there was virtually no resistance. Castelo Branco instituted a military dictatorship with many arrests, tortures, disappearances, and death squads. The Brazilian coup was perhaps the largest and one of the most significant rollback operations ever undertaken by the United States; with Brazil's size and importance in Latin America, this event had a major impact on subsequent South American history.[54]

Dominican Republic, 1965

In December 1962, liberal Juan Bosch was elected president with 60 percent of the vote. Kennedy initially supported Bosch but turned against him when he initiated modest land reform and minor nationalizations. In fact, Bosch was supportive of foreign investment, and was opposed by the communists as overly friendly to the United States. Because of Bosch's apparent independence in a nation long under tight U.S. control, a press campaign was started against Bosch, inaccurately linking him with communists. Kennedy turned off any new aid to the Bosch government; the CIA and U.S. military were in contact with right-wing military officers opposing Bosch. The CIA-created union federation publicly supported a coup against Bosch. In September 1963, after only seven months in office, Bosch was overthrown and Colonel Wessin y Wessin took over.

Younger elements in the armed forces, the constitutionalists, worked with Bosch's political party in a campaign to return Bosch to the presidency. On April 24, 1965, the constitutionalists initiated a revolt which spread rapidly throughout the armed forces and the population. The United States immediately persuaded pro-U.S. officers, especially in the air force, to bomb the capital city. By April 25, it was universally recognized that the pro-Bosch forces were victorious. But that afternoon the Dominican air force attacked the national palace. A bloody battle broke out which the constitutionalists, supported by masses of people in the streets, were on the verge of winning. On April 28, President Johnson ordered in the Marines, a total of 23,000. Johnson's major justification for the action was to prevent a communist takeover, though the communists were minimally involved in the revolution. The revolution was put down, 2,500 civilians died in the fighting, and the Marines occupied the country until a sufficiently pro-U.S. government could be found to take over.[55]

Indonesia, 1958-1965

On December 17, 1965, *Time Magazine* ran the following story on Indonesia:

> Communists, red sympathizers and their families are being massacred by the thousands. Backlands army units are reported to have executed thousands of Communists after interrogation in remote jails. Armed with wide-bladed knives called parangs, Moslem bands crept at night into the homes of Communists, killing

entire families and burying the bodies in shallow graves...The killings have been on such a scale that the disposal of the corpses has created a serious sanitation problem in East Java and Northern Sumatra where the humid air bears the reek of decaying flesh. Travellers from those areas tell of small rivers and streams that have been literally clogged with bodies.

Estimates indicate that perhaps 500,000 to one million people were killed during the military coup in which General Suharto overthrew the government of President Sukarno, a nationalist who had the support of several political parties including the Communists. This slaughter was based on U.S. policy—initiated during the Eisenhower administration—to roll back the Sukarno government.

Bolstered by CIA successes in Iran and Guatemala, John Foster Dulles had wanted to rid Indonesia of President Sukarno. By the mid-1950s, the CIA was spending millions to finance two parties in opposition to Sukarno. The CIA supplied weapons and advice to anti-Sukarno rebels on the island of Sumatra and sponsored their 1958 revolt, providing bombing missions in support. Planes and pilots for the bombings came from Civil Air Transport, the CIA proprietary airline. However, CIA pilot Allen Pope was shot down during a May 18 1958 bombing raid, the U.S. involvement was exposed, the CIA pulled out, and the rebellion fizzled.

A CIA memo of June 18, 1962, reveals that Kennedy wanted to continue efforts to oust Sukarno. Following the failed rollback attempt of 1958, the United States switched to the strategy of winning over the Indonesian military. By 1965, almost half the officer corps had received training from North Americans. Economic aid to Sukarno was cut off but direct aid to the military was increased—a pattern used in Chile after 1970. According to the *New York Times* of April 27, 1966, the CIA had thoroughly infiltrated the Indonesian government and army.

While the U.S. military kept an extremely low profile during the 1965 coup itself, James Reston wrote in the *New York Times* on June 19, 1966: "it is doubtful if the coup would ever have been attempted without...the clandestine aid it has received indirectly from here." Following the coup, Marshall Green, U.S. Ambassador to Indonesia in 1965, said: "what we did we had to do, and you'd better be glad we did because if we hadn't Asia would be a different place today."[56]

Greece, 1967

In 1964, liberal George Papandreou was elected prime minister of Greece; in July 1965, he was maneuvered out of office by a coalition of rightists assisted by the CIA. Two years later, the Right consolidated its power in a military coup. Of the five officers taking power, four were intimately connected with the U.S. military or CIA. The leader, George Papadopoulos, worked with the Nazis in World War II, was trained in the United States, and had been on the CIA payroll for fifteen years. Since 1947, the Greek army and the U.S. military aid group in Athens had worked as part of the same team. Following the 1967 coup, the Papadopoulos dictatorship instituted widespread repression; Amnesty International documented not less than two thousand people tortured.[57]

Southeast Asia, 1958-1970

In Laos, the U.S. government almost certainly engineered coups during the period 1958-60, and possibly again in 1964, to ensure that the Laotian government would not take a neutralist stand in the Southeast Asian conflict, and to keep the leftist Pathet Lao out of coalition governments. For many years, Laos was one of the major sites of CIA covert activity in the affairs of China, Vietnam, Cambodia, and Thailand.

In March 1958, the National Security Council adopted a rollback policy document on Vietnam calling for its eventual reunification under anti-communist leadership. The Vietnam War had aspects of both containment and rollback: while the land war in South Vietnam was a containment action, the air war on North Vietnam had strong elements of rollback.[58]

Prince Sihanouk of Cambodia represented a major problem for the United States in Vietnam due to his neutralist stance. Cambodia was a vital supply line from North to South Vietnam and the United States wanted the supplies shut down. The Pentagon wanted to get rid of Sihanouk, and, in March 1970, he was ousted by former Defense Minister Lon Nol, a man with close ties to the U.S. military.

In 1969, Lon Nol was approached by agents of U.S. military intelligence and asked to overthrow Sihanouk. The CIA-financed Khmer Serai and the Khmer Krom were anti-Sihanouk Cambodian groups working under direct U.S. military command in the Green Beret special forces. The United States had a plan code-named "Dirty Tricks" to infiltrate mercenaries from both groups into the Cambodian army which was generally loyal to Sihanouk. By the end of 1969, 4,000 Khmer Serai and Khmer Krom members—presumably still under U.S. command— had joined Lon Nol's forces. The U.S. military had several days notice of the coup and a request for assistance if needed.[59]

Because of the interrelatedness of the 1958-70 events in Southeast Asia, and the resolve of the United States to keep control of all governments in that region, the rollback activities in Southeast Asia can be considered as one complex, prolonged, major covert operation working in conjunction with the overt Vietnam War.

Chile, 1970-1973

On September 4, 1970, socialist candidate Salvador Allende received the plurality of votes in the Chilean election. A congressional runoff election was required to decide between the top two candidates, and Allende's victory in Congress was assured because he had the support of the third-place candidate. On September 8, Henry Kissinger ordered a "cold-blooded assessment" of "the pros and cons and problems and prospects involved should a Chilean military coup be organized now with U.S. assistance...." On September 15, President Nixon told CIA Director Richard Helms and Henry Kissinger that they must do everything possible to prevent Allende from assuming power.[60]

As a result of the Nixon order, CIA operatives were sent into Chile to pass money and weapons to right-wing Chilean military officers to assassinate Allende. A quarter of a million dollars was authorized to bribe members of the Chilean Congress to vote against Allende. The CIA and U.S. Army attaché Col. Paul Wimert contacted two groups of right-wing Chilean officers, headed by Gens. Roberto Viaux and Camilo Valenzuela, to arrange a coup or assassination. U.S. Ambassador Edward Korry, who advised against such action, was not told of the U.S. plots. On October 22, Gen. René Schneider was murdered by Viaux's people in the hopes that the resultant upheavals in the military would precipitate action against Allende; Schneider was a moderate and opposed any military action against Allende. However the Schneider killing angered Chilean moderates, thus ensuring Allende's election in the October 24 congressional vote.

Following this failure, the United States began a policy of economic destabilization. National Security Decision Memorandum 93, of November 9, 1970, called for an end to guarantees for U.S. private investment in Chile, a limitation on international credit for Chile, a ban on bilateral economic aid, and a plan for adversely affecting the world price of copper which is critical to the Chilean economy. The World Bank, the Export-Import Bank, and the Inter-American Development Bank—all run or heavily influenced by the United States—shut Chile out of international credit markets. U.S. suppliers refused to sell needed parts to Chile, causing buses and taxis to remain out of commission for months, and ensuring prolonged breakdowns in the copper, steel, electricity, and petroleum industries. International Telephone and Telegraph (ITT), which owned the Chilean telephone company and which had given large sums of money to prevent Allende's election, stated in 1970, "A more realistic hope among those who want to block Allende is that a swiftly-deteriorating economy will touch off a wave of violence leading to a military coup."

While U.S. economic aid disappeared, aid to the military and U.S. training of military personnel increased. CIA covert tactics continued at the cost of several million dollars per year. The CIA financed long strikes, particularly in the trucking industry, disrupting distribution of consumer goods and creating shortages of necessities. The CIA trained members of the extreme rightist organization *Patria y Libertad* in bombing and guerrilla warfare. The CIA recruited agents within the Chilean military. The CIA sponsored the spreading of false rumors about the government. Right-wing newspaper *El Mercurio* received considerable CIA funds. The CIA collected names of pro-Allende individuals to be targeted for arrest after a coup and supplied plans for which installations should be occupied during a coup. During the September 1973 coup, U.S. military attachés were in the field with the Chilean army, a Navy commando team landed in Chile, U.S. ships were in Chilean waters, and U.S. fighter planes were at an Argentine base just across the Chilean border.

Following the coup which installed Gen. Augusto Pinochet's military dictatorship, Richard Helms, CIA Director during the Chilean operation, denied in sworn testimony that the CIA had tried to overthrow Allende. Helms was later indicted for perjury and pleaded no contest.[61]

Jamaica, 1974-1980

In 1972, democratic socialist Michael Manley was elected prime minister of Jamaica. Henry Kissinger initiated measures to destabilize the government, including a withdrawal of U.S. aid and the sending of CIA-trained Cuban exiles to Jamaica to instigate violent incidents which had a devastating effect on the tourist business, critical to the Jamaican economy. CIA-trained labor leaders engaged in anti-government strikes and U.S. aluminum companies reduced their Jamaican production, further damaging the economy. The United States closed Jamaica out of the international public and private lending market. Economic austerity measures initiated by the U.S.-dominated International Monetary Fund led to price increases and wage freezes. While Manley won re-election in 1976, he was defeated in 1980 as the deterioration of the economy turned the public against his government. The Jamaican operation introduced a sophisticated form of economic destabilization/electoral rollback which could become a pattern for the future.[62]

Containment = Selective Rollback

We have listed thirteen major rollback operations between 1950 and 1980: Korea, China, Iran, Guatemala, Congo, Cuba, Brazil, Dominican Republic, Indonesia, Greece, Southeast Asia, Chile, and Jamaica. The criteria for listing these thirteen episodes are: 1) there is clear evidence of significant U.S. participation in the overthrow or attempted overthrow of a government, 2) the outcome or attempted outcome was or would have been significant to the political development of the involved region, and 3) the overthrow was of a government (whether communist or nationalist) believed to be overly independent from U.S. influence. In making this listing, we have left out coups meeting the above criteria. The purpose of our history is to make the point that the official policy of containment included as a major feature the policy of selective rollback.

It is noteworthy that these rollback operations did not coincide with Republican presidents; in fact, they were equally associated with Democrats and Republicans. Four of the thirteen rollback operations took place in the 1950s, six in the 1960s, and three in the 1970s. Four were conducted by Democrats, three by Republicans, and six by both parties.

A number of the operations stretched across one or more administrations: Cuba between Eisenhower and Kennedy, Indonesia from Eisenhower to Kennedy to Johnson, Brazil from Kennedy to Johnson, Cambodia from Johnson to Nixon, Jamaica from Nixon through Carter. Underlying changes in the presidency was an apparatus that conducted rollback. According to Schurmann, the locus of rollback in the U.S.

government has been the CIA and to some degree the military, and the power of these establishments cannot be disregarded by the president. Schurmann also makes the point that a deal was made between the presidency and the national security apparatus by which the president would have power over nuclear weapons and the U.S.-USSR relationship, which would be governed by a policy of containment; and in return, the military-CIA-right wing would have freedom to conduct regional policy, including covert operations and rollback.[63]

The specific interests behind the rollback operations differed from case to case. Guatemala in 1954 was by and large a business deal on behalf of United Fruit Company. The Chilean rollback was strongly related to the interests of ITT and U.S. copper companies. Indonesia and Brazil had geopolitical motivations, keeping entire regions of the world within the U.S. orbit.

U.S. postwar policy, generally called containment, on closer inspection is actually a hidden policy of selective, deliberate overthrow of governments in the Third World, with the ultimate long-term goal of disintegration or "mellowing" of socialism in the Soviet Union. In other words, containment in practice has meant selective rollback. In essence, containment is realist rollback: overthrow unfriendly governments when feasible without risking major war. The main historical debates between the traditional conservative elites and the right wing have not really been about containment vs. rollback, but about realist or selective rollback vs. global rollback.

$\boxed{2}$

How to Roll Back the "Evil Empire"

The right wing sees the world as a simple, bipolar battleground between the forces of freedom and justice led by the United States and the "evil empire" of the Soviet Union. The Soviet empire is bent on world conquest; thus, in order to protect and defend freedom, the Soviet empire must be destroyed. There is no room for negotiation. There is no room for compromise. There is no room for two social systems on the face of this earth.

The Expanding Soviet Empire Theory

In its popular expression, the right-wing view of the world is highlighted by Ronald Reagan's statement: "The Soviet Union underlies all the unrest that is going on. If they weren't engaged in this game of dominoes, there wouldn't be any hotspots in the world."[1] In 1982, at the United Nations, Reagan denounced Soviet "tyranny," "repression," "aggression," and "atrocities."[2] In 1983, he warned that the Soviets "are the focus of evil in the modern world."[3]

This worldview is not simply overblown rhetoric; it is backed by an entire academic analysis, a theory we call the Expanding Soviet Empire Theory (ExSET). According to Vernon Aspaturian, an expert on the Soviet Union and a former Rand consultant,

> Three distinct components or rings of the empire can be
> delineated, with the Russian nation at the center. The first and
> most integrated component consists of the non-Russian
> nationalities within the USSR, which can be designated as the *inner
> empire*. The second component consists of other Communist
> states, which will be designated as the *outer empire;* the third com-
> ponent consists of Third World countries and will be designated
> as the *extended empire*. The Soviet empire is still very fluid....
> Some former parts of the outer empire (Yugoslavia, Albania,
> China) have defected, although Yugoslavia's relationship with the
> Soviet Union is akin to being a member of the extended empire.
> Afghanistan provides a vivid illustration of the dynamic fluidity of
> the Soviet imperial system. Given the Soviet military occupation
> of Afghanistan, the country is being treated as if it were a part of
> the Soviet outer empire, whereas before the invasion it was a part
> of the extended empire.[4]

Aspaturian lists the religious and ethnic minorities within the USSR
as the inner empire (e.g., the Ukranians, Estonians, Latvians,
Lithuanians, Georgians, and Moslems). Eastern Europe (East Germany,
Poland, Czechoslovakia, Hungary, Romania, and Bulgaria), Mongolia,
Cuba, and Vietnam make up the outer empire. The extended empire
is generally listed as including Afghanistan, Laos, Cambodia, South
Yemen, Ethiopia, Mozambique, and Angola. Other authors also include
Tanzania, Zimbabwe, and Nicaragua. Aspaturian discusses the weaknesses of the Soviet empire and what strategies could be taken to
"wean" (i.e., rollback) nations from the empire or to weaken the empire. He says there is a Russian proverb that "the cloth unravels at its
edge," meaning that the unraveling process for the Soviet empire is
most easily initiated at its margins.[5]

According to ExSET, the Soviet Union is not simply an empire; it
is an *expanding* empire. As the Heritage Foundation puts it, "Expansionism is endemic to Marxist-Leninist ideology and Soviet state interest."[6] The concept of expansion is critical to the right-wing view because
it justifies rollback as a defense of the United States. Were the Soviet
empire simply static, with its policy to defend itself rather than to seek
new areas of domination, then mutual co-existence would be possible.
To argue against mutual co-existence, the right wing affirms that the
Soviet empire is expanding and, in fact, wishes to take over the entire
world. Either socialism or capitalism will rule the world, and those who
support capitalism must roll back the dangerous and expanding Soviet
empire.

One theorist of the Expanding Soviet Empire, a former Reagan
National Security Council advisor, is Harvard Professor Richard Pipes

whose description of the Soviet empire matches that of Aspaturian's. In his book *Survival is Not Enough,* Pipes stays away from an objective global balance sheet (which shows that the USSR has made both new friends and new enemies in the past thirty years—see Chapter Ten), and moves to more theoretical arguments to demonstrate Soviet expansionism. According to Pipes, the elite class that runs the Soviet government *must* have an expansionist policy in order to impress fear upon the large dissatisfied minority populations of the USSR. Pipes states that Soviet rulers "require permanent international tension and ceaseless territorial aggrandizement." For Pipes, the elites' drive for power is so strong that the average Soviet official views democratic or religious dissenters as mentally deranged.[7]

ExSET is by no means confined to right-wing Reaganites. President Carter's National Security Advisor Zbigniew Brzezinski is a sophisticated ExSET advocate, as indicated by his recent book *Game Plan*:

> Russian history is, consequently, a history of sustained territorial expansionism.... Both in scale and in duration such territorial expansion is doubtless one of the most ambitious examples of a relentless imperial drive in known history.... The drive to global preeminence, for decades measured by competition with the United States, has become the central energizing impulse.[8]

Not all Soviet empire theorists find Soviet expansionism to be inexorably aggressive; Aspaturian, for example, feels that the Soviets expand in order to defend their borders, and that the Third World portion of the Soviet empire represents "voluntary adhesions to the Soviet empire" whose value to the Soviet Union "remains dubious."[9]

Pipes tries to prove that the elimination of capitalism worldwide is the objective of the USSR.[10] Pipes explains that this presumed goal is conducted by the tactics of divide and conquer, by "exploiting the contradictions in the enemy camp." For example, the Soviets look for "useful idiots," such as U.S. businessmen, who may not like the USSR but, by doing business with it, are "making common cause with Moscow."[11]

The Third World is regarded as the main focus of Soviet divide and conquer strategy because the nations there are politically unstable and torn by social strife. Here Pipes is providing intellectual support for such Reagan pronouncements as "The Soviet Union underlies all the unrest that is going on," even though virtually every serious scholar of the Third World understands that poverty, malnutrition, unfair land ownership and political repression are main causes of Third World strife. Even Pipes' ideological ally Irving Kristol calls it oversimplistic to attribute the problems of the Third World to the Soviet Union, admitting a strong autonomous impulse in Third World movements: "Indeed, the Third World can often be as much of a headache for the Soviets as it is for us."[12] On the other hand, right-wing intellectual guru Jeane Kirkpatrick tells us that "the 'deep historical forces' at work in such diverse places as Iran, the Horn of Africa, Southeast Asia, Central America, and the United Nations look a lot like Russians or Cubans."[13]

Pipes and Brzezinski are not the only pied pipers of ExSET; they have much company in right-wing policy-making circles, for example, Michael Ledeen of the Center for Strategic and International Studies; Edward Luttwak, also of the CSIS; and former Reagan advisor Colin Gray who believes, "The Soviet commitment to world dominion is non-negotiable."[14]

Like the "creeping socialism" it abhors, ExSET has infiltrated from academia into policy-influencing organizations, into the speeches of aspiring politicians and the policy statements of their parties, and finally into the councils of the U.S. foreign policy apparatus. In attempting to make their theory official U.S. policy toward the Soviet Union, ExSET proponents do battle with their very distinguished opponents who disagree with the ExSET conclusions; a 1986 article in the Heritage Foundation's *Policy Review* condemns Soviet specialist George Kennan for rejecting ExSET, virtually accusing him of being a communist.[15]

At the level of the public opinion-influencing groups, ExSET is most clearly expressed by the influential Committee on the Present Danger (CPD): "No empire in history has expanded so persistently as the Russian.... [The Soviet Union] is driven by internal, historical and ideological pressures toward an expansionist policy which, given its enormous military might, makes it a uniquely dangerous adversary."[16] The accession of CPD leaders into the Reagan government made ExSET the conventional wisdom of the 1980s. A powerful commission of the Democratic Party, the Democratic Policy Commission, put forth ExSET in its 1986 statement of policy:

> [The USSR] is a totalitarian society that remains an empire in the classical sense.... The expansion of Soviet influence continues to pose the major threat to U.S. interests and world peace. We must not and cannot relax our vigilance against Soviet imperialism.[17]

An entire right-wing school of thought, the neoconservatives, bases its foreign policy on ExSET. Furthermore, a type of intellectual journalism of the Right has sprung up that evokes a popular politics of hatred toward the USSR, for example, Kristol's description of the Soviet leaders (presumably all of them) as "liars and thugs," a Mafia that is "inefficient, unpopular, and in total, ruthless control of the country."[18] Ronald Reagan's statement that the Soviets "reserve unto themselves the right to commit any crime, to lie, to cheat" is of the same journalistic tradition.[19]

Global Rollback

With the popularity of ExSET, the stage was set for the revival of global rollback as a legitimate foreign policy. As we saw in Chapter One, global rollback had not been welcome in the highest circles of the traditional conservative elite. While selective rollback actions have taken place within an overall doctrine of containment, global rollback—turning the entire socialist and nationalist world into pro-U.S. capitalist states—has remained on the fringe of acceptable policy options.

The ExSET justification for global rollback makes it appear as a logical policy. Ronald Reagan stated in 1976 that the "final step" in "the Communist master plan is to conquer the United States."[20] In this view, the two social systems cannot cohabit the planet because socialism wants to roll back capitalism rather than coexist with it. The only remedy, as stated by Reagan, is that "The march of freedom and democracy...will leave Marxism-Leninism on the ash heap of history as it has left other tyrannies which stifle the freedom and muzzle the self-expression of the people."[21] Rollback is the march that Ronald Reagan led during the first six years of his presidency before he retreated at the end of his second term. (See Chapter Nine.)

Because the Soviet empire is one entity, the ultimate goal must be to roll it back in its entirety. Thus the rollback of a particular Third World nation, Nicaragua for example, is not simply a bilateral matter concerning the United States and Nicaragua, but is a step in the defeat of the entire Soviet empire. A U.S. war to overthrow the Nicaraguan government would accomplish U.S. aims in Nicaragua and at the same time pressure the USSR to use scarce resources to assist Nicaragua, thereby weakening the economy of the USSR itself. In fact, hostility toward Soviet Third World allies is a prime example of making sure that "the cloth unravels at its edge."

Among the ideological Right, rollback means the destruction of socialism by any means necessary. In the words of Lawrence Beilenson, a longtime Reagan friend and foreign policy advisor: "We ought to try to overthrow any communist government. I go all the way. I include Yugoslavia...I'd try to overthrow the government of China, too."[22] Right-wing American Security Council president John Fisher's preferred method of dealing with the Soviet Union, according to an ASC researcher, was "to go blow it up right now."[23] The Committee of Santa Fe, which made recommendations on foreign policy to candidate Reagan in 1980, issued a dramatic call for rollback:

> Containment of the Soviet Union is not enough. Détente is dead.... America must seize the initiative or perish. For World War III is almost over.... America is everywhere in retreat. The impending loss of the petroleum of the Middle East and potential interdiction of the sea routes spanning the Indian Ocean, along with the Soviet satellization of the mineral zone of Southern Africa, foreshadow the Finlandization of Western Europe and the alienation of Japan. Even the Caribbean, America's maritime crossroad and petroleum refining center, is becoming a Marxist-Leninist lake. Never before has the Republic been in such jeopardy from its exposed southern flank. It is time to seize the initiative.[24]

Global rollback (defeating the *entire* Soviet empire rather than just particular nations) has served as a clarion call not just for the right wing; it was also a goal of important sectors of the Reagan administration. According to the prestigious policy document of the Heritage Foundation, *Mandate for Leadership II,* "The president and other high Administration officials have emphasized that the U.S. does not accept the current expanse of the Soviet empire as a permanent and irreversible feature of the historic landscape."[25] A secret five-year defense guidance plan from Secretary of Defense Weinberger ordered Special Forces to be ready "to exploit political, economic, and military weaknesses with the Soviet bloc" and that "other opportunities for counteroffensives against the Soviet interests, forces, and proxy forces worldwide will be exploited to the extent possible."[26] An eight-page national security document, approved by Reagan in 1982, was reported to endorse "a campaign aimed at internal reform in the Soviet Union and shrinkage of the Soviet empire."[27]

The Heritage Foundation, one of the main foreign policy advisory bodies to the Reagan administration, has stated its "refusal to accept the permanency of...Central Europe," a polite way of saying that Eastern Europe should be brought back into the capitalist camp.[28] In 1984, Reagan and Secretary of State Shultz clarified that the United States does not forever recognize Soviet domination over Eastern Europe. There has been a general repudiation of the "Sonnenfeldt Doctrine" even by the author himself, a former National Security Council advisor for Eastern European affairs. The doctrine stated that trying to remove Eastern Europe from the Soviet orbit would be counterproductive because of the reaction it would provoke in the Soviet Union. Brzezinski has published a sophisticated rollback program for Eastern Europe.[29] In the fall of 1986, the editor of Heritage's *Policy Review* suggested "the next challenge for conservative strategic thinking: how to roll back Communism in Eastern Europe and the Soviet Union itself, without provoking a world war in which all our freedoms would be destroyed."[30]

The Heritage Foundation has also called for nine governments (Nicaragua, Angola, Cambodia, Afghanistan, Laos, Vietnam, Libya, Ethiopia, and Iran) to be targeted for overthrow.[31] Other rightists have added Cuba. In 1980, Reagan said, "I do not believe relations can be normalized until Cuba is out from under Soviet domination.... My policy would be based on my longtime view that captive nations must once again know freedom."[32] And arch-conservative William Buckley, Jr. stated, "We have got to get at Cuba.... A declaration of war...could plausibly be framed."[33]

The Right has varying timelines for the implementation of global rollback. The overthrow of Nicaragua should take place as soon as possible; rollback of the Soviet Union is a longer-term project.

If the world is a battlefield between freedom and evil, what are the means by which the evil empire is to be destroyed? The remainder of this chapter explores the methods of global rollback: economic, by placing such economic pressure on targeted nations that they internally collapse; military, by initiating or threatening force; and political, by organizing dissident movements within targeted nations. These methods are closely interrelated, since the worse the economic situation, the easier to organize internal opposition and the easier to launch a successful military attack. In the following discussion of rollback strategies, we will look at: 1) economic-military rollback directed against the Soviet Union, 2) economic rollback of the Soviet Union through the isolation of the Soviet economy, and 3) economic/military/political insurgency against Third World countries, destabilizing those countries and thereby undermining the USSR itself.

Methods of Rollback

Economic-Military Rollback of the USSR

One of the most powerful methods of destabilizing the USSR is to make it dedicate a large portion of its scarce resources to the military sector. This is done by an aggressive U.S. military buildup which requires a response by the USSR, taking funds away from civilian economic development. At the same time, the U.S. buildup could gain the related objective of military superiority. The result would be a reduction in the Soviet standard of living, creating fertile ground for fomenting political unrest. In addition, the crippling of the Soviet economic infrastructure would prevent the USSR from economically competing with capitalist nations, thereby furthering internal economic crisis and stagnation. As an important byproduct, such an arms race feeds the military-industrial complex in the United States, thereby providing profits and political support for the policy from significant sectors of business and labor.

This policy is nothing new, but in the 1980s the right wing sponsored a major new variant: the Strategic Defense Initiative (SDI), otherwise known as Star Wars. The plans for SDI were hatched in 1981, at the Heritage Foundation. By 1987, the program had been budgeted for more than $26 billion over the next five years; it is estimated to have an ultimate cost of $1 trillion.

Star Wars has great potential for economic destabilization of the USSR. As Edward Luttwak, a Reagan administration advisor, stated in a Heritage Foundation symposium:

> The real payoff of an American SDI would be its stimulation of Soviet spending on similar defenses, thereby soaking up rubles that would otherwise go for more dangerous purposes....[34]

According to right-wing Congressman Jack Kemp:

> The one area where the Soviets cannot compete at all with the United States is in technology and the industrial capacity to meet a challenge. SDI would force them to divert huge amounts of resources away from expanding their current offensive posture trying to overcome our defenses, and developing defense of their own.[35]

As Soviet scholar Jerry Hough sees it, SDI would be particularly damaging to the Soviets because they are far behind in high technology capability and would need to divert immeasurable economic resources into catching up. One of Star Wars' major advocates, Edward Teller, feels that SDI would have a "devastating impact" on the Soviet economy.[36]

SDI critic Isaac Asimov puts it this way:

> I don't think Star Wars is feasible and I don't think anyone takes it seriously. It's just a device to make the Russians go broke. But we'll go broke too. It's very much of a John Wayne standoff.[37]

The right wing recognizes that the escalating arms race hurts the USSR not only at home but also abroad, forcing the Soviets into an emphasis on politico-military rather than on the more productive economic relations with other nations. According to former CIA director William Casey:

> Yet the Soviet Union is crippled. It is crippled in having only a military dimension.... But in the long run it is economic, financial, scientific, technical and cultural exchanges which attract, deliver benefits, and maintain close relationships with Third World countries. The Soviet Union cannot compete in these areas.[38]

A prominent commentator from the socialist world agrees: the Soviets, unable to compete with the West economically, have turned to "politico-military methods to exert their influence in world affairs," and these methods cannot work. The Soviets need a safe international environment to "shift from military buildup to economic restructuring."[39] Clearly the U.S. right wing does not want to allow such a safe international environment to exist.

It would be a great mistake to view economic-military rollback as purely economic in its goals. The byproduct of the military buildup is military superiority, and that means nuclear superiority. As we will see in Chapter Five, a basic plank in the right-wing platform is nuclear superiority. The doctrine of military superiority fits perfectly with the strategy of economic destabilization through military buildup, because the drive for superiority implies a never-ending, massively expensive arms race, with SDI as the ultimate weapon in both military and economic destabilization.

Rollback Through Economic Isolation

A second major method of destabilizing the USSR—adding to the economic effects of the arms race—is the denial of East-West trade. The right wing is united in its opposition to any action that would improve economic relations with the Soviet Union; such actions aid the Soviet economy and, in certain cases, its military capabilities. Jeane Kirkpatrick has argued against any credit terms, money, or technology for the Soviets and has said, "I don't think we should do anything to take the strain off the Soviet people under conditions of the chronic failure of Soviet agriculture."[40]

Richard Pipes, director for Eastern European and Soviet affairs at the National Security Council from 1981-82, has been more than blunt in his support for such economic warfare:

> ...under normal conditions, economic policy is the only field where we are able to exert pressure. Since you do not want to resort to military means for fear of getting into a war, and since there are severe limits to what you can do politically, economic countermeasures remain the only effective instruments at our disposal. Their use can be very painful to the other side.[41]

According to Pipes, industrial assistance provided to the USSR through commercial trade helps the Soviet military effort either directly or indirectly. "So it happens that while the West busily arms itself, it also helps arm its opponent." Pipes asks: "Does it make sense...for private enterprise to make profit by helping the potential enemy improve his military capabilities?"[42] In his answer, he implies that those who trade with the USSR are traitors to the cause.

> The most unabashed voice in the West favoring accommodation with the Soviet Union, however, belongs to the business community. On the face of it, pro-Soviet sympathies on the part of a group that the Soviet Union is committed to destroying may seem absurd.... Leading business executives...vigorously oppose punitive sanctions and embargoes; and they are the most vociferous champions of arms control and summit meetings.[43]

Lewis Tambs, from the Committee of Santa Fe, put it equally strongly:

> Western bankers and businessmen, unable or unwilling to understand that their capital investments in the Soviet Union are hostages at the mercy of Moscow, have helped construct a military machine which will crush them in the end.[44]

Midge Decter, executive director of the Committee for the Free World and also a trustee of the Heritage Foundation, is opposed to all trade with the Soviet Union. "The most important thing we can do now is stop helping the Soviets keep their regimes stable. Whatever lightens the economic burden of the Soviet Union frees the Soviet regime by that much for its military buildup."[45]

Reagan's first National Security Advisor, Richard V. Allen, also a member of the Committee on the Present Danger (CPD), criticizes the arguments made by proponents of détente:

> ...I believe that our long-range objective in conducting trade should be to make the Soviet Union pay the price of its own in-efficiency. Whether trade can, as former President Nixon and many others argue, serve as an incentive to alter behavior is a highly dubious proposition. After all, this was the basis of the détente theory—that one could entice the Soviet Union into a web of self-enforcing agreements that would involve the transfer of technology, know-how and credits to the Soviet Union in return for which the Soviet dependence would grow and therefore its behavior improve. That, of course, has been demonstrated to be nonsense.[46]

In the public glare of the nuclear arms race, the low-key, day-by-day economic destabilization is often forgotten; this type of warfare is designed to make the Soviet people lay the entire blame for their economic failures on their own government rather than to see the hostility of the United States as one factor.

Hand in hand with economic destabilization go political methods to incite dissension within socialist nations. Two bases for these methods are natural tensions developing from existing nationalist differences within socialist nations and economic dissatisfaction based on the effects of economic destabilization.

During an anti-Soviet speech Reagan talked about his crusade for freedom, for which he requested $65 million to intensify the broadcasting of information programs into communist countries.[47] In addition, his administration took steps to increase the budgets and improve the capabilities of Radio Free Europe and Radio Liberty, which broadcast into the Soviet Union, including its national minority regions, and into Eastern Europe. Under the glasnost program of Soviet General Secretary Gorbachev, U.S. opportunities for political destabilization increase; during the August 1987 anti-Soviet demonstrations in the three Baltic countries, U.S. radio broadcasts were a key factor in organizing the protests.[48]

Richard Viguerie, a prominent New Right leader, has proposed that the only way to get rid of the Soviet Union is by supporting dissension from within. He suggests actively helping to build insurgencies within the Soviet Union primarily among the non-Russian population using increased propaganda and economic warfare.[49] The Heritage Foundation has called for the broadcasting of programs to Soviet-Bloc inhabitants about the nature and extent of internal failings of the communist system.[50] This policy of activating insurgency is the means through which economic warfare can ultimately lead to rollback. At more advanced stages, such political insurgency can be armed by the United States and become a military operation.

Destabilization Through Insurgency in the Third World

The final, and perhaps most important, global rollback strategy is the organizing and financing of military insurgencies, mainly against Third World nations. This has two major effects: 1) it threatens the economies of the Third World nations, thereby contributing to their overthrow; and 2) in the case of nations friendly to the USSR, it attempts to place the USSR into the position of providing funds to assist these nations, thereby creating an economic drain on the USSR itself. Examples of the right wing and the Reagan administration's use of this tactic are Nicaragua, Afghanistan, and Angola. Third World insurgency has been so closely identified with the Reagan administration that it is now called the "Reagan Doctrine." (See Chapter Four.)

Afghanistan represented the clearest example that the Reagan Doctrine is aimed both at Third World nations and at the USSR. The United States spent at least $625 million to finance the Afghan insurgency against the Soviet-allied Afghan government.[51] This money assisted in tying down Soviet troops in Afghanistan, thereby creating both an economic drain and a major internal political problem for the Soviets.

In addition to the economic drain on the Soviets, the policy of Third World insurgency could, according to neoconservative Irving Kristol, have a direct political impact on the destabilization of the USSR. In a *Wall Street Journal* article entitled "Coping with an 'Evil Empire'," Kristol hopes to provoke a split within the Soviet ruling circles, as

> ...that is the way Leninist parties change.... And this will only occur when the party finds itself stalemated and dispirited. So long as the Soviet Union enjoys the kind of success it has had in foreign

policy, the party's legitimacy remains unruptured, its usurpation of national pride unchallenged, and a crisis can be indefinitely postponed. The thrust of American foreign policy, therefore, should be to inflict a series of defeats, however minor, on the Soviets. This is the significance of our support, or lack thereof, of liberation movements in Angola, Nicaragua, Afghanistan, and wherever else they emerge. The success of such rebellions would bring into question the basic assumption of all Leninist parties as to their 'historic mission,' and their inevitable victory. Only in this way can the possibility of 'liberalization' become a reality.[52]

The Reagan Doctrine, then, represents the full implementation of the proverb that "the cloth unravels at its edge"; that the Soviet empire must be attacked at its weakest link. Both Richard Pipes and Vernon Aspaturian emphasize that the extended empire economically drains the USSR, requiring far more assistance than it provides economic benefits in return. The more the extended empire is under attack, the more it drains the Soviets.

The Reagan Doctrine is also looking for specific successes in rolling back particular Third World nations. Its goal of international counterrevolution faithfully articulates the recommendations contained within the Heritage Foundation's *Mandate for Leadership II* that call for developing a coordinated "low intensity warfare" policy to deal with "Soviet and Soviet proxy involvement in the developing world."[53]

The Right's argument to justify rollback policies in the Third World is the ExSET conception that the expansionist Soviet empire, rather than specific conditions of poverty and repression, is responsible for all unrest in the world. The other major argument of the right wing holds that insurgent armies are forces of democracy, or so-called "freedom fighters."[54] This particular argument is the contribution of Jeane Kirkpatrick, the Democrat turned neoconservative turned Reaganite. Kirkpatrick, in *Dictatorships and Double Standards,* justifies U.S. support for right-wing dictators by widely generalizing that "traditional authoritarian governments are less repressive than revolutionary autocracies," and that right-wing dictatorships can be transformed into democracies. From her vantage point as an affluent North American, she claims that "because the miseries of traditional life [in Third World right-wing dictatorships] are familiar, they are bearable to ordinary people." On the other hand, revolutionary "totalitarian" regimes such as the USSR, Cuba, and Vietnam are far worse, and can never evolve into democratic governments.[55] Under the Kirkpatrick Doctrine, insurgent leaders, whether supporters of former dictator Somoza among the Nicaraguan contras, or rich and autocratic mullahs in the Afghan resistance, can be considered democrats or freedom fighters because they are attempting to overthrow "totalitarian" governments.

Escalation Dominance

In summarizing the right-wing methods of rollback, it is important to remember that these methods—economic, military, and political—are closely interrelated. One such relationship deserves special mention because it is so easily overlooked: the link between "low intensity" warfare in the Third World and the nuclear arms race. These levels of military competition, seemingly in widely separate realms, come together in the concept of "escalation dominance." Escalation dominance is the ability to prevail in a war at each stage of potential or actual escalation of that war. For example, if a "low intensity" conflict erupts into a larger regional conventional war, the United States must be capable of winning that larger war. If the regional war spreads to other areas of the world, the United States must be able to win all the wars at the same time. And if a regional or conventional worldwide conflict escalates into nuclear war, the United States must be capable of winning the nuclear confrontation. Logic would ultimately dictate that guaranteed success in rollback through Third World insurgencies depends on nuclear superiority.

The importance of escalation dominance was established by two of the main movers of the Committee on the Present Danger (CPD), Paul Nitze and Eugene Rostow. In 1979, Nitze wrote:

> It is copybook principle in strategy that, in actual war, advantage tends to go to the side in a better position to raise the stakes by expanding the scope, duration or destructive intensity of the conflict. By the same token, at junctures of high contention short of war, the side better able to cope with the potential consequences of raising the stakes has the advantage. The other side is the one under greater pressure to scramble for a peaceful way out. To have the advantage at the utmost level of violence helps at every lesser level. In the Korean war, the Berlin blockades, and the Cuban missile crisis the United States had the ultimate edge because of our superiority at the strategic nuclear level.[56]

In 1978, Rostow made a similar point:

In the late sixties and early seventies, our nuclear superiority was no longer so evident as it had been at the time of the Cuban Missile Crisis; indeed, superiority had given way to stalemate. Therefore the hints which brought the Korean War to an end could no longer determine the course of events in Indo-China.[57]

The point both men were making is, of course, that the United States did threaten (hint) at the use of nuclear weapons in the Korean War and the Berlin and Cuban crises, and these threats worked because of U.S. nuclear superiority. In Vietnam, with superiority lost, no such threat could be credibly used, though Nixon tried it in 1969. By the mid-'60s, the United States no longer had escalation dominance. In the 1980s, the right wing was determined to get it back.

3

The Global Rollback Network from Chiang Kai-shek to Oliver North

No political movement can take place without cadres to carry it out. Cadres are those people who are committed to taking control and working for a cause, whatever that cause might be. Chapters One and Two reviewed the history and ideas of an international movement—the campaign for global rollback. In this chapter we will examine the people and institutions dedicated to making rollback a reality.

The revelations of Contragate focused the public on a covert network carrying out foreign policy operations. Yet little attention has been placed on the historical context of Contragate. In fact, the prosecution of a secret foreign policy by a mixture of governmental and quasi-private operatives is not a new development. Contragate is simply another chapter in a forty-year pursuit of global rollback by a committed cadre of U.S. covert operatives in conjunction with a growing domestic and international right-wing network.

This network, activated in the early postwar rollback activities of Eastern Europe and the Far East, has gradually developed a strong constituent interest in maintaining and fortifying an active program of global counterrevolution. At times such a program has dovetailed with the strategies of traditional conservative policy-setting elites; on other occasions it has conflicted with the traditional conservatives. When such contradictions become intense, as took place over China, Vietnam, and most recently Contragate, the infighting has exploded to occupy center stage in the domestic political arena.

Whereas some authors have described the international right-wing network, thus far this institution has not received a generally accepted name. *Global rollback network* is an accurate description because the network is global in scope and its political goal is likewise global. For the purposes of this book we will use that name, and call it *Rollnet* for short. Rollnet refers to the cadres—the most dedicated members—of the much larger political movement, the international right wing.

It is important to think of Rollnet as an international institution separate from, though interlinked with, the government of the United States. Rollnet cadres, such as those central to Contragate, circulated in and out of the official U.S. government. Those cadres—most prominently Oliver North—who had gained influential U.S. governmental positions were in effect using these positions to further their Rollnet cause; the Constitution and laws of the United States were secondary considerations. They equated the goals of the United States with the goals of Rollnet.

This chapter will proceed in two sections: 1) brief descriptions of the actors in Rollnet, and 2) an historical sketch of some Rollnet activities in relation to U.S. foreign policy.

Covert Cronyism: Who are the Actors?

The CIA and "ex"-CIA Old Boys Network

CIA and supposedly *ex*-CIA operatives, the world's specialists in covert action, constitute the heart of the global rollback network. Perhaps the best known of these people (publicized during the Contragate hearings) are the groupings of operatives involving retired Maj. Gen. Richard Secord, Theodore Shackley and Thomas Clines,[1] and the overlapping entourage surrounding retired Gen. John Singlaub.[2] In the work of these operatives, it is difficult to distinguish what is governmental activity, what is private, and what is a public-private meld. Similarly, it is difficult to determine whether a particular person in a particular operation is on the CIA payroll or not. In their private functions some individuals in these groupings appear sometimes to have conflicting motives: the rollback of unwanted governments and the accumulation of personal profit. As we will see later in this chapter, the past and present activities of these individuals and their contacts reads like a review course of major U.S. covert operations.

The book *The Iran-Contra Connection* provides an important analysis to explain the centrality of ex-CIA operatives in Rollnet. The explanation is called "the disposal problem": what to do with troops no longer needed.[3] In the late 1970s, 820 positions were eliminated from the CIA's clandestine services, producing a group of unemployed covert war specialists.[4] Such an elite corps would not simply fade into the suburban United States; their way of life was anti-communism, secrecy, and, on occasion, shady financial deals involving arms and/or drugs. Some of these ex-CIA operatives worked for the election of Ronald Reagan; after his victory they insinuated themselves back into newly revived covert operations, whether in governmental, private, or mixed roles.

The Military-Industrial Complex

The military-industrial complex includes both the Pentagon and the corporations who develop and manufacture weapons under Pentagon contract. Whereas some military officers act as professional soldiers without an overriding political agenda, others—like their CIA counterparts—are committed right-wing cadres whose governmental and private political activities are difficult to keep separate. Individuals and corporations representing the military contractors have also acted as key members of Rollnet. General Electric, one of the top ten Pentagon contractors, played an important role in starting Ronald Reagan's political career. David Packard (of Hewlett-Packard) has raised funds for three major right-wing think tanks: the American Enterprise Institute, the Hoover Institution, and the Center for Strategic and International Studies.[5]

Three interlocking organizations speaking for the military-industrial complex have been the American Security Council, the Coalition for Peace Through Strength, and the Committee on the Present Danger. Generals John Singlaub and Daniel Graham, with lengthy covert careers in both the military and the CIA, have been co-chairmen of the Coalition for Peace Through Strength.

The American Security Council (ASC), established in 1955, has been led by a number of high-ranking military officers and prime defense contractors; three retired chairs of the Joint Chiefs of Staff were at one time co-chairs of its national strategy committee. The ASC has spent millions to "educate voters" on the need for a stronger military.

Its president, John Fisher, has stated the need for "clear military superiority." ASC has actively supported Third World rollback in Nicaragua and Angola.[6] The two men most responsible for the Strategic Defense Initiative (Star Wars), Gen. Daniel Graham and physicist Edward Teller, have both worked with the American Security Council.[7]

Right-wing Foreign Governments

Critically important support for Rollnet has always come from certain governments that for one reason or another have a stake in rollback. A major rollback government, not surprisingly, has been Taiwan, which has always wanted to roll back the Chinese Revolution and has actively assisted right-wing operations in other countries. South Korea, South Africa, Saudi Arabia, and Israel have also acted as rollback regimes. Of course, these governments often act in their own direct national interest, for example Taiwan *vis-a-vis* the Chinese mainland. But at other times they seem to provide assistance as part of more complicated deals such as Saudi Arabia sending money to U.S.-backed insurgencies in Nicaragua, Angola, and Afghanistan in return for receiving sophisticated U.S. weapons.[8] Sometimes these governments have acted through ostensibly private organizations; for example Chiang Kai-shek and South Korean intelligence agents created and operated through the Asian People's Anti-Communist League (APACL).[9]

In an example of rollback regime behavior, South Africa illegally provided $450,000 in campaign contributions to defeat liberal Sens. John Tunney and Dick Clark in the 1970s; Clark was author of the amendment prohibiting U.S. aid to the South African-backed Angolan contras. South Africa also donated to conservative Senator Hayakawa who sat on the Senate Foreign Relations Committee Subcommittee on Africa and contributed $40,000 to a research institute headed by Gen. Daniel Graham.[10]

The case of Israel is complex because it is a major arms exporter for economic reasons, selling arms to many nations and groups throughout the world. However, U.S. intelligence officials have claimed that Israel has secretly provided several million dollars of aid to the Nicaraguan contras as a political action in support of rollback.[11]

Eastern European Emigrés and Fascists

Among the first covert operations attempted by the reformulated U.S. military/intelligence network in the postwar period were those against the USSR and its satellite Eastern European states. Recruited into these operations were a host of people who ranged from social democrats, disaffected with Stalin's incorporation of Eastern Europe, to native fascists who actively collaborated with the Nazis during the war. In addition, German Nazi leaders were recruited into Western intelligence circles.

Some groups in the Eastern European fascist network joined together to form an anti-Soviet front known as the Anti-Bolshevik Nations (ABN). Members of this organization aided U.S. military actions and propaganda efforts such as Radio Free Europe and Radio Liberty against the Soviet Bloc. In general, they have taken the most extreme rollback position against the USSR and Eastern Europe.[12]

The Knights of Malta is a European organization which played a role facilitating Hitler's assumption of power in Germany. Former CIA Director William Casey belonged to the Knights of Malta as did James Angleton, at one time chief of the Counterintelligence Division of the CIA. The Knights of Malta also had links with the fascist P-2 Masonic Lodge, members of which were responsible for many terrorist actions in Italy during the 1970s.[13]

The World Anti-Communist League

The World Anti-Communist League (WACL) was formed with the merger of the Anti-Bolshevik Nations (ABN) and the Asian People's Anti-Communist League (APACL) in 1966.[14] In addition to ABN and APACL, WACL embraces disparate national right-wing formations that include:

- Latin American right-wing nationalist and/or fascist parties, some of which have at times been in power, some of which have sponsored death squads and/or narcotics-related activities. (Examples are the Guatemalan National Liberation Movement (MLN) and the El Salvadoran Arena Party.) Organized within the regional WACL chapter, the Latin American Anti-Communist Confederation (CAL), these groups have provided much of the Latin American support for the Nicaraguan contras.[15]

- Members of the U.S. Right, represented over the years within the U.S. affiliate U.S. Council for World Freedom (USCWF). The membership has had strong representation by notables from the military/intelligence community including Singlaub and Graham, who have been USCWF's top two officers, with Singlaub having served as WACL's Chairman in 1984.[16]

- Representatives of right-wing governments in power including Taiwan, South Korea, South Africa, Chile, and Saudi Arabia.[17]

Roger Pearson, a known neo-Nazi and WACL's world chairman in 1978, was removed as head of the U.S. WACL chapter because his views were too extreme even for WACL. Pearson was editor of the *Journal of International Relations* in the 1970s; the journal's publisher was John Fisher, president of the American Security Council; the associate editors were Gen. Robert Richardson (also of ASC) and ex-CIA counterintelligence chief and Knight of Malta James Angleton.[18]

The "Moonie Empire"

The Unification Church headed by Reverend Sun Myung Moon is closely interrelated with WACL. The Moon organization has known ties to the Korean Central Intelligence Agency (KCIA), itself an offshoot of U.S. intelligence agencies. Moon served the interests of the Japanese Right and its U.S. military allies when he set up campus study groups called Collegiate Association for the Research of Principles (CARP); by the early 1960s, these were used by school authorities to counter the strong anti-militarist radical student movement. These Japanese groups prefigured the Moonie CARP movement set up on U.S. campuses to promote right-wing causes among students. In addition to its close relationship with the right-wing South Korean government, the Moonie Empire has received $4.5 million from the government of South Africa.[19]

A notable Rollnet-related organization in the Moonie Empire is the Unification Church's political arm, Confederation of Associations for the Unity of the Societies of America (CAUSA). This organization has worked in close coordination with the U.S. Right to support Reagan policy in El Salvador and Nicaragua. In Nicaragua, it was part of Singlaub's private contra supply network. The Moonies have also promoted their right-wing views with such publications as the *Washington Times* and the weekly glossy *Insight,* offered free to business executives and other elite opinion makers.

CAUSA USA's president has been retired Air Force Gen. E. David Woellner, who also held high positions in the American Security Council and the Coalition for Peace Through Strength. CAUSA has also worked closely with the Council for Inter-American Security, the organization sponsoring the Santa Fe Committee whose influential 1980 report recommended a global rollback policy.[20]

Rollback Intellectuals and Government Officials

A respectable veneer for Rollnet has been supplied by a number of U.S. intellectuals. In fact, the ExSET theory can be viewed as the intellectual justification for Rollnet's activities. During the Reagan administration, some of these people became important government officials. One key link of Rollnet with intellectuals is the CIA. Leading neoconservative Irving Kristol was publisher of a 1950s journal *Encounter* which was financed by the CIA.[21] Former CIA deputy director Ray Cline has more recently served as a foreign policy "analyst" at the conservative Center for Strategic and International Studies. Cline helped initiate APACL during his CIA days in Taiwan and also assisted in organizing the U.S. WACL chapter while also serving as a representative of the related Moonie CAUSA organization.[22]

The Committee on the Present Danger (CPD) has provided important links between rollback-oriented intellectuals such as Eugene Rostow, Jeane Kirkpatrick, and Norman Podhoretz, and military-industrial figures including David Packard, Adm. Elmo Zumwalt, and ex-Chair of the Joint Chiefs of Staff General Lyman Lemnitzer. Thirty-three CPD members received appointments in the Reagan administration; among them were John Lehman, Secretary of the Navy and Richard Perle, Assistant Secretary of Defense for International Security Policy, both of whom had performed consulting work for large military contractors.[23] Foremost ExSET theorist Richard Pipes was a Reagan National Security Council advisor, and Fred Iklé, formerly from the Air Force's Rand Corporation think tank, became Under Secretary of Defense for Policy. Clare Booth Luce, former China Lobby mainstay, was also on the CPD and became a member of Reagan's Foreign Intelligence Advisory Board.

Right-wing think tanks have also had Rollnet links. Professor Stefan Possony has worked at the Hoover Institution and has also been active in WACL and the American Security Council.[24] The ubiquitous Gen. Daniel Graham has been associated with the Heritage Foundation. The Nicaraguan contras also have their supporting group of intellectuals, called Prodemca (Friends of the Democratic Center in Central America), including such prestigious people as Jeane Kirkpatrick, right-wing patron William Simon, and Ben Wattenberg of the influential Coalition for a Democratic Majority.[25]

Anti-Castro Cubans and other Assorted Contras

The word *contra* means counterrevolutionary. Every social revolution creates a group of individuals or economic groups that have lost their power, wealth, or economic stability. These groups are fertile soil for the recruitment of professional contras who hope to regain their previous positions in society via armed insurgency. The leaders of these groups are often military or police officers supportive of the dictator deposed by the revolution. If their insurgency fails, they often become permanent exiles, available for other counterrevolutionary causes around the world. Along with CIA and ex-CIA operatives, contra leaders are key Rollnet cadres.

While the Nationalist Chinese contras have played a major Rollnet role, the grouping most significant in modern U.S. politics has been the Cuban contras or anti-Castro Cubans. Following the failed Bay of Pigs rollback attempt, some Cuban exiles have been willing CIA mercenaries, signing up for CIA actions in the Congo, Bolivia, Vietnam, and Central America. At the same time, a number of Cuban contras have been convicted of drug smuggling and accused of bombings and other terrorist acts.[26]

As with CIA operatives, failed contra insurgents constitute a major disposal problem. With the spate of contra operations of the 1980s, this problem is likely to increase. In particular, if the Nicaraguan contras fail in their rollback efforts, they could become the next generation of unemployed Rollnet mercenaries. As *The Iran-Contra Connection* puts it, "The $100 million in U.S. aid now flowing to the contras is a mere down payment for violence yet to come."[27]

Organized Crime and Drug Smugglers

Covert action networks have had working relationships with organized crime from the time of World War II, when U.S. military intelligence arranged to release Mafia kingpins Lucky Luciano and Vito Genovese from prison in return for their cooperation in facilitating Allied landings in Italy. This U.S. government-initiated bailout of the drug-dealing Mafia allowed the European heroin trade to revive at a time when it was in disarray and heroin could possibly have been eliminated as a major social problem in the United States.[28]

With the onset of the Cold War, the covert intelligence community worked with criminal elements in a mutually beneficial way, based on the rationale that such tactical alliances were necessary in the global crusade against communism. In addition, the high profitability of drug trafficking has proved useful for generating cash flows for secret operations. According to one theory, CIA-related "trafficking in drugs in Southeast Asia was used as a self-financing device to pay for services and persons whose hire would not have been approved by Washington."[29] The Afghan resistance has partially financed its war by selling opium; Afghanistan and bordering areas of Pakistan are the world's leading source of illicit heroin exports to the United States and Europe.[30] Drug smuggling has also had an intimate relation with gun running; in both Southeast Asia and Central America, pilots have ferried weapons into battle zones and brought drugs back out.[31] The close relationship between narcotics dealing and contra armies in such places as Latin America and Afghanistan has led one observer to call the armies *narcocontras*.[32]

Banks and Airlines

Since Rollnet is like a government unto itself, it requires an infrastructure and large funding sources. Some shady banks and CIA-related airlines have been key parts of Rollnet's infrastructure. The Castle Bank & Trust and the Mercantile Bank and Trust were created by Paul Helliwell, former OSS chief in China and operator of the CIA-controlled Sea Supply Corporation which was involved in gun and drug trading in Thailand. The Castle Bank was one of the CIA's conduits to finance Cuban rollback operations and held the accounts of several organized crime figures.[33] The Nugan Hand Bank in Australia had close ties to the CIA and was probably used to launder drug profits from Laos and Thailand. Funds through the Nugan Hand Bank were alleged to have been channeled to the CIA-backed rebels in Angola.[34]

CIA-run airlines have been used to transport personnel, ship arms, and traffic drugs. The CIA supplied the rollback-oriented Nationalist Chinese army in Burma via Civil Air Transport, later changed into Air America. Air America crews supplied the pro-U.S. Montagnard tribes in Vietnam and Hmong tribes in Laos; the CIA airline also flew opium out of northeastern Laos.[35] Southern Air Transport was a CIA company that became "privately" owned in 1973; it was used to transport arms to the Nicaraguan contras and·to deliver U.S. arms to Iran in 1985-86. The FBI received at least one report that cocaine had been loaded onto Southern

Air Transport planes in Colombia.[36] CBS News journalist Leslie Cockburn, in her recent book *Out of Control,* convincingly documented extensive drugs-for-guns trafficking utilizing current and "ex"-CIA proprietaries within the contra supply network.[37]

International Arms Merchants

As the diversion of profits from Iranian arms sales to the contras demonstrated, international arms sales are an excellent method for financing Rollnet's activities. The other purpose of the arms trade for Rollnet, of course, is to obtain arms for Rollnet insurgent fighters. One clever method used to supply the Nicaraguan contras was reported to be the transfer of weapons to them after each major U.S. military exercise in Honduras.[38] Clearly an international movement can accrue enormous power and wealth based on arms transactions and—with the addition of Saudi Arabia to the right-wing club—from oil. Arms, drugs, airlines, banks, and governments work together in the implementation and financing of Rollnet operations.

The U.S. New Right and Religious Right

A network of 1970s-vintage right-wing organizations generally associated with the New Right are connected with or part of the global rollback network. Howard Phillips, who has been chairman of the Conservative Caucus, and Andy Messing, former Caucus executive director, have been on the advisory board of the U.S. WACL affiliate, and General Singlaub has been active in Conservative Caucus activities.[39] Fred Schlafly, the husband of Phyllis Schlafly who spearheaded the New Right anti-ERA campaign, has been on the board of directors of the U.S. WACL chapter.[40] The Unification Church has raised $500,000 for the National Conservative Political Action Committee (NCPAC).[41] The *Conservative Digest,* formerly published by Richard Viguerie, is a major supporter of Rollnet causes.

Accuracy in Media (AIM), right-wing critic of the *New York Times,* CBS and other "liberal establishment media," was co-founded by Bernard Yoh who served under the CIA's Gen. Edward Lansdale in Vietnam and advised Spanish dictator Francisco Franco and right-wing regimes in South Korea and the Philippines; a number of CIA and military figures have been on AIM's advisory board. AIM chairman Reed Irvine has had a regular column in the Moonie-run *Washington Times.*[42]

An important umbrella organization of the religious Right, the National Religious Broadcasters (which has included Jerry Falwell, Pat Robertson, and Jimmy Swaggert on its board of directors) has worked with the Moonies and WACL. The Council for National Policy provides a link between the Christian Right and other right-wing groups; CNP recently had on its board General Singlaub, Oliver North, Pat Robertson, and General Graham. Oliver North arranged for the Florida-based Gospel Crusade to assist in supplying the Nicaraguan contras. Right-wing evangelist and presidential candidate Pat Robertson has also helped raise funds for the contras.[43]

Right-wing Funding Sources

The global rollback network did not just happen; it needed money. Right-wing businesses saw the usefulness of Rollnet for their economic interests and provided much of the funds to create and sustain the network through a small number of ultraconservative foundations. Richard Mellon Scaife has contributed over $100 million in recent years, with beneficiaries including CPD, Center for Strategic and International Studies, Heritage Foundation, Accuracy in Media, and the American Security Council. The Smith Richardson Foundation, the Coors Foundation, the Olin Foundation, and the Pew Freedom Trust have financed many of the same groups. Texas millionaire Nelson Bunker Hunt donated funds to WACL.[44] The CIA operations naturally have received their funding from the U.S. taxpayers, and contra groups are funded by the U.S. government, other rollback regimes, and private sources. Drug trafficking and arms sales are other key sources of Rollnet money.

Rollnet

Clearly, Rollnet is a highly complex institution with multiple interrelated parts. Who runs it? Is it ultimately a CIA creation? Or is it controlled by certain right-wing individuals or corporations, possibly within the military-industrial complex, who have succeeded in pressuring the U.S. government to let them use the CIA for their own purposes? The latter is probably closer to the truth. In any case, each part of the network has particular interests in global rollback. These interests might be the regaining of personal power lost in a revolution or the earning of profits by a military contractor thriving on the Cold War. In the next section, we will summarize some of Rollnet's activities in various regions of the world.

Rollnet and U.S. Foreign Policy: 1945-1980

The history of the global rollback network lies far beyond the scope of this single chapter. Our aim here is to provide some examples of how Rollnet has functioned to influence and implement U.S. foreign policy.

Rollnet's Origins: U.S. Covert Operations

The global rollback network derives in part from the expanded use of covert operations to support U.S foreign policy objectives after World War II. With the onset of the Cold War, the Soviet Union and its "satellites" became a central target for these operations. U.S. capability for covert action grew directly out of the experiences of the Office of Strategic Services (OSS) and related military agencies that ran "special operations" to anti-fascist resistance groups during World War II. Subsequent to the signing by President Truman of the 1947 National Security Act, covert operations derived a strict line (albeit changing over the years) of authorization from the president and top leadership represented in the National Security Council.

With technological developments causing more intelligence to be collected by machines rather than spies, the CIA was reorganized to devote more of its activities to covert action. Starting in the late 1940s, skilled operatives from the ranks of the old OSS were recruited into the CIA's Office of Policy Coordination (OPC) and subsequently into the Deputy Directorate of Plans (DDP), coordinating with special operatives in the military services to conduct covert and overt operations throughout the world. Such old-time covert warriors include John Singlaub, Thomas Clines, Paul Helliwell, Richard Stilwell, and Ray Cline, all of whom worked in the OSS operation in the Burmese-China theater during World War II, and who over the next forty years would be involved in operations ranging from Cuba to Southeast Asia to Central America. Reagan's CIA Director William Casey was a member of the OSS "band of brothers," the "club that didn't meet," the old-timers who were "the dedicated secretive operatives who did the dirty work."[45]

These early days established the basis for personal and political relationships that would form a major nexus of power within the covert community. Although tremendous battles would continue to be waged among U.S. foreign policymakers over issues such as containment versus rollback of a nuclear-armed USSR, the covert warriors were primed for an aggressive global mission. As expressed in President Eisenhower's 1955 directive NSC-5412/2, the general guidelines for covert operations aimed to:

> Create and exploit troublesome problems for International Communism, impair relations between the USSR and Communist China and between them and their satellites, complicate control within the USSR, Communist China and their satellites...Counter any threat of a party or individuals directly or indirectly responsive to Communist control to achieve dominant power in a free world country...In areas dominated or threatened by International Communism, develop underground resistance and facilitate covert and guerrilla operations...[46]

The ideology expressed in these guidelines, differing little from the precepts of the modern Reagan Doctrine, would increasingly constitute the worldview of covert activists. The total commitment against "international communism" would inevitably generate its own set of policy objectives and political alliances that would impact greatly on the international and the domestic U.S. political scene.

Western European Restraint, Eastern European Frustration

As the Cold War took hold, the traditional conservative establishment was predominantly Atlanticist, preoccupied with restraining Soviet power in Europe. Within Western Europe, particularly France and Italy where communist parties active in the anti-Nazi resistance commanded widespread popular support, containment involved numerous covert activities on behalf of pro-Western political parties and labor unions. In 1948, the CIA worked with the Corsican underworld to provide the shock troops to defeat communist-led strikes in Marseilles. Consequently, the Corsicans gained a foothold enabling them to set up heroin processing labs in southern France that would provide the bulk of street heroin to the United States.[47]

In the same year, covert relationships were worked out with the Mafia in Italy to counteract the strength of the Italian Communist Party, which threatened a victory at the polls. This continuation of previous understandings reached with Luciano guaranteed the Mafia the powerful position it has maintained within Italian politics to this day.

The CIA conducted numerous operations against the Western European communist parties, including financing a family of antisocialist intellectual journals sponsored by the Congress for Cultural Freedom.[48]

The combination of covert activities and Marshall Plan economic aid was highly successful in keeping Western Europe in the U.S. camp. Eastern Europe was another matter. While the basic policy was to contain the Soviets within the limits agreed to at the 1945 Yalta Conference, it was considered fair game to take cautious advantage of any Soviet weaknesses in Eastern Europe. Direct military rollback under the nose of the Soviets was far too dangerous, especially after the USSR became a nuclear power. Thus most covert activities against the Eastern Bloc were centered on intelligence collection and psychological warfare. Chapter One summarized the failed Albanian venture; of note is that Rollnet figure E. Howard Hunt of Watergate fame served as chief of covert operations for the Balkans during this operation. After Albania, practical recognition of the dangers of fighting the Soviets constrained the United States from giving direct military aid to rebellious Hungarians, East Germans, and Poles.

East European emigrés and Nazis were particularly useful as sources of intelligence. After the war, Gen. Reinhard Gehlen, head of Nazi counterintelligence on the Eastern front, transferred his extensive files and network of anti-Soviet spies and collaborators to the U.S. intelligence services. The U.S. government actively aided and abetted the escape of numerous Eastern European fascists after World War II, sometimes in conjunction with the efforts of right-wing Vatican elements, allowing such Nazis as Klaus Barbie to flee to South America. These activities were carried out in conjuction with the Anti-Bolshevik Nations (ABN) and were justified as serving the anti-Soviet cause.[49]

With the merger of ABN and the Asian People's Anti-Communist League (APACL) in 1966 to form the World Anti-Communist League (WACL), a major actor in the global rollback network was born. ABN provided links to those Nazis who had escaped to South America, many of whom subsequently attained positions of influence within various Latin American military dictatorships such as Gen. Alfredo Stroessner's Paraguay. Klaus Barbie was allegedly in a cocaine smuggling ring in Bolivia while serving as a close advisor to its right-wing government. Though organized rollback attempts in their own countries were impossible, the frustrated Eastern European fascists committed numerous terrorist murders, a TWA hijacking in 1976, and a Yugoslav airline bombing in 1972 that killed twenty-seven people. A failed movement, they became a disposal problem, and some fought as mercenaries on other continents while others became cadres of WACL.[50]

Rollnet's Crucible: Far Eastern Rollback

In Chapter One we reviewed the rise of a new interventionist Right, attuned to the potential of U.S. expansion into the Pacific Rim and bankrolled by a Sunbelt-based military-industrial complex providing the technological muscle for Pacific air and naval power. The traditional elite Atlanticists, as represented in the Council on Foreign Relations (CFR), recognized Chiang Kai-shek's lack of any political base in China and preferred to adopt a wait-and-see attitude toward the 1949 Chinese Revolution. The Asia-first economic interests lost their bid for direct military confrontation with China during the Korean War, but successfully pressured for a covert policy to roll back China in the 1950s. While the rollback attempts were never serious enough to gain victory, the organization of Far Eastern covert operations laid the groundwork for the next forty years of Rollnet actions, both within the United States and internationally. The major domestic movement growing out of the China issue became known as the China Lobby.

The China Lobby

Allied with those traders and missionaries oriented to satisfying the economic and spiritual needs of a mass Asian market, the China Lobby sprang forth to reclaim a China "lost" by traditionally conservative, equally anti-communist Atlanticists. The conservative elites could barely protect their own State Department from the ravages of a McCarthyism that was ultimately nurtured by the very anti-communist climate the elites had created to sell their European Truman Doctrine. With no nuclear threat from China, the traditional elites "signed on" to rollback in the Far East as long as war with Russia could be prevented.

The China Lobby in its most populist expression took on a strong bipartisanship exemplified by the activities of the Committee of One Million, organized by Marvin Liebman. While controlled by the right wing, the Committee was backed by a notable number of Atlanticist cold warriors.[51] The Committee of One Million launched numerous campaigns persuading the majority of Congress to oppose diplomatic and trade relations with communist China and to prevent Chinese admission to the UN.

Most important for the development of Rollnet domestically were the movers behind the China Lobby. The politico-economic base for the China Lobby was the classical triad of frontier expansionism: the entrepreneur, the soldier, and the missionary. In the case of China, this involved Protestant church people (in particular Henry Luce, publisher of *Time* and *Life*, born in China of missionary parents), shipping and aviation interests (including Gen. Claire Chennault and Sen. William Knowland from Oakland, California, a major port), import-export traders, and the Navy and Air Force, who wanted to maintain the Pacific as the American lake it had become following the defeat of Japan.[52] But transcending these narrow considerations, the China issue was one that could rally reactionary opposition to the Atlanticist conservative elite.

The major political figure benefiting from the China Lobby's intense criticism of the Truman administration was Sen. Joseph McCarthy, who used the China issue to purge anti-rollback elements from the State Department. But for long-range right-wing organization building, more important was conservative fundraiser and Committee of One Million organizer Marvin Liebman, who conducted his campaigns in close contact with the Taiwanese government. Liebman, who prefigured Richard Viguerie as the predominant right-wing fundraiser of his time, in turn coordinated his activities with the numerous other right-wing groups he worked with, providing them with more clout and more organizational capabilities. Some groups benefiting from their association with China Lobby leaders have been Young Americans for Freedom, the American Security Council, Accuracy in Media, the Moonie Empire, and the Committee on the Present Danger. WACL was closely related with the China Lobby; Marvin Liebman was general secretary of WACL's first steering committee and Liebman's successor at the Committee of One Million organized the first U.S. chapter of WACL.[53]

Chiang Kai-shek, APACL and the Moonies

Domestically the China Lobby was an important precursor of the modern rollback Right, but far more important were the international linkages developed between the CIA and the first major contra army, the Nationalist Chinese.

After being routed from the Chinese mainland, Chiang Kai-shek and his troops (described by U.S. Army Gen. Joseph Stilwell as "a Gestapo") had established themselves on Taiwan by a massacre of perhaps 20,000 Taiwanese.[54] From 1950 to 1970, Chiang and his Nationalist

Chinese played major roles in the U.S.-directed covert warfare programs in East Asia. Wherever the CIA went, they were able to make use of the natural networks of Chinese businessmen all over the Pacific. According to Asia scholar Franz Schurmann, the Chinese supplied the CIA with saboteurs, commandos, agents, smugglers, spies, and "businessmen" to help out in the complex world of East Asian transactions.[55]

Close cooperation between U.S. covert intelligence agencies and the Taiwanese government continued in this period. This included the establishment of the Political Warfare Cadres Academy, allegedly with the help of Ray Cline, who was Taiwan CIA Station Chief from 1958-62. This school provided warfare training to thousands of Third World military figures. Prominent graduates include El Salvador's Roberto d'-Aubuisson, widely viewed as the mastermind of his country's death squads; Lieutenant Colonel Domingo Monterrosa, a Salvadoran military commander whose troops massacred an estimated one thousand civilians at Mozote in December 1981; Amilcar Santamaria, a rightist Honduran political figure; and numerous other intelligence officers in the armies of Latin American dictators.[56]

Concurrently, the United States collaborated with Chiang Kai-shek and South Korean intelligence in founding the Asian People's Anti-Communist League (APACL) in 1954. Ex-Nazi collaborators from Eastern Europe also helped set up APACL.[57] This organization had the purpose of uniting conservatives from all over the Asian continent to battle communism. Possibly arranged through Taiwanese CIA station chief Ray Cline, U.S. funds seem to have helped start APACL.[58] APACL also drew sustenence from the coffers of the Japanese Right. Ryoichi Sasakawa and Yoshio Kodama were prominant members of the wartime fascist Tojo clique who had been convicted of war crimes. In a manner analogous to the rehabilitation of German Nazi war criminals to serve the interests of the West, these individuals were freed in 1948 and helped to bankroll APACL.[59]

Intertwined with APACL was the Unification Church of right-wing Korean Reverend Sun Myung Moon. Moon received major financing from Sasakawa (who has called himself the world's wealthiest fascist) and Kodama. The Korean CIA (whose precursor may have been set up in part by General Singlaub, CIA deputy chief in South Korea in the 1950s[60]), organized by South Korean dictator Park Chung Hee to support his 1961 military coup, adopted the Unification Church as its political arm.[61] Park, as head of one of the world's chief rollback governments, was also a major actor in APACL. In both Korea and Japan, the Moonies and APACL were closely interrelated.

Two important rollback activities in Asia were the Nationalist Chinese attempt to overthrow the Chinese government and the multiple coups in Laos to prevent neutralist governments from gaining power. (See Chapter One.) These two related operations, spanning the 1950 to 1970 period, were the true moments of birth for Rollnet; individuals joined in covert warfare in Asia then spread out as rollback operatives throughout the world.

Arms and Drugs in Burma

The Burma-based Nationalist Chinese operations directed against communist China in the 1950s were supplied by the CIA airline Civil Air Transport (CAT), with some pilots drawn from the ranks of ex-Nazis recruited by the United States. CAT was originally organized by Gen. Claire Chennault in consultation with Colonel Richard Stilwell, the CIA's Office of Policy Coordination chief for the Far East. Also used in these activities was the CIA-run Sea Supply Corporation, which brought arms to the Chinese contras. Sea Supply was run by Paul Helliwell who, as chief of the OSS mission in China during World War II, had used opium bricks to pay off local informants, initiating intelligence-related involvement with drug traffic. Continuing this tradition, Nationalist Chinese trafficked in Burmese opium, using CAT planes delivering arms to ship the opium out, to ultimately reach the world market.[62] These GIDO (guns in, drugs out) operations persisted in Laos and later in Vietnam and Central America.

During this period the China Lobby was taking out full-page ads asserting (without evidence) that communist China was behind the heroin trade. But the truth about the Burmese operation leaked, causing a scandal leading to Stilwell's dismissal and the cessation of direct CIA support for the Chinese contras. However, APACL, probably using the same CAT planes, took over the supply operation.[63]

Arms and Drugs in Laos

The Chinese contras were driven from Burma into Laos in 1961, and the CIA, after changing the name of CAT to Air America, took over a revived arms/drug trade. The political objectives of the Laotian operation were several: the organizing of the Hmong (who inhabited parts of China, Vietnam, Laos, Thailand, and Burma) into a pro-U.S. force in Southeast Asia, the prevention of a neutralist Laotian government, the development of a capacity to disrupt the supply lines of the Ho Chi Minh Trail that ran along the Laotian-Vietnamese border, and the securing of a base from which to launch paramilitary raids against North Vietnam. Rollnet cadres Ted Shackley, Thomas Clines, Richard Stilwell, John Singlaub, Richard Secord, and Felix Rodriguez worked together in the Laotian secret war.[64]

As usual, politics is never pure. Franz Schurmann explains that

> One need not believe that the CIA had some grand design for flooding the world with dope to believe that it got entrapped in the dope business. If [the Hmong] raised opium as their main cash crop, then one would have to put aside one's puritanical beliefs about opium in order to gain their support for more important causes. If Chinese businessmen in Bangkok and Hong Kong helped to process and smuggle the opium to various parts of the world, it was exceedingly deplorable. But since they formed an invaluable intelligence network...that too had to be overlooked. If Air America was supposed to help the anticommunist covert war in Laos, who could prevent its Asian and American operatives from making some money on the side?[65]

Arms and Drugs in Vietnam

As regular U.S. forces became progressively involved in the Vietnam conflict in the later 1960s, many of the personnel associated with the secret war in Laos shifted over to Vietnam. Some members of the U.S. intelligence team in Vietnam were Ted Shackley as head of the CIA station, John Singlaub, Richard Secord, Oliver North, Felix Rodriguez, Edward Lansdale, Harry Aderholt, and William Colby, who directed the Pheonix assassination program that resulted in the deaths of 20,000 to 40,000 Vietnamese.[66]

Besides Burma and Laos, a third Southeast Asian GIDO operation involved the pro-U.S. Montagnards in South Vietnam, whose loyalty was to some extent bought by Air America assistance in bringing the Montagnards' opium crop to the world market.[67] Mafioso Santos Trafficante, fresh from his covert work against Cuba, was also a key organizer of this drug network.[68] The multiple purposes of the drug smuggling were to gain the favor of opium growers, to generate funds for the secret operations themselves, and to gain personal profit. The networks created by GIDO operations formed the basis of Rollnet: U.S. military and intelligence personnel, contra armies, airlines, banks, arms, and drug dealers.

The drug trade run through Air America blossomed. As well as supplying the habits of the addicts that at one point comprised over 5 percent of the U.S. armed forces, heroin from the "Golden Triangle" came home to hook tens of thousands of U.S. citizens. Most of the drugs came through Florida via anti-Castro Cuban networks working with the Trafficante organization, with Trafficante himself visiting Southeast Asia to coordinate the setting up of regional heroin factories to supplement the Corsican networks that heretofore had provided the only source of street heroin.[69]

With the fall of the Saigon regime in 1975, the covert assets that had been carefully nurtured over the years were removed for future use. Under the direction of Assistant Secretary of Defense Erich von Marbod and the CIA apparatus headed by Shackley, millions of dollars worth of arms and profits from the heroin trade were transferred out of Vietnam. Money was deposited in secret accounts around the world. Of special note was the use of the Nugan Hand Bank in Australia, which would provide a secret source of funding over the next few years for U.S. covert operations, including the destabilization of the Australian Labor Party and possibly the South Africa-backed Savimbi insurgency in Angola.[70]

Nugan Hand's connection with the entire Rollnet web is underscored by the people intimately involved with its activities. Individuals associated with the bank included Theodore Shackley, Thomas Clines, and Edwin Wilson, later convicted of selling arms to Libya. The president of the bank, which stole the savings of low-level military personnel, was retired Rear Adm. "Buddy" Yates, who had been the chief of staff for planning for U.S. forces in Asia and the Pacific. The head of the bank's Hawaiian operations was retired Gen. Edwin Black, who had been the commander of U.S. troops in Thailand as well as assistant army chief of staff in the Pacific. Former CIA Director William Colby served as a lawyer for Nugan Hand. The bank reportedly laundered money for Suharto of Indonesia, provided services for Marcos of the Philippines, and assisted the Shah in shifting money out of Iran.[71]

Southeast Asia, then, was the cradle of the global rollback network. Close behind in importance was Latin America, in particular the operations involving Cuba.

The Latin American Death Squad Network

Eight major rollback operations have been mounted in Latin America since World War II: Guatemala in 1954, Cuba in 1961 (failed),

Brazil in 1964, Dominican Republic in 1965, Chile in 1973, Jamaica in 1980, Grenada in 1983, and Nicaragua in 1981-present. In addition, large counterinsurgency campaigns have been conducted in Guatemala, El Salvador, Argentina, Uruguay, and elsewhere. In most of these nations, various elements of the global rollback network have been in evidence. We will describe only a few examples.

Guatemala

The overthrow of the Arbenz government in 1954 involved a full-scale psychological warfare campaign organized by Guatemala CIA station chief E. Howard Hunt. Bombing raids were carried out by Civil Air Transport planes flown by Nationalist Chinese pilots. Following the coup, U.S.-picked Colonel Castillo Armas took over the government. The Guatemalan episode saw the cooperation of neighboring allied dictatorships that prefigured the later campaigns against Cuba and Nicaragua. Somoza's Nicaragua was used for training the insurgents and they staged their invasion from Honduras. Howard Hunt built upon this relationship to organize the Interamerican Council for the Defense of the Continent (CIADC), the first Latin American affiliate of APACL, in Mexico City in 1954.

Castillo Armas' personal secretary was Mario Sandoval Alarcon, the future "godfather" of the Guatemalan death squads. By the late 1950s, Sandoval had become leader of the right-wing party the National Liberation Movement (MLN), which in the 1960s initiated the death squads to eliminate any serious opposition to military rule. By 1970, it was difficult to distinguish the death squads from the Guatemalan military. One observer explained: "People ask if the death squads are controlled by the Army. They are the Army."[72]

Sandoval has reportedly worked for the CIA, and the CIA was involved in the creation of the Guatemalan death squads.[73] Sandoval also had close ties with Taiwan and arranged for fifty to seventy Guatemalan officers to receive training at the Political Warfare Cadres Academy there. Sandoval was also head of the Guatemalan chapter of WACL and helped create a death squad apparatus in El Salvador and Honduras.[74] During the Carter administration, aid to Guatemala was cut off as a result of the unfettered death squad activities; in 1979, Generals Singlaub and Graham headed an American Security Council delegation to Guatemala with the aim of re-establishing U.S. aid. By 1980, aid to Guatemala had become an interest of the U.S. New Right. Leaders from the Heritage Foundation, Moral Majority, Young Americans for Freedom, and the Conservative Caucus visited Guatemala. Ronald

Reagan is reported to have received an estimated $10 million in campaign contributions from rightist Guatemalans,[75] and Sandoval "mixed with the Reagan inner circle during inauguration week."[76]

Cuba

Rollnet cadres involved in planning the overthrow of Fidel Castro included Ted Shackley and Thomas Clines, who ran the CIA office overseeing the Bay of Pigs invasion and the susequent secret war against Castro. Central European ex-Nazis helped train the Cubans for the Bay of Pigs.[77] Paul Helliwell's Sea Supply Corporation and Castle Bank were used in the financing of the Cuban operations.[78]

It was during the anti-Castro operations, organized by the CIA's largest station in the world, that numerous right-wing Cubans received training that would provide an indispensible reserve for U.S. covert activities in years to come. Cuban contra veterans have seen action in the Congo, South America, Southeast Asia, Southern Africa, the Middle East, not to mention the Watergate complex in Washington, D.C. With the winding-down of the CIA station in 1965, many of these Cubans were set loose, and some used their talents in the netherworld of crime, drugs and right-wing politics.[79] A number of anti-Castro Cubans had been criminal elements, running prostitution and gambling rackets for the Mafia under the pre-Castro Batista regime; this involvement persisted in the United States. According to the book *The Fish is Red,* a great deal of evidence implicates a coalition of Cuban contras and the Mafia in the events surrounding President John Kennedy's assassination.[80] In the attempts to assassinate Castro, the CIA worked directly with organized crime figures Sam Giancana, Johnny Roselli, and Santos Trafficante, Mafia boss of Southern Florida.[81] While these activities were intermittently prosecuted by U.S. authorities, in the main the Cubans continued to support the larger aims of U.S. policy in the hemisphere and elsewhere. The Cuban contras were a disposal problem, but a useful disposal problem indeed.

It is useful to review the careers of two active members of the Bay of Pigs graduating class. Cuban contra Felix Rodriguez worked under Shackley and Clines in Southeast Asia, setting up the secret army in Laos. He also served in the Congo in 1965 to help mercenaries supporting pro-U.S. Mobutu against an insurrection. Afterwards he spearheaded CIA efforts to track down Che Guevara in Bolivia, and was at Guevara's interrogation before his murder. (Rodriguez reportedly wears Guevara's watch today.) Rodriguez went back to Vietnam as a counterinsurgency expert, working under Shackley after the latter became CIA station chief for South Vietnam. In 1981, he served in the CIA-supported Nicaraguan contra training camp run by the Argentinians in Honduras, and at the time of Contragate was in charge of logistics at the Salvadoran Ilopongo airbase supplying the contras.[82]

The second Contragate figure, Luis Posada, supposedly took part in a CIA-inspired assassination attempt against Castro in 1971. He has been identified as a member of Operation 40, an elite force recruited by the CIA, which had to be closed down after one of its planes crashed with several kilos of cocaine and heroin aboard. Posada's close friend and Operation 40 member Eugenio Martinez was arrested as one of the Watergate burglars and later pardoned by President Reagan.[83] In 1976, Posada attended the founding meeting of the Congress of United Revolutionary Organizations (CORU), a Cuban terrorist alliance supported by the Chilean and Argentine dictatorships. CORU was financed by gunrunning and narcotics trafficking. One of the organizations working in CORU was the Cuban terrorist group Alpha 66, which was closely connected with WACL.[84] Posada and fellow Cuban Orlando Bosch were indicted in Venezuela for the 1976 bombing of a Cubana Airlines plane, killing seventy-three people.[85] After getting out of prison, Posada ended up at Ilopongo with Felix Rodriguez to help supply the Nicaraguan contras.

Chile

Two assassinations following the Chilean coup of 1973 demonstrate the international workings of Rollnet. The Pinochet dictatorship that took over after the coup initiated Operation Condor to coordinate the security forces of Latin American right-wing governments, enabling them to hunt down their enemies. After Condor was dismantled as an official operation, its work was contracted to private groups including WACL. This international murder network was responsible for the 1975 assassination of an anti-Pinochet Chilean, Bernardo Leighton; the killing was planned by the Chilean government, carried out by a Cuban contra group, and took place in Italy.[86] The following year, anti-Pinochet Chilean Orlando Letelier was assassinated in Washington, D.C. by a mix of Rollnet actors: the crime was ordered by the Chilean dictatorship and carried out by Cuban contras assisted by a member of the Mafia-connected Italian fascist group P-2. One of the chief right-wing groups behind the 1973 Chilean coup was *Patria y Libertad,* which apparently gained the contacts needed to undertake these assassinations under the auspices of WACL.[87]

El Salvador

El Salvador has suffered heavily under the influence of Rollnet. Maj. Roberto d'Aubuisson, trained at the Political Warfare Academy in Taiwan, and his ARENA Party bore a remarkable resemblance to Chiang Kai-shek's Kuomintang.[88] Guatemala's Mario Sandoval Alarcon took d'Aubuisson as his protégé, reorganized and assisted the Salvadoran death squads which are widely believed to be led by d'Aubuisson.[89] Through WACL, Sandoval recruited fifty Argentine military advisors, veterans of the Argentine fascist terror campaign of the late 1970s, to assist in training Salvadoran death squads.[90]

According to former U.S. Ambassador to El Salvador Robert White, testifying before the House Subcommittee on Western Hemispheric Affairs,

> From the first day in office, the Reagan White House knew—beyond any reasonable doubt—that Roberto d'Aubuisson planned and ordered the assassination of Archbishop Oscar Arnulfo Romero.... The administration of President Carter classified ex-Maj. Roberto d'Aubuisson, accurately, as a terrorist, a murderer, and a leader of death squads.[91]

In November 1987, Salvadoran President Jose Napolean Duarte formally accused d'Aubuisson of planning the Romero murder.[92] But death squads were no obstacle to d'Aubuisson's gaining respectability in Rollnet circles, not only through WACL, but also via the U.S. New Right, to which he became something of a hero. Sen. Jesse Helms and New Right organizer Paul Weyrich have been d'Aubuisson supporters, as is the American Security Council where d'Aubuisson has given two speeches.[93]

The El Salvador-Guatemala-Argentina death squad nexus did become an image problem for WACL in the early 1980s, in part due to a Jack Anderson column linking WACL's Latin American affiliate CAL (Latin American Anti-Communist Confederation) with death squads. WACL chairman Singlaub wrote to right-wing journalist Reed Irvine, now head of Accuracy in Media, asking for help in combating the Jack Anderson "articles which link WACL with the death squad activity."[94]

Argentina

The period of military terror in Argentina in the late 1970s is often called the "dirty war." The repression of any liberal or left-wing dissent led to an estimated 9,000 people murdered or disappeared. The Argentine government joined Chile, Guatemala, and El Salvador as a death squad regime. In doing so, it became a positive example to CAL, WACL's Latin American branch.[95] Argentine interrogators and torture specialists, coordinated through CAL, taught their methods to other Latin militaries. The Argentines, working with the CIA, were also the first to train the Nicaraguan contras.

The Argentine junta also had a connection with European fascism and the Mafia through the Italian-Argentine Masonic lodge P-2, which supported the junta. P-2 veteran Stefano delle Chiaie was involved in the murder of Chilean Orlando Letelier, helped train death squads in El Salvador, and his associate Klaus Barbie provided German and Austrian gunmen for death squad operations.[96]

In Latin America, the global rollback network shows its true face: death squads, tortures, terrorism, repression—all coordinated with European and Asian links. In the 1980s, the Nicaraguan contras were trained by the death squad organizers of the 1970s to become—as Chapter Four will show—a celebrated death squad of the 1980s.

Rollnet Reaches Southern Africa

In Southern Africa, U.S. goals have been to keep the region pro-Western without appearing too closely linked with South Africa, an international outlaw because of its apartheid policies, but also the dominant regional power. One mechanism for carrying out this policy has been to utilize Rollnet in implementing U.S. objectives, enabling the official U.S. position to appear at least mildly critical of South Africa.

Besides South Africa, the Belgian Congo was important as a large nation that gained independence in 1960. Now named Zaire, this nation fought a post-independence struggle in which the United States helped eliminate popular leader Patrice Lumumba. But after a pro-U.S. government had been installed, insurgency continued, and the CIA brought in its Bay of Pigs Cuban veterans and South Africans to put down the rebellion.[97] By 1965, Zaire was safely in the hands of dictator Mobutu Sese Seko. The United States now had friends at both the northern and southern ends of the Southern African region.

When revolutions erupted in the Portuguese colonies of Angola, Mozambique, and Guinea-Bissau, the United States provided counterinsurgency assistance to the Portuguese Salazar dictatorship.[98] Cuban Bay of Pigs veterans flew missions for the Portuguese.[99] At the same time—playing both sides of the field so as to win whatever the outcome—the

CIA kept insurgent leaders Holden Roberto (Mobutu's son-in-law) and Jonas Savimbi on retainer.[100]

With the 1974 revolt of progressive officers against the decades-old Salazar dictatorship, the colonialist war in Africa was effectively over. The United States authorized about $30 million through the CIA to unseat the Popular Movement for the Liberation of Angola (MPLA).[101] Finally, Sen. Dick Clark succeeded in passing an amendment forbidding covert actions in Angola, thereby forcing the United States to rely on South Africa to carry on.

South Africa, with tacit collusion of the United States, permitted terrorist attacks against the leftist government of Mozambique, and propped up the Savimbi insurgency in Angola, possibly aided by secret funds flowing from the coffers of the Nugan Hand Bank. As we noted earlier, South Africa spent considerable sums attempting to defeat Senator Clark and to reverse U.S. public opinion.[102] The upshot of these activities was that the newly independent governments of Southern Africa were the first to suffer the effects of modern *contra* war, presaging the future unleashing of the Reagan Doctrine on the Third World.

Rollnet Profiteering in the Middle East

Only a few points will be made about the enormously complex Middle East. First, this region contained three important pro-U.S. nations: Iran prior to the fall of the Shah in 1979, Saudi Arabia, and Israel. Even before the Soviet invasion of Afghanistan, the Shah and the Saudis were aiding the Afghan rebels against the pro-Soviet regime.

Second, these three Middle East nations were closely linked with the U.S. military-industrial complex. Because Israel received billions of dollars each year in military aid, it bought many weapons from the United States. Because the Shah's Iran and Saudi Arabia were rich, oil-producing nations, they could afford billions in arms purchases. In just one of many arms deals, Rockwell International, assisted by the CIA, paid large bribes to the Shah's air force commander (and brother-in-law) to gain approval to sell to Iran a $500 million electronic spying and communication system of little value. Admiral Thomas Moorer, on the board of directors of the American Security Council, was also involved in a major arms transaction with the Shah, as was Richard Secord, who at that time headed the Pentagon's military assistance program to Iran.[103]

Third, it was in the money-laden labyrinth of the Middle East that profit came close to exceeding anticommunism as motivation for some

Rollnet operatives. Ted Shackley, Thomas Clines, Richard Secord, and Edwin Wilson had formed the private firm EATSCO to transport arms to Egypt, a deal that allegedly skimmed $8 million from U.S. government funds. Center for Strategic and International Studies "intellectual" Michael Ledeen intervened on behalf of Shackley and Secord in this case.[104] Secord and Oliver North had also been involved in the $3.5 billion AWACS radar plane sales to the Saudis, following which Saudi funds were sent to the Nicaraguan contras.[105]

For most of these operatives/entrepreneurs, patriotism and profit were designed to overlap. But for Edwin Wilson, this may not have been the case. Wilson was convicted of supplying Libya's Qaddafi with advanced explosives, timing devices, and military training.[106] Regarding Contragate, Wilson has said, "If I wasn't in jail I'd have headed up this operation."

Poised and Ready

By 1980, the global rollback network was poised and ready for action. They had a candidate, Ronald Reagan, with many Rollnet ties. The military-industrial complex wing of Rollnet led by CPD had scored major victories against the SALT II arms control pact and in favor of greater military budgets. Revolutionary changes on three continents had spawned resistance movements that tied into Rollnet. Old time CIA operatives and Cuban exiles felt betrayed, abandoned, and unemployed by the Carter administration and were mad. And the actions of the Soviet Union in Afghanistan, plus the taking of hostages in Iran, created the ideal climate for a resurgence of global rollback.

During this transition period, the global rollback network was very active both in lobbying for the U.S. government to support their causes and in modernizing their networks. Less than two months after Ronald Reagan's inauguration, Rollnet was back in business.

The Reagan Doctrine: Third World Rollback

Nowhere is rollback more evident than in U.S. policy toward the Third World. Third World rollback has come to be named the *Reagan Doctrine*. However, it is inaccurate to attribute this Doctrine solely to Ronald Reagan or the Right. Third World rollback in the 1980s is little more than an extension of postwar era policy. As the preceding chapters show, this policy transcends which party holds the office of president or the balance of power in Congress.

In this chapter we will make the following points: 1) The Reagan Doctrine affirms that Third World rollback is justified as the American contribution to a *worldwide democratic revolution;* but in fact, the major groups supported by the Reagan Doctrine are anything but democratic. 2) Third World rollback plus Third World containment are being carried out through a total program of political, economic, military and psychological warfare called *"low intensity" conflict.* 3) The right wing was unable to pressure the Reagan administration into pursuing comprehensive Third World rollback on every possible front because such a policy is not realistic.

Roots of the Reagan Doctrine

As Chapter One shows, U.S. government policy in the 1945-1980 period was containment *vis-a-vis* the USSR and rollback toward the Third World. In the late 1970s, intense pressure built from the global rollback network, particularly the military-industrial complex and ex-CIA operatives, to reinstate a more aggressive foreign policy. Around 1980, the right wing publicly formulated a resurgent *global rollback* doctrine meant to supplant rather than supplement containment. The rallying cry for the new rollback came from the Committee of Santa Fe:

> Containment of the Soviet Union is not enough…. It is time to sound a clarion call for freedom, dignity and national self interest which will echo the spirit of the people of the United States. Either a Pax Sovietica or a worldwide counter-projection of American power is in the offing. The hour of decision can no longer be postponed.[1]

If the Santa Fe Committee was the cheerleader of the rollback team and Rollnet cadres the players, the Expanding Soviet Empire (ExSET) theorists were its coaches. According to ExSET, since the Soviet Union is relentlessly expanding, it takes rollback (offense), not simply containment (defense), to bring victory. Because rollback of the USSR itself was not immediately feasible, the Reagan Doctrine came to mean the rollback of the outposts of the Soviet Empire in the Third World as a first step toward global rollback.

An ExSET intellectual who made rollback politically respectable was neoconservative Jeane Kirkpatrick. She argued in 1979 that Third World revolutions are illegitimate, the products of Soviet expansion rather than of local historical forces opposed to repressive dictatorships. It should be noted that nowhere in her famous *Dictatorships and Double Standards* does Kirkpatrick empirically prove that left-wing regimes are more repressive than right-wing dictatorships. Notwithstanding this factual weakness, Kirkpatrick had solved the moral problem of the rollbackers: why it is fine to overthrow left-wing governments and make friends with rightist dictators. The Kirkpatrick Doctrine held that right-wing dictatorships can evolve into democratic governments while left-wing nations cannot.[2] Under this Doctrine, Marcos, Pinochet, and P.W. Botha were leading their countries down the path to democracy.

With global rollback newly respectable, it was the Heritage Foundation that translated theory into concrete policy. Heritage targeted nine nations for rollback: Afghanistan, Angola, Cambodia, Ethiopia, Iran, Laos, Libya, Nicaragua, and Vietnam.[3]

The Reagan government's initial implementation of the Heritage plan was done covertly, following the longstanding custom that containment can be overt but rollback should be covert. In March 1981,

CIA Director William Casey presented proposals for covert actions against Nicaragua, Afghanistan, Laos, Cambodia, Grenada, Iran, Libya, and Cuba.[4] On March 9, 1981, six weeks after taking office, Reagan authorized covert military actions against the Nicaraguan government, and on December 1, 1981, he signed a covert action plan calling for the creation of a 500-commando force and the expenditure of $19 million to conduct paramilitary operations against Nicaragua.[5] On March 19, 1981, Reagan formally asked Congress to repeal the 1976 Clark Amendment prohibiting U.S. aid to the rebels attempting to overthrow the government in Angola. The CIA reportedly violated the Clark ban by training, funding, and arming the rebels.[6] The Reagan administration increased the covert supply of arms to the resistance in Afghanistan, a policy begun in the Carter administration.[7] In December 1982, the CIA informed Congress that the Nicaraguan commandos, called counterrevolutionaries or "contras" by the Sandinistas, had grown to 4,000 men.[8] By late 1982, the U.S. media reported that the goal of Reagan's Nicaragua policy was indeed rollback: the overthrow of the Sandinista government.[9] In 1984, Congress repealed the Clark Amendment; in 1985 and 1986, the administration provided $15 million per year for Jonas Savimbi's Angolan insurgents. The number of covert actions jumped from a dozen small ones in 1980, to about forty major operations in 1986.[10]

In all probability, the Reagan government was planning to keep its rollback operations covert, but leaks in Washington made that option impossible. On May 4, 1983, Reagan officially made the Nicaraguan venture public, calling the contras "freedom fighters," but he stopped short of admitting his rollback goal.[11] On October 25, 1983, 1,900 U.S. troops invaded Grenada; the first edge of the evil empire had been unraveled.

The Selling of Rollback as "Democracy"

When Ronald Reagan entered the White House, his policy appeared to fit the historic scenario of anti-communist military interventions of containment and rollback, both covert and overt, and support for pro-U.S. right-wing dictatorships. This traditional "support your local dictator" policy had a new intellectual rationale: the Kirkpatrick Doctrine, mentioned above. But even with Kirkpatrick's intellectual blessings, this classic right-wing policy ran into major roadblocks.

In Nicaragua, the covert rollback activities were unearthed, and such CIA actions as the mining of the harbors became embarrassments. Counterinsurgency in El Salvador was seen as propping up a regime condoning death squads. "Constructive engagement" in South Africa was attacked by the president's own party as incompatible with the gaining of any black domestic electoral support. And the growing unpopularity of the Philippines' Marcos, which was spawning an increasingly strong leftist insurgency, reminded too many people of Somoza and the Shah. The final blow was the 1984 congressional cutoff of aid to the Nicaraguan contras.

To meet this crisis of foreign policy legitimacy, the administration brought out its modern version of an old ideological weapon: democracy. The test case was El Salvador. The administration needed a Salvadoran president to be elected with a "moderate" image who would be acceptable to a Congress that was balking on the provision of military aid. José Napoleon Duarte was the man, and after his 1984 election—in which the United States provided funds on his behalf—Duarte came to Washington to be hailed as the answer for democracy in Central America. A few days later, Congress approved $61.7 million in military and economic aid for El Salvador.

Nicaragua presented more problems. Initially the U.S.-run contra operation was covert, but by 1982, its cover had been blown. The operation was then justified as simply the interdiction of Nicaraguan arms to the guerrillas in El Salvador. But in 1984, former CIA Central America analyst David MacMichael revealed that this rationale was bogus.[12] The explanation for the aggression against Nicaragua then became the need to pressure the Sandinistas to negotiate. But again credibility was lost when it was the United States who did not negotiate. A new justification was needed.

In February 1985, Reagan met the problem head on. Starting in his State of the Union address, escalating in a radio message, and peaking at a press conference, he proudly stated what everyone knew: his policy was to support "freedom fighters" trying to overthrow Third World "communist tyranny."[13] This was the Reagan Doctrine: overt and unashamed support for Third World rollback.

How was the Reagan Doctrine different from the multiple well-known interventions by the United States in the past? In many respects, it was a continuation of selective rollback, but there were some changes. First, it was not simply case-by-case intervention, but a worldwide rollback policy whose aim was to shrink the "Soviet empire" at its periphery. Second, it was an openly stated policy, a clear difference from previous rollback activities that had generally been covert and denied. Third, its justification went beyond the negative goal of defeating communism and took the moral high ground by espousing worldwide democracy.

This was not the first time the United States used democracy to promote interventionist actions. Truman's March 12, 1947 speech announcing the Truman Doctrine pledged, "it must be the policy of the United States to support free peoples who are resisting attempted subjugation...." Kennedy similarly pledged to "bear any burden...to assure...the success of liberty." Over the past twenty years, the national platforms of both the Democratic and Republican parties have given prominence to the strengthening of freedom worldwide.

But apart from such general rhetoric, a look at specific interventions shows that the usual justification was not the establishment of democracies but the overthrow of "communists." Guatemala was an elected democracy in 1954; that year, the United States put a military regime into power. In Vietnam, the United States supported the cancellation of the 1956 elections and backed one after another repressive South Vietnamese leader who took power through coups and assassinations.[14] The 1965 Dominican Republic intervention (to prevent a previously elected president from re-assuming power after he had been ousted by a coup) was initially justified as protecting U.S. citizens from civil unrest and later was sold to the public as a necessary act to prevent a new communist state in the hemisphere.[15] Chile's Allende was democratically elected and the United States covertly installed a bloody military dictatorship in his place in 1973. It was simply not credible to mouth "democracy" and then install a military dictator.

Prior to the Vietnam War, the justification of anti-communism was sufficient to sell foreign interventions to the U.S. population and to the non-communist world. In the 1970s, with the Vietnam Syndrome at home and the decline of U.S. influence abroad, this argument no longer worked. Large percentages of the population opposed military involvement in Southern Africa and Central America. Foreign policy analysts and policymakers, aware of the potency of the Vietnam Syndrome in the United States were—according to 1976 and 1980 surveys—strongly split over whether the United States should take an interventionary posture in the world.[16] Thus, under the guise of supporting a genuine Third World movement for democracy, the Reagan administration tried to make the policy of global rollback respectable. The U.S. government can no longer get away with the crushing of democracy around the world directly; to justify its actions it now works with authentic democratic movements or graces its rollback actions with the terminology of democracy.

While in the long run, the new reliance on "democracy" was designed to help solve the problem of the Vietnam Syndrome, in the short run, "democracy" was to get Democratic congressional support for Reagan's policies in El Salvador and Nicaragua. Rather than trying to hide its support for the Nicaraguan contras, the Reagan administration was now proudly trumpeting its support for them as freedom fighters, the moral equivalent of Thomas Jefferson and George Washington.[17] The Reagan Doctrine spells it out: it is OK to overthrow governments we call communist. In fact, it is our responsibility to do so.[18]

The Success of
the Democracy Argument

Reagan hit the jackpot with his worldwide "democratic revolution." Most of the right wing accepted the argument, as did center and center-right Democrats. In the Contragate hearings, the terminology "freedom fighters" was applied to the Nicaraguan contras by Congressional interrogators and witnesses alike as though this designation was an established fact.

Speaking for the right wing, Jeane Kirkpatrick has said, "The point of departure of Reagan Doctrine...is the idea of freedom." Right-wing presidential candidate Jack Kemp wrote that the guiding force in U.S. foreign policy is to protect freedom where it exists, and to advance freedom where it is denied.[19] Right-wing ideologue and Reagan consultant Michael Ledeen has stated that the organizing theme of U.S. foreign policy must be to support the movement for a democratic revolution around the world.[20]

Some far rightists did not support the democracy adventure if it meant challenging dictators who were Rollnet actors. Democracy was a slap in the face to much of the World Anti-Communist League (WACL), an organization including ex-Nazis, death squad organizers, and right-wing dictators. Sen. Jesse Helms chastised the State Department for its (mild) criticisms of the Pinochet government in Chile. The right-wing periodical *Human Events* strongly supported South Africa, calling it a "pro-Western bulwark that provides more in the way of freedom and wealth to its blacks than the vast majority of black African states."[21]

Some would have preferred death squad organizer Roberto d'Aubuisson over moderate Duarte as El Salvador's president. But more and more of the Right came to support the Reagan administration on this issue.

The Democrats bought Reagan's newly found commitment to democracy *en masse*. They began to support Reagan on El Salvador after the Duarte election.[22] In 1983 and 1984, House and Senate Democrats voted three times by margins of more than 75 percent to prohibit aid to the contras. In 1985 and 1986, when the contras were transformed into founding fathers and freedom fighters battling the Reagan-labeled "totalitarian dungeon" of Nicaragua, the Democrats became more positive toward contra aid. The Democratic Policy Commission, composed of centrist Democrats, stated, "The promotion of our democratic principles is one of the most effective ways of protecting our strategic interests."[23]

Is "Democracy" New Policy or New Rhetoric?

Is the verbal support for freedom and democracy simply a justification for U.S.-supported insurgencies or is it an actual change in policy? *The New Republic,* which supports the Reagan Doctrine, sees a real change:

> The Reagan Doctrine has a Philippine corollary.... President Reagan's March 14 [1986] message to Congress on regional conflicts amplifies the doctrine. And it adds a corollary pledging 'to oppose tyranny in whatever form, whether of the left or the right.' The struggle for democracy, it seems, is to be supported not only in Communist countries but also in right-wing dictatorships.[24]

In *The New Republic's* view, this policy started with El Salvador, then was applied in Haiti and the Philippines. It was then initiated in Chile by mild U.S. pressure against Pinochet. The Reagan administration seemed to recognize that dictatorships (even Kirkpatrick's "good" dictatorships) do not serve U.S. long-term interests.[25]

How much the "Philippine Corollary" is a true change in Reagan policy is questionable.[26] The timing of Reagan's March 14, 1986 statement was no accident; it was to bolster contra aid by putting it in the context of a global pro-democratic strategy. The United States abandoned the dictatorships in Haiti and the Philippines less as a great gesture for freedom and more as a rat leaving two sinking ships. *New York Times* writer Bernard Weinraub observed, "Mr. Reagan seemed to be saying that the United States will promote ballots for dealing with right-wing regimes, such as Mr. Marcos's in the Philippines, but bullets for left-wing dictatorships like that in Nicaragua."[27] While the March 14 statement may have meant little change in policy, it marked a major potential domestic development: the post-Marcos Reagan Doctrine attempted to revive the bipartisan foreign policy consensus that was weakened by the Vietnam War.

A 1986 *Wall Street Journal* article cites the conservative authority Robert Tucker of the Johns Hopkins School of Advanced International Studies: "What is happening in this country is the reconstitution of the consensus in foreign policy." Tucker argues that portions of the right wing have moved away from their Marcoses, D'Aubuissons, and Bothas while liberal Democrats have become more willing to project U.S. power in the world.[28] Whether or not the Reagan administration believed its espousal of democracy as the goal of foreign policy, many other government officials and news analysts moved toward that position.

What Kind of Democracy?

What are the characteristics of Reagan Doctrine democracy? For the far Right, democracy is equivalent to Kirkpatrick's authoritarian regimes. Michael Ledeen, who writes about the importance of the Reagan Doctrine as part of the worldwide "democratic revolution," believes that "in the context of the Middle East, Iran was a remarkably decent place" under the Shah. He adds, "The Salvadoran army has been a driving force behind the successful democratization of the country."[29] Democracy crusader Ledeen has also advocated the assassination of Sandinista leaders in Nicaragua.[30]

It may not be surprising that the right wing makes the simple equation between democracy and anti-communism. More disturbing is that in the case of the Nicaraguan contras, most Republicans and Democrats have stripped the word democracy of all its meaning. The Contragate hearings were devoid of any investigation into the actual practices of the contras.

Democracy and the Contras

The Nicaraguan contras are the prototype "freedom fighters," leaders in the worldwide democratic revolution. What is the nature of the democracy they practice?

Arturo Cruz was one of the three leaders of the contra movement from 1985 until he resigned on March 9, 1987. Upon his resignation he condemned the Reagan administration for allowing the contras to be controlled by military commanders and right-wing politicians originally chosen by the CIA. He called the contra leaders puppets of the United States, and said it was impossible to turn the contras into a democratic movement.[31]

Edgar Chamorro is a former member of the directorate of the main contra organization, the Nicaraguan Democratic Force (FDN). In a 1986 interview, Chamorro said he "resigned rather than continue as a Central Intelligence Agency puppet." Citing a U.S. congressional study of April 1985, that forty-six of the forty-eight positions in the FDN's military leadership were held by ex-Somoza National Guardsmen, he stated:

> It is a gross fabrication to claim that the 'contras' are composed of 'democratic groups'.... As I can attest, the 'contra' military force is directed and controlled by officers of Somoza's National Guard.... During my four years as a 'contra' director, it was premeditated policy to terrorize civilian noncombatants to prevent them from cooperating with the Government. Hundreds of civilian murders, tortures and rapes were committed in pursuit of this policy, of which the 'contra' leaders and their CIA superiors were well aware.[32]

Oliver North's aide Robert W. Owen wrote a memo to North in March 1986, calling contra leader Adolfo Calero a "creation" of the U.S. government. Owen said that Calero surrounded himself with aides who were "liars and greed- and power-motivated," adding, "This war has become a business to many of them." Regarding contra aid in 1986, Owen wrote that without improvements it "will be like pouring money down a sinkhole."[33]

The contras' terrorist methods have been directly taught by the United States. The CIA manual *Psychological Operations in Guerrilla War,* written for the contras, includes sections on "implicit and explicit terror" including "neutralizing" Sandinista officials and coercing individuals to join the contras.

On October 13, 1983, Oliver North's heroes in the "Nicaraguan democratic resistance" attacked the town of Pantasma, murdering forty-seven people. There was not one target of military significance in Pantasma. In November 1984, these same contras attacked the coffee farm La Sorpresa, killing seventeen residents including four women and two children. During the contra raid on El Nispero on November 9, 1986, two Sandinista soldiers, two elderly women, a young mother, and two infants were killed. On June 18, 1987, a band of contras attacked a farming settlement in eastern Nicaragua killing eight civilians and wounding ten others.[34] Episodes of this nature have been documented over and over since 1983.

Human rights groups and journalists from the United States have reported the regular occurrence of contras going to people's houses to kill entire families. This practice is not mindless brutality. Because the contras are not popular in Nicaragua, they are forced to kill civilians they think are pro-Sandinista to prevent those civilians from reporting their location to the Nicaraguan army. The United States cannot simply tell the contras to clean up their human rights act; the brutality is necessary for their survival.[35]

When Congress granted the contras $100 million in 1986, a portion of the funds were earmarked for the U.S.-created Nicaraguan Association for Human Rights. High-ranking contra commanders including contra military chief Enrique Bermudez have attempted to block the work of this organization, denying it information. In July 1987, the Association reported that the contras not only execute prisoners and murder civilians; they also forcibly kidnap Nicaraguan peasants as contra recruits.[36] The *New York Times* reported a mass kidnapping by the contras of fifteen to twenty Nicaraguans near the town of Siuna on April 27, 1987. At least 400 Nicaraguan families have had a relative kidnapped by the contras, and the practice was on the increase in 1987.[37]

Other "freedom fighters" around the world treat civilians similarly. On February 8, 1986, several hundred of Jonas Savimbi's Angolan insurgents (who were supported by South Africa and the CIA as far back as the 1975 Angolan war[38]) attacked Camabatela in northern Angola, killing 107 villagers, most of them civilians, including women and children. The insurgents routinely plant mines in farming areas to drive farmers off the land and reduce food production. Thousands of Angolan farmers have lost their legs from these mines.[39]

The Mozambican "freedom fighters" of the Mozambique National Resistance (Renamo) are another example of the right wing's worldwide democratic revolution. While they have not received direct U.S. government support, South Africa has been the key source of their arms, ammunition, and supplies. Renamo's Washington office shared an address with the Heritage Foundation. Tactics used by Renamo have included murdering civilians, capturing peasants and cutting off their ears, burning clinics and schools, attacking medical teams carrying out vaccination campaigns, and employing terror to drive farmers from their land thereby creating food shortages. A UNICEF report concluded that Renamo violence was the main cause of the famine that has killed 100,000 Mozambicans since 1983. In the summer of 1987, Renamo carried out two massacres killing over 400 people. Like the Nicaraguan contras, Renamo kidnapped civilians as a recruitment device. Renamo demolished 718 clinics and attacked twelve CARE food deliveries. The viciousness and common banditry of Renamo prevented even conservatives such as Margaret Thatcher and Ronald Reagan from supporting them. But right-wing pressure in 1987 brought Senate Minority Leader Robert Dole into the pro-Renamo camp.[40]

The U.S. government defines terrorists as individuals or groups seeking to further a political objective through violence, generally directed against innocent civilians.[41] The freedom fighters of the right wing's worldwide democratic revolution are not a democratic resistance; they are terrorists. In the case of the Nicaraguan contras, they are terrorists run by the U.S. government.

A Tale of Two Elections

For most people, the right wing included, elections are a major defining characteristic of democracy. According to Jeane Kirkpatrick, democratic governments are defined as "governments whose rulers are chosen in periodic, competitive elections that feature widespread suffrage, free speech, and free assembly."[42] This is a reasonable definition; however Kirkpatrick and her associates do not follow it. For the Right, elections are not valid if they are won by leftists. By these standards, the 1984 Nicaraguan elections were not legitimate, while the 1982 and 1984 Salvadoran elections were.

On November 4, 1984, Nicaragua held an election while under attack by the U.S.-directed contras. The United States had constantly criticized the Nicaraguan government for refusing to hold elections. But once the elections were called, the U.S. role was to sabotage the vote. According to John Oakes, former senior editor of the *New York Times,*

> The most fraudulent thing about the Nicaraguan election was the part the Reagan administration played in it. By their own admission, United States Embassy officials in Managua pressured opposition politicians to withdraw from the ballot in order to isolate

the Sandinistas and to discredit the regime...Instead of encouraging the democratic opposition to fight within the system, the Reagan administration did just the opposite. It tried to torpedo the election, thus helping to lose for its clients the considerable influence they otherwise would have had.[43]

In addition to the administration's political sabotage, the contras attempted military sabotage of the election. In Matagalpa they attacked voter registration tables, slit the throats of eight farmers in front of their families, and kidnapped fourteen others. In another town they murdered two people registering voters. Prior to the election they made numerous attacks on civilians and kidnapped Ray Hooker, a Sandinista candidate for National Assembly.[44]

In the election, the Sandinista presidential candidate Daniel Ortega won 67 percent of the vote, and sixty-one National Assembly seats went to the Sandinistas, with opposition parties receiving thirty-five seats. Many foreign observers were present during the election, and while some criticisms of the electoral process were made, the overall process was deemed to be fair. The prestigious Latin American Studies Association's observer team concluded that

> The Nicaraguan electoral law of 1984 provided a broad array of protections to assure fair access, procedural honesty, and an accurate vote count. The actual voting process was meticulously designed to minimize the potential for abuses. The vote was truly a secret ballot, and was generally perceived as such by voters. We observed no evidence of irregularities in the voting or vote-counting process.[45]

The Reagan administration's response to the election? It was called a sham. According to the *Washington Post,* a secret National Security Council document revealed that the U.S. goal all along had been to convince the world that the elections were illegitimate.[46] Immediately after the Nicaraguan election the United States fabricated a major news story about Soviet MiGs in Nicaragua, thereby blacking out any news on the election itself.

A comparison of the Salvadoran and the Nicaraguan elections, however, does not show a greater degree of democracy practiced in the former as compared with the latter:

- In Nicaragua, any opposition party could safely run candidates; those who did not participate made this choice themselves. In El Salvador, the center-left coalition was intimidated from participating by threats of assassination and reprisal.[47] Thus the range of choices to voters was far broader in Nicaragua than in El Salvador.

- In Nicaragua, people were free to abstain from voting, while in El Salvador voting was compulsory, and the government made statements that anyone not voting was committing an "act of treason."[48]

- In El Salvador the ballot boxes were transparent, thereby reducing secrecy; in Nicaragua this was not the case.[49]

- The United States interfered in both elections: in Nicaragua to coerce opposition parties not to participate; in El Salvador to ensure the victory of the centrist Duarte over the right-wing D'Aubuisson. For example, the CIA spent $2 million to assist Duarte in the 1984 election. The *Wall Street Journal* stated that such interference was "allowing the principle of free elections to be debased."[50]

There is no factual evidence that would lead any objective observer to annoint the Salvadoran election as democratic while condemning the Nicaraguan election as a sham. Yet the bipartisan consensus in the United States holds Nicaragua to be a totalitarian state while El Salvador is a democracy. During Contragate's congressional hearings, the foundation of Oliver North's activities—that Nicaragua is a totalitarian dictatorship—was never questioned.

Democracy and the Military

Many nations considered democracies by the Reagan administration do, indeed, contain strong democratic currents; however democracy is not an easy goal to achieve. Deficiencies present in "totalitarian" Nicaragua must be viewed in the context of similar deficiencies in countries labeled democracies. The topic of democracy and the Third World is an enormous one; for our purposes here we will simply look at a few examples from the nations most publicized by the Reagan Doctrinists as U.S.-inspired democracies—El Salvador, Guatemala, Haiti, South America in general, and the Philippines.

Freedom of the press is a major item in U.S. condemnations of Nicaragua. Until censorship relaxed in 1987, Nicaragua placed strict controls on its press, a situation engendered by the contra war. However, when have U.S. politicians condemned lack of free speech in El Salvador? Prior to the 1982 Salvadoran election, the only two Salvadoran newspapers critical of the government were closed, all remaining papers were subject to censorship, twenty-six journalists were murdered, and a death squad published a list of thirty-five more journalists targeted for assassination.[51]

Human rights is another important matter related to democracy, and a source of major criticism of Nicaragua by Republicans and Democrats alike. But according to the authoritative human rights organization Amnesty International, Nicaragua's main human rights violations were conducted by the contras, not the government.[52] El Salvador, on the other hand, was given the following description by Amnesty International in 1985:

> Amnesty International continued to be concerned about massive human rights violations, including arbitrary arrest and prolonged detention without trial, torture, 'disappearances,' and individual and mass extrajudicial executions...[done by] government forces, sometimes in uniform, and sometimes in plain clothes in the guise of so-called 'death squads'....[53]

Similarly with U.S. ally Guatemala:

> Amnesty International continued to be concerned that the regular security and military forces—as well as paramilitary groups acting under government orders or with official complicity (the so-called 'death squads')—were responsible for massive human rights violations, including arbitrary arrest, torture, 'disappearance' and extrajudicial executions.[54]

Amnesty International has estimated that 40,000 Salvadorans were murdered, mainly by government forces, between 1979 and 1984. This figure is confirmed by El Salvador's President Duarte.[55] For Guatemala, Amnesty International states that the government has killed tens of thousands of people since 1966.[56] The death squads in El Salvador, and possibly in Guatemala, were created with the assistance of the CIA and of Rollnet.[57] While Guatemala is touted as finally having elected a civilian government in 1986, U.S. Embassy sources say that 425 political assassinations were recorded by the local press in the first two months of 1987. After sixteen months in office, President Vinicio Cerezo had not managed to wrest significant power from the army.[58]

Fundamental to this anti-human rights tradition in Guatemala, El Salvador, and many democracy-seeking nations is the overriding power of the military. One senior Western diplomat in San Salvador claimed: "I would say that the biggest long-term threat to civilian government in El Salvador is the army, not the guerrillas." Central American analysts have made it clear that the governments there, including in El Salvador, are in power at the pleasure of their militaries, which have traditionally been anti-democratic, brutal, and corrupt.[59]

In Haiti, which the Reagan government claimed as one of its democratic triumphs, the military government that took over from dictator Duvalier was handpicked by Duvalier himself. Though U.S. policy toward Haiti has been publicly "to help Haiti move to democracy through elections," the United States has sent substantial military aid to this Duvalier-linked government. The November 1987 election was disrupted by murder and intimidation created by the government and by Duvalier's thugs, and was cancelled. When the farcical and fraudulent January 1988 election followed, the United States simply deplored the situation and extended an aid cutoff.[60] At the same time, the United States proceeded with its contra attacks on Nicaragua, a nation that did hold fair elections, the outcome of which the United States did not approve.

Secretary of State George Shultz boasted that more than nine-tenths of Latin America lived under democratic governments in 1985 compared with one-third in 1979.[61] In fact, this trend had little to do with the United States, and the Latin democracies have been extraordinarily fragile. *New York Times* editorials lament that from Argentina to Guatemala, elected officials are beholden to military officers and incipient democracies are slipping away. These realities were hidden by the Reagan government which wanted to splash its democratic accomplishments around the world.[62]

In the newly democratic Philippines, the military also holds the keys to the nation. At the time of this writing, President Aquino has already faced five attempted military coups, each one more serious than the last. The only thing keeping Aquino in power is the support of a portion of the army. If sufficient military forces join Aquino's opposition, democracy in the Philippines will prove to be shortlived.

To conclude the discussion of the Reagan Doctrine and Third World democracy, several points can be made: 1) The "freedom fighters" supported by the Reagan Doctrine have generally been terrorists without a popular base. 2) In some cases the Reagan administration lessened its support for right-wing leaders in the Third World, backing Aquino rather than Marcos, Duarte rather than d'Aubuisson. 3) This move toward Third World democracy was done for pragmatic reasons rather than love of freedom: in El Salvador and Guatemala, to enable military and economic aid to get through Congress; in Haiti and the Philippines to gain more control over anti-dictator movements on the verge of success so as not to "lose" those nations as Iran and Nicaragua were "lost" in 1979. 4) U.S. support for democratic developments in the Third World (for example the Philippines and South Korea) was more a reaction to world events beyond U.S. control than a U.S.-generated policy. The United States did not initiate most of these developments, though Reagan enjoyed taking credit for them. 5) Third World democracies are often fragile, operating at the whim of their militaries. 6) Many right-wing dictatorships are still supported by the United States, such as Pakistan, Saudi Arabia, and Indonesia. 7) The main goal of the United States in the Third World is to maintain imperial control. As we will see later in this chapter, Third World democracy can be useful in the prosecution of "low intensity" counter-insurgency warfare. Democratic governments with submerged control by the military can be more effective than overt military dictatorships in combatting popular movements seen as unfriendly to U.S. interests.

The Global Rollback Network Implements the Reagan Doctrine

In 1980, the global rollback network was primed for action. With the accession of Ronald Reagan to the presidency in 1981, Rollnet seemed to have unambiguous support at the highest levels of the government. President Reagan depended on right-wing think tanks for his foreign policy advice, and when Reverend Moon's *Washington Times* started up in 1982, Reagan relied on it to keep up with the news. Rollnet intellectuals thought up the Reagan Doctrine and Rollnet operatives made it happen.

Central to the global rollback network is the CIA. Between 1981 and 1984, the CIA's budget more than doubled. CIA personnel saw a one-third increase, placing the agency back near its Vietnam era strength. Eight hundred of the 2,800 CIA officers who left the agency between 1977 and 1981 were hired back on short-term contracts.[63] In addition, throughout the Reagan presidency, the CIA drew on the expertise of the covert cadre veterans of the past. As we saw in Chapter Three, this grouping could be counted on to conduct rollback actions through private companies, using well-hidden methods to raise funds both for the covert operations and for their own personal enrichment. The Reagan government needed supersecrecy because in the 1970s, Congress had acquired increased power to monitor CIA covert actions and was skeptical about some of what it found. Thus the mixed governmental-private conduct of rollback policy was made to order, using Rollnet cadres to conduct operations far from the probing eyes of Congress.

Covert Cadres of the 1980s

What is so astounding about the covert personalities of the Reagan era is their forty-year history as an "old boys" network. A brief look at the personalities gives a flavor of the real Reagan Doctrine, far from the democratic ideals of the president's speeches. Theodore Shackley is one central figure in forging the secret public-private implementation of the Reagan Doctrine. Shackley, an ex-head of the CIA's Directorate of Plans, was central to the development of the covert network during his direction of the Cuban and Southeast Asian ventures. Shackley and his erstwhile assistant Thomas Clines had been involved in the CIA- and drug-connected Nugan Hand Bank.[64] They had also continued to work with the now-imprisoned Edwin Wilson, who was putting together arms sales schemes including the provision of arms and equipment to Libya under Qaddafi.[65] The contra war in Nicaragua reportedly got its earliest impetus from the activities of Clines when he approached Nicaraguan dictator Anastasio Somoza in 1978 with an offer to organize "search and destroy" missions to eradicate the Sandinista leadership.[66]

Shackley was linked to Wilson's EATSCO company, an Iran-contra-type operation that reaped $8 million in false billings from arms sales to Egypt funneled through it by the Defense Department.[67] In 1980, Shackley moved on to consult with Stanford Technology, the arms trading firm run by Albert Hakim and Richard Secord that would later figure so prominently in the Contragate scandal.[68] In 1984, Shackley himself held talks with Iranian arms merchant Ghorbanifar to facilitate the Iran arms sale whose profits were secretly siphoned to the Nicaraguan contras.[69]

Clines, who had previously supervised Wilson during the Cuban operations, was heavily involved in the EATSCO scandal.[70] But this did not keep him from becoming Richard Secord's deputy in the Iran-Contra covert arms network. Clines directed arms deliveries to the contras, and oversaw the activities of Bay of Pigs veterans Felix Rodriguez and Luis Posada (see Chapter Three) in addition to Rafael "Chi Chi" Quintero, a professional assassination expert who had worked with Wilson.[71]

These individuals coordinated supply runs to the contras from places like the Ilopongo airbase in El Salvador, utilizing "former" CIA proprietary firms such as Southern Air Transport, the successor to the old Civil Air Transport and Air America fronts in Southeast Asia.[72] Reminiscent of the covert GIDO (guns-in, drugs-out) escapades of the Far East were the well-substantiated reports of drug-running by contra supporters as an integral element of the supply operation.[73]

Ultimately supervising all of these activities was retired Maj. Gen. Richard Secord, the chief "private" organizer of the Iranian and contra arms deals. Secord has a long covert warrior history including work for Shackley and Clines in Southeast Asia, the overseeing of arms sales to the Shah of Iran, and other covert operations intertwined with Edwin Wilson. Secord was reportedly shielded from the Nugan Hand Bank scandal through the intervention of Clines, and from prosecution for the EATSCO dealings with the help of Frank Carlucci, later Reagan's Secretary of Defense. Secord also helped steer the AWACS airplane sale to Saudi Arabia through Congress, an action that served as a *quid pro quo* for Saudi financial support to the Nicaraguan contras.[74]

Secord may have been a key figure (reportedly along with Oliver North) in the Army's Intelligence Support Activity (ISA), a secret group of at least 250 officers created in 1981. ISA, disbanded after revelations of financial fraud, engaged in classified missions in Central America, Africa, and Southeast Asia. As president of Stanford Technology Trading Group, Secord designed and operated the logistics for supplying the Nicaraguan contras. In his activities, he worked closely with partner Albert Hakim to launder money through a variety of Swiss bank accounts and other financial entities. In his dual public-private persona, Secord served until 1985 as a member of the Pentagon's Special Operations Policy Advisory Group.[75]

General Harry Aderholt, Secord's deputy in Laos, was also active in private covert aid in Central America. Head of the Air Commandos Association of 1,500 special warfare veterans, and an editor of the mercenaries' magazine *Soldier of Fortune,* Aderholt flew missions to aid counterinsurgency activities in Guatemala. He also served as military advisor to the National Defense Council and worked with Refugee Relief International, a World Anti-Communist League (WACL) affiliate which has supplied the Nicaraguan contras. Another public-private figure, Aderholt was picked by Under Secretary of Defense for Policy Fred Iklé to advise the military about "low intensity" warfare in Central America.[76]

From the start of the Reagan administration, Gen. Richard Stilwell, who helped form the ISA, promoted the build-up of Special Operations Forces, the official military supplement to the "private" covert networks. Stilwell, another Asian OSS veteran, took charge of the Far East Division of the CIA's Office of Policy Coordination during the early 1950s' raids against China, but was dismissed when the Nationalist Chinese drug-running through Civil Air Transport was exposed. He returned to Southeast Asia to direct the secret war in Laos as commander of U.S. forces in Thailand, where the military leadership had been heavily involved in the opium trade.[77]

The Revitalization of WACL

In concert with the covert warriors, a revitalized WACL, with its related domestic and international organizations took on an important role in implementing the Reagan Doctrine. The U.S. WACL chapter had as leaders or advisors Maj. Gen. John Singlaub; Lt. Gen. Daniel O. Graham; John Fisher, president of the American Security Council; Conservative Caucus chairman Howard Phillips; Gen. Lewis Walt, ex-Marine Corp commander in Vietnam; National Defense Council leader Andy Messing; and Anthony Kubek, a veteran of the China Lobby.[78]

The new influence of WACL was due in good measure to Singlaub, who from his days with the OSS in China, has thrived in the rollback intrigues in the Far East. From 1950 to 1952, he was deputy CIA station chief in South Korea and he may have had a role in the formation of the Korean CIA which is itself strongly linked to WACL and Rev. Moon's Unification Church. During the Vietnam War, Singlaub was one of the major organizers of Operation Phoenix which killed between 20,000 and 40,000 South Vietnamese.[79] He later headed UN forces in South Korea until he was recalled after quarreling publicly with President Carter over announced plans to reduce the level of U.S. forces there. Because of this, Singlaub—reminiscent of General MacArthur's dismissal over Korea policy—became a *cause célébre* of the ascendant New Right.[80]

WACL played a critical role in the early development of the Nicaraguan contras. Following Somoza's fall, a group of the dictator's supporters trained in Guatemala with the help of WACL leader and death squad organizer Mario Sandoval Alarcon.[81] In late 1980, WACL member nation Argentina began to train the contras.[82] From 1981 through 1984, the U.S. government took over the main supporting role for the contras, but when Congress turned off the funds in 1984, WACL and other Rollnet cadres stepped in with alternate funding sources. In addition to the domestic fundraising work of Singlaub and CAUSA, several WACL countries raised funds or contributed to the Nicaragua rollback crusade:

- Saudi Arabia, through the negotiating efforts of William Casey and Richard Secord, and partly in response to Secord's successful management of the $8.5 billion AWACS sale, reportedly donated $30 million to the contras. The Saudis have also generously donated to the insurgent forces in Angola and Afghanistan.[83]

- South Korea donated funds to the contras and was involved in shipment of arms, including acting as a back-channel for shipments to Iran.[84]

- Taiwan, which has provided training to death squad members throughout Latin America, reportedly donated $2 million to the contras in 1985 after a solicitation by National Security Council staff member Gaston Sigur.[85]

- South Africa has been the main prop to the insurgencies in Mozambique and Angola. Secretary of State Shultz and CIA Director Casey approved a plan by which South Africa would pay for Nicaraguan contra training and equipment. South Africa's international pariah status made this politically problematic, and the deal was dropped. However, South Africa did give 200,000 pounds of materials to contra leader Eden Pastora.[86]

- Israel, although not itself a WACL member, provided assistance to Somoza at the end of his regime, and has secretly sent aid to the contras.[87]

In his private role Singlaub raised millions of dollars to support the Nicaraguan contras while in his public role he was chairing a Pentagon panel on "low intensity" warfare.[88] Singlaub coordinated arms shipments and training through such organizations as Friends of the Americas, organized by New Right Louisiana State Rep. Woody Jenkins; *Soldier of Fortune,* headed by Robert K. Brown; and Civilian Military Assistance, led by Tom Posey.[89] Other domestic right-wing groups with WACL links assisting the contra movements in Nicaragua, Angola, and Mozambique included the Christian Broadcasting Network, the Conservative Caucus, the Council for Inter-American Security (CIS) (which sponsored the Committee of Santa Fe), and Western Goals.[90] Carl "Spitz"

Channell, who admitted to conspiring with Oliver North to operate a complex of nonprofit firms to engage in fundraising, lobbying, and propaganda for the contras, was a key Western Goals member.[91]

The Reagan Doctrine, then, was not simply a U.S. government undertaking. It was a program of the global rollback network that included the U.S. government as one among many participants. Despite the setback to the Reagan Doctrine created by Contragate, Rollnet is continuing its work in support of aggressive Third World rollback. In addition, though the U.S. government commitment to rollback projects is currently undergoing reevaluation, the U.S. government has in place a vast infrastructure—lobbied for by the same Rollnet cadres—for pursuing rollback policy. We now turn to that infrastructure, which contains the capacity for *"low intensity" conflict.*

Tactics of the Reagan Doctrine: "Low Intensity" Conflict

The military tactics most appropriate for Third World rollback belong to the category of warfare called *"low intensity" conflict.* Such warfare, while "low-intensity" for the United States, is of very high intensity for the unfortunate Third World target nations. "Low intensity" conflict (LIC) is not strictly military, but includes such elements as economic destabilization, political interference, and psychological operations. A recently proposed definition of LIC for the revised U.S. Army field manual on the subject reads:

> The limited use of power for political purposes by nations or organizations...to coerce, control or defend a population, to control or defend a territory or establish or defend rights. It includes military operations by or against irregular forces, peacekeeping operations, terrorism, counter-terrorism, rescue operations and military assistance under conditions of armed conflict.[92]

The roots of "low intensity" conflict can be traced to the late 1950s and early 1960s, with full expression in the counterinsurgency doctrines of the Kennedy administration. In order to accomplish its containment tasks, the United States had to adopt a novel approach involving the entire civilian and military foreign affairs apparatus.[93] The bulk of "low intensity" conflict has been carried out by Special Operations Forces such as the Green Berets, with intensive training in insurgency or counterinsurgency warfare.[94]

Psychological operations ("psyops") is accorded a particular role within LIC. *Army Field Manual 33-5* defines psyops as the use of propaganda and other means to influence opinions, attitudes, emotions, and behavior of friendly, neutral, or hostile groups. According to psyops teachings,

> Military deception is an aspect of strategy and tactics that is often used but seldom acknowledged…deception is the deliberate misrepresentation of reality done to gain a competitive advantage.[95]

One way to determine if a doctrine is truly being put into practice is to look at the budget implementing that doctrine. One area of budgetary support for the Reagan Doctrine lies in the Pentagon's Special Operations Forces (SOF), the military commando units specially trained to carry out the frequently covert operations of LIC. After the military failure of U.S. forces in Vietnam, SOF funding fell from its peak of over $1 billion per year to less than $100 million in FY 1975. As recommended by the Heritage Foundation, the Reagan administration initiated an unprecedented peacetime expansion of SOF. According to Defense Secretary Caspar Weinberger,

> The high priority we have assigned to SOF revitalization reflects our recognition that low-level conflict—for which the SOF are uniquely suited—will pose the threat we are most likely to encounter throughout the end of this century.[96]

Since 1981, money for SOF has more than tripled, with total FY 1986 funds for special operations at about $1.5 billion. Future Pentagon plans call for spending $7.6 billion in the five years beginning in 1988.[97] By 1990, active duty SOF personnel will be 80 percent higher than in 1981, with the total forces numbering 38,400.[98] Psyops troops, including three active duty battalions and nine reserve battalions, will be increased with another active duty battalion by 1990. SOF units are targeted for the Pacific, Latin America, the Persian Gulf, and North Africa.[99] With bipartisan support, Congress has passed measures calling for the beefing up of special operations forces.[100]

An important aspect of LIC is the use of proxy military forces, which avoids the unpopularity of sending U.S. troops abroad. One aspect of proxy armies is the sale of weapons to governments and movements which carry out U.S. aims in the Third World; such arms sales increased markedly under the Reagan administration. As part of the proxy tactic, SOF personnel are heavily involved in Military Training Teams (MTT) in Latin America, Africa, the Middle East, Asia, and Europe. Under the Reagan government, the number of MTT personnel-weeks abroad increased more than five-fold since 1980.

SOF affords the Reagan Doctrine a distinct advantage over the CIA's covert operations; the Pentagon is not required to report details of the SOF's activities to Congress, and therefore can be used in clandestine activities to avoid Congressional oversight. The use of LIC tactics in Central America is consistent with recommendations of a 1984 panel convened by right-wing Under Secretary of Defense for Policy Fred Iklé and headed by WACL leader Gen. John Singlaub. SOF have been more active in Central America than in any other region; Special Forces military advisors have trained over 5,000 Salvadoran and 5,000 Honduran troops, and SOF have been deployed in an almost continuous series of Central American military exercises.[101] The 1986 Congressional contra aid package allowed Special Forces to provide direct training to the contra forces in Honduras and in the United States.

To understand the complex workings of "low intensity" conflict, we will briefly describe three examples: Nicaragua, Libya, and the Philippines.

Rollback and Economic War: The Case of Nicaragua

Economic destabilization of unwanted governments is a well known Third World rollback tactic and is inextricably linked with "low intensity" conflict. It is a powerful weapon for destroying a government by causing disaffection among its population. The strong point of covert economic warfare is that—as compared with an invading army—the enemy is invisible so that the people are likely to blame their own government rather than the United States for their difficulties. Also, economic destabilization is designed to prevent the need for direct U.S. military intervention, thereby avoiding the political resistance within the United States created by such intervention.

In 1980, the Heritage Foundation recommended a policy of economic warfare against Nicaragua.[102] This policy has been conducted on two fronts: the U.S.-financed contra war and international economic pressure to cut off trade, loans, and credits. With this economic warfare, the United States hoped to create a dissatisfied middle-class fifth column within Nicaragua that would link up with the contras, weakening the society internally such that the government would either collapse, become a more susceptible target to military intervention, or succumb to electoral defeat.

The United States has damaged the Nicaraguan economy through economic actions (e.g., the 90 percent reduction in the sugar quota, extreme pressure on lending institutions to cut off loans, the economic boycott) that cost Nicaragua $1 billion in lost credits and exports between 1981 and 1985. But far more destabilizing has been the contra war. Even the Pentagon has admitted that the contras cannot overthrow the Nicaraguan government militarily.[103] Their purpose is to disrupt the country economically.

The contra operation forced the Nicaraguan government to increase defense spending from 7 percent to 40 percent of the total budget, diverting precious funds, food, medications, and personnel into the defense sector, and producing shortages in the civilian sector. In 1984, the contras destroyed ninety-two coffee farms, thereby reducing Nicaragua's main export crop and creating a severe shortage of foreign exchange.[104] During January 1985, the contras made repeated raids through the coffee-growing Jinotega province, burning trucks, blowing up bridges, interrupting power lines, attacking coffee farms, and ambushing vehicles of government officials. Peasants in many areas could not pick coffee without armed guard.

The attack on major crops dropped Nicaragua's export earnings to less than half what was required to buy necessary imports.[105] The country has been unable to make sufficient payments on its $4 billion foreign debt (a large portion of which was inherited from Somoza), and was the first nation ever to fall six months behind in repaying loans to the World Bank. One Latin American economic consultant described Nicaragua's position as created by U.S. economic warfare:

> I don't see how the Nicaraguans will be able to pay their debts unless they get external financing. And I don't see how they will get external financing unless they pay their debts.[106]

The CIA's mining of Nicaragua's harbors was another attempt to blockade and intimidate ships from carrying Nicaraguan exports and imports, both military and domestic. Carter national security advisor Zbigniew Brzezinski proposed in 1986 that if the contra policy fails in Nicaragua, the United States might have to impose a sea and air blockade.[107]

Basic grains for internal consumption have been the target of contra destruction. Also, people entering military service have been unable
to work the fields, thereby reducing the yield of basic grains by as much
as 25 percent. Adding to these problems, 40 percent of all basic necessities produced in Nicaragua—staple foods, shoes, soap—supply the
soldiers at the front. These factors have led to major price increases and
shortages of basic foods.[108]

Disinformation, the deliberate misrepresentation of reality for
political purposes, is part of psyops, and has been extensively conducted against the Nicaraguan and U.S. populations. The infamous CIA
"assassination manual," *Psychological Operations in Guerrilla War,* includes chapters on "Combatant-Propagandist Guerrillas," and "Armed
Propaganda." The Reagan rhetoric labeling Nicaragua a threat to its
neighbors and a Soviet outpost in the Western Hemisphere is conscious
deception aimed to gain the support of the U.S. public. The facts from
U.S. defense and intelligence sources reveal that Nicaragua's military
capacity is primarily defensive and incapable of attacking neighboring
nations, and that Soviet influence and assistance to Nicaragua has been
limited and reluctant.[109] Another wild story designed to play on the fears
of U.S. citizens was the assertion by Reagan that "top Nicaraguan
Government officials are deeply involved in drug trafficking. There is
no crime to which the Sandinistas will not stoop." Reagan's own Drug
Enforcement Agency disputed this statement as lacking any evidence.[110]
In fact, it is the contras, with connections to the Colombian cocaine
cartel, who have been involved in the guns for drugs trafficking, using
U.S. government facilities and aided and abetted by U.S. authorities.[111]

Whether or not the international Right succeeds in overthrowing
the Nicaraguan government, it has been highly successful in blunting
the major threat of the 1979 Nicaraguan Revolution: the "threat of a
good example."[112] It is this threat, rather than rifles and bullets, that con-
stitutes the "export of revolution" feared by U.S. policymakers.
Nicaraguan Vice President Sergio Ramirez has argued that the export
of revolution—from 1776 to 1979—is nothing but the free international circulation of new ideas:

> Without the revolution of the thirteen North American colonies,
> there would never have been a French Revolution...the revolu-
> tion which gave rise to the United States' nationhood has been the
> most exported revolution in modern history.

> How can one prevent a peasant from another Central American
> country from hearing, from finding out, from realizing that in

Nicaragua land is given to other poor and barefoot peasants like him? How can you avoid his realizing that here children—not his children—are being vaccinated while his children still die of gastroenteritis and polio?...In that sense, we export our revolution.[113]

This threat, that news of the domestic successes of a revolution will spread throughout a continent, has led the U.S.-run contras to ruin the greatest achievements of the Nicaraguan experiment, the internationally recognized gains in health and education.[114] The contras have deliberately targeted health centers and schools for attack. The transfer of budgetary resources from health and education to the military has also created major problems for these programs. U.S. officials have openly stated that while they doubt the contras can depose the government, "they are content to see the contras debilitate the Sandinistas by forcing them to divert scarce resources toward the war and away from social programs."[115]

In the same vein, the restrictions on civil liberties in Nicaragua, such as the closing of the U.S.-funded, pro-contra newspaper *La Prensa*,[116] have been turned into major victories by the United States, even more significant than a victorious military battle by the contras. It is the war-created press restrictions, food shortages, population relocations, and military draft that erode support for Nicaragua around the world. They show other countries that Nicaragua's socio-economic experiment is not a model to follow. For the United States, the first choice is to overthrow Nicaragua; second best is to ruin it.

Psyops, Rollback and Terrorism: The Case of Libya

Libya represents an entirely different use of LIC to rollback an unfriendly government. In July 1981, a CIA plan was made to overthrow Libyan leader Muammar Qaddafi.[117] Prior to 1986, Reagan authorized covert programs to depose Qaddafi. The United States tried to recruit Egypt to a joint U.S.-Egyptian military operation to oust the Libyan leader but Egypt failed to go along.[118] Libya appeared on the Heritage Foundation hit list of rollback targets and on CIA Director Casey's rollback list. Lacking the potential of an insurgent army or of any credible organized opposition to Qaddafi, Libyan rollback presented major military problems. Psychological warfare was chosen as the major tool.

For several years, the Reagan administration advertised Qaddafi as the world's leading terrorist. The truth is that Qaddafi has been a relatively minor and unimportant terrorist.[119] When terrorists shot up the Vienna and Rome airports on December 27, 1985, the administration blamed Qaddafi though the incident was probably related to Iran, not Libya.[120] In March 1986, the United States bombed Libyan ships in the Gulf of Sidra with the intent of producing discontent in the Libyan army and provoking Libyan terrorist retaliation that could justify further military moves. The subsequent April 5, 1986 bombing of La Belle discotheque in West Berlin was again blamed on Libya, though the chief of the German investigating team later admitted there was no evidence of Libya's connection to the bombing. The Berlin incident was then used as pretext for the April 14 bombing of Qaddafi's headquarters in Libya, killing Qaddafi's daughter; the goal of the bombing was to assassinate Qaddafi or to encourage a coup against him. Because of almost unanimous negative foreign reaction, the United States stopped the escalation. In the words of columnist Jack Anderson, "The administration set up Libya's erratic Moammar Khadafy as a scapegoat, portraying him as the chief terrorist menace, at the same time that it was selling arms to the real menace, Iran's implacable Ayatollah Khomeini."[121]

Following the April bombing, the United States continued its psyops campaign against Qaddafi, finally causing State Department spokesman and highly regarded journalist Bernard Kalb to resign in protest against the deliberate deceptions of the U.S. press.

The Libya operation had a major goal besides that of rollback. Libya became the center of a program of deception to support the entire Reagan Doctrine by linking Mideast terrorism to Nicaragua, Cuba, and the Soviet Union. In 1985, Reagan spoke to the American Bar Association, claiming, "Most of the terrorists who are kidnapping and murdering American citizens and attacking American installations are being trained, financed and directly or indirectly controlled by a core group of radical and totalitarian governments, a new international version of Murder, Inc." Reagan considered these governments—Iran, Libya, North Korea, Cuba and Nicaragua—a confederation of outlaw terrorist states engaged in outright war against the United States; he noted the support for this terrorist network provided by the Soviet Union.[122] Right-wing Sen. Jeremiah Denton, Chair of the Subcommittee on Security and Terrorism, claimed that a vast terrorist network is controlled by the

Soviet Union and allied with the international narcotics trade.[123] The Republican platform of 1984 states,

> The international links among terrorist groups are now clearly understood; and the Soviet link, direct and indirect, is also clearly understood. The Soviets use terrorist groups to weaken democracy and undermine world stability.

This entire construction is factually incorrect as Professor Edward Herman shows in *The Real Terror Network*.[124] The characterization has two purposes. First, it makes the Reagan Doctrine of rollback into a defense of the United States against terrorist aggressors. Second, it distracts attention from the U.S.-sponsored contra terrorism in countries like Nicaragua. The entire anti-terrorism campaign has been an example of psychological operations as part of LIC on a worldwide basis, building support for more and more Special Operations Forces funding.

For example, the Reagan government manipulated popular outrage about violence conducted against innocent victims (e.g., the Achille Lauro hijacking) by extending the "terrorist" label to left-wing governments such as Nicaragua and Cuba with no evidence to support such claims. The Reagan government portrayed Managua as a place where Palestinians, Libyans, Cubans, and Iranians plot against innocent U.S. citizens. A *Conservative Digest* article (June 1986) claims that Nicaragua is a major base for Libyan operations in the Western hemisphere. There is no denying that terrorism has become an important weapon for some groups. What is hidden by the right-wing anti-terrorist campaign is the fact that the United States sponsors terrorism in its rollback actions.

"Low Intensity" Conflict and the Philippines

The Reagan Doctrine's espousal of Third World democracy is closely related to its employment of "low intensity" conflict in its counterinsurgency face. LIC heavily relies on political factors in addition to military, economic, and psychological warfare. The Philippines provides the clearest example.

Both the Republican and Democratic parties turned against Marcos, not for moral reasons, but out of pragmatic anti-communist concerns. Senate Select Committee on Intelligence chair Dave Durenberger, a Republican, initially called on Marcos to resign because he was unable to contain the communist insurgency. Liberal Democrat Stephen Solarz called Marcos the number one recruiting agent for the Communists.[125]

By early 1984, the State Department was distancing itself from Marcos for the same reason; the Pentagon and White House disagreed. But by 1985, new successes of the insurgent New People's Army brought Reagan to the State Department view. In October 1985, Sen. Paul Laxalt carried Marcos a message from Reagan telling him to stop "screwing up" the counterinsurgency effort.[126] Conservatives in the United States would have preferred a smooth transition from Marcos to a more effective conservative successor, but Cory Aquino appeared on the scene, requiring a highly flexible U.S. response. Fortunately for the United States, Defense Minister Enrile and Armed Forces Chief of Staff Ramos became key bridges between the old regime and a moderate, pro-Western new government.[127] According to former CIA analyst Ray Cline, the only reason why Corazon Aquino ousted Ferdinand Marcos was that many military officers were fed up by Marcos' corruption and inaction in defeating the communists.[128]

The anti-Marcos strategy was initially successful; many insurgents lay down their arms in response to Aquino's amnesty. The United States had learned its lesson from Nicaragua and Iran: do not stick too long with a failing dictator.

By the later years of the Reagan regime, a preferred nomenclature suited to U.S. interests became standardized for the Third World. In the case of nations to be rolled back (e.g., Nicaragua), governments were called terrorist and the insurgents were labeled democratic. In the case of countries to be supported against "communist" insurgencies (e.g., El Salvador and the Philippines), the governments were called democratic and the insurgents were labeled terrorists.

The "Strategy of Worldwide War"

While "low intensity" conflict represents the military tactics of the Reagan Doctrine (the Third World component of global rollback), a more all-embracing military strategy for global rollback is called *horizontal escalation*. Military expert Jeffrey Record calls horizontal escalation "the strategy of worldwide war."[129]

Under the doctrine of horizontal escalation, at one time adopted by Reagan's Secretary of Defense,[130] "no area of the world is beyond the scope of American interest...[we must have] sufficient military standing to cope with any level of violence" around the globe.[131] Horizontal escalation, then, is the military doctrine related to ExSET; if the Soviet empire is one global entity, the military approach to that entity must be globally unified. Horizontal escalation teaches that if the USSR expands in one area of the world, the United States can move somewhere else to attack an asset highly valued by the Soviets.[132] According to Defense Secretary Weinberger, the United States "might choose not to restrict ourselves to meeting one immediate front. We might decide to stretch our capabilities, to engage the enemy in many places...."[133] One proponent of horizontal escalation, former Rand corporation analyst Vernon Aspaturian, proposes that the best defense of Europe may be to threaten valued Soviet assets outside of Europe, for example Cuba or Vietnam. Aspaturian suggests that it is most prudent to attack the Soviet empire at its weakest point.[134]

The "strategy of worldwide war" through the methods of "low intensity" conflict indicates the degree to which the Reagan Doctrine places the United States at war with the Third World. Forty areas of the world have been considered to be potential "low intensity" battlefields.[135]

Prior to the Reagan administration, foreign and military policy analysts, recognizing the limitations of U.S. power, generally set priorities to determine which regions of the world would be allocated the finite quantity of military resources. In its extreme form, horizontal escalation holds that the United States must be militarily prepared in all areas of the world at once. Under this view, the forty-year debate between the Atlanticists and the Asia-firsters becomes moot; both are priorities. When asked which areas of the world the Reagan administration would stress in its efforts to reassert the U.S. international position, then Defense Secretary Weinberger answered "All of them."[136] Such a strategy requires massive armed forces; the original Reagan military buildup proposed to develop the capacity to conduct horizontal escalation.[137]

It is precisely the problem of desires vs. realities that has placed the Reagan Doctrine in a vise. Military and foreign policy analysts of the realist school feel that the United States lacks the military and political power to pull off the ambitious rollback program. The right wing counters that the Reagan administration has not matched its rollback goals with sufficient action. It is to these contradictory critiques of the Reagan Doctrine that we now turn.

Did Ronald Reagan Betray His Doctrine?

According to some critics, not only was Ronald Reagan a hypocrite, he was a coward as well. He talked about rollback, but only rolled back a tiny island in the Caribbean—Grenada. He boasted he could take on the Russians, but the only countries he went after were small and weak, Grenada and Libya. He gave up before he beat Libya. Sounds more like a bully going after the little kids on the block than a world leader.

This criticism comes from Ronald Reagan's old supporters on the Right.

Michael Johns, assistant editor of the Heritage Foundation's journal *Policy Review,* wrote in 1987:

> ...seven years after Ronald Reagan's arrival in Washington, the United States government and its allies are still dominated by the culture of appeasement that drove Neville Chamberlain to Munich in 1938.... [An] example of appeasement is the unsteady commitment to freedom in many parts of the world...the administration permits American oil companies to pump 300,000 barrels a day at Angola's Cabinda facility, financing the presence of 40,000 Soviet, Cuban and East German troops in that country. In Mozambique, the administration is not only denying funds to the resistance, it is sending $78 million in assistance to the pro-Soviet Frelimo government.... In South Africa, the State Department has established casual diplomatic contact with a Soviet-backed terrorist group, the African National Congress.... Even the Reagan Administration's Nicaragua policy has been governed by a spirit of appeasement...and has continued to embrace negotiations with Nicaragua as if anything good could come of them.[138]

Right-wing analyst Edward Luttwak, in a 1985 interview, complained that

> The president, after the election, has come to the conclusion that the little cold war we just had is the most his nerves are willing to take.... The administration's level of what they can eat is Grenada. It is all they are capable of absorbing. I don't want it to be so bel-

licose as to eat eastern Europe, but I'm not satisfied with the eating of Grenada. I would like to be able to do Nicaragua.[139]

Following the 1984 election, the *Conservative Digest* (November/December 1984) proposed a new cabinet for Reagan's second term. While Defense Secretary Weinberger was slated for a new four-year contract, Secretary of State George Shultz was to be replaced by Jeane Kirkpatrick. For Undersecretary of State for Political Affairs, the right-wing nominee was ExSET theorist Edward Luttwak, and for National Security Advisor archconservative Navy Secretary John Lehman. The right-wing "action agenda" for the first 100 days of the new term included overt and covert action to support liberation movements in the USSR, Eastern Europe, Afghanistan, Angola, Mozambique, Nicaragua, and elsewhere. A specific item was to begin a political, economic, and psychological campaign to remove Fidel Castro.

A *Conservative Digest* article (August 1986) announced: "The Freedom Fighters of Mozambique are Being Betrayed by the State Department." Conservative Caucus chairman Howard Phillips complained that the Reagan administration is propping up the Soviet puppet regime in Mozambique. The World Anti-Communist League and *Conservative Digest* were unhappy that Reagan failed to sever diplomatic relations with Nicaragua and extend recognition to the contras.[140] Howard Phillips advocated the severing of diplomatic relations, declarations of war, and naval and air blockades of both Nicaragua and Cuba.[141]

On many issues the Right was united in its disappointment with Reagan's failure to match his rhetoric with action. But on other issues, the Right became divided, particularly after the 1985 emphasis on "democracy" in the Reagan Doctrine. One split in the right wing was over South Africa. Apartheid was so unpopular that right-wing politicians hoping to get elected were forced to moderate their pro-South Africa stand. In 1984, thirty-five Republicans, including some prominent rightists, signed a strong anti-apartheid statement. They were castigated in *Human Events* (December 29, 1984) for assisting Soviet expansion into Africa.

The Philippines was another puzzle for the Right. On the one hand, dictator Ferdinand Marcos, a well-connected member of the WACL-Moonie network, was a traditional friend of the Right; on the other, he had become counterproductive in fighting the leftist insurgency. Since Aquino's election, the Right has gradually moved away from Marcos and has been supporting military elements such as former

Defense Minister Juan Enrile, who recently said he regrets having helped overthrow Marcos.[142] According to right-wing analyst Ray Cline,

> Cory [Aquino] is the Jimmy Carter of the Philippines, full of good thoughts and words but naive. It is very important that Enrile wield great influence with Aquino to avoid a civil war, an anti-American regime, and a communist presence—a disaster the dimensions of Iran.[143]

The Right and traditional conservatives appear to agree that the main hope for the Philippines lies with the new vigilante groups such as Alsa Masa, set up by Lieutenant Colonel Franco Calida who trained at Fort Bragg in "low intensity" and psychological warfare.[144] U.S. Secretary of State Shultz personally endorsed the vigilante groups, which are also supported by Philippine President Corazon Aquino.[145] Veteran Rollnet operative Gen. Richard Stilwell wrote in early 1988 that vigilante groups are extremely important as a counterinsurgency adjunct to the military as long as they are controlled by the military.[146] The CIA has a $10 million covert program that includes the establishment of such vigilante groups, and John Singlaub was reportedly traveling around the archipelago organizing paramilitary squads in 1987.[147] CAUSA, the political arm of the Reverend Moon's Unification Church, is involved in the vigilante movement which has carried out killings of suspected communists. One CAUSA manifesto read on a local radio station stated: "Just one order to our anti-Communist forces, your…brains will be scattered in the streets."[148]

Another example of right-wing disunity over Third World policy concerns Iran. It was right-wing elements in and around the Reagan administration that masterminded the Iran arms sales: Casey, Poindexter, North, Secord, and Michael Ledeen. The moderates in the administration such as Shultz opposed the move. Yet when the arms sales became public, the Right was very unhappy. How could their hero Ronald Reagan help their villain Khomeini?

In fact, the arms sales were initially a rollback operation designed to overthrow Khomeini and his followers rather than to assist them. Iran is on the Heritage Foundation's rollback list. *Mandate for Leadership II* proposed opening "backdoor channels" to gain influence in Iran.[149] Ledeen felt that the Iran operation had great potential for undermining the regime.[150] The Reaganites intended to provide arms to formerly pro-Shah military officers in the hopes that they would challenge Khomeini's followers after the Ayatollah's death. Such a policy is similar to the supplying of arms to the Indonesian army under Sukarno, the Brazilian army under Goulart, and the Chilean army under Allende. In each case, the pro-U.S. military overthrew the anti-U.S. head of state. However the complicating factor of the hostages gave Reagan an incentive to provide the arms to his enemy Khomeini, rather than to his enemy's enemies. Thus the rollback operation was botched.

The Iran, Philippines, and South Africa cases demonstrate how complex international relations are, and how inadequate the simplistic right-wing formulas have become. It is precisely these complexities that made Ronald Reagan as president—as opposed to Ronald Reagan as right-wing hero—unable to carry out the wishes of the Right. As president, Reagan had to face up to reality.

The Limits of the Reagan Doctrine

While the right wing went after Reagan for doing too little, the foreign affairs and military professionals—both conservative and liberal—criticized him for doing too much. Realism has always taken precedence over idealism in U.S. foreign policy. Since 1947, when he telegraphed in the containment era, George Kennan has been the archtypical realist. For Kennan and for influential realist Robert Tucker, a critical principle of foreign policy is the recognition of one's limitations.[151]

Military realists have been similarly unhappy about horizontal escalation, the military strategy behind global rollback. Military analyst Jeffrey Record claims that to meet all U.S. commitments in the world would require greater expenditures than even the Reagan military build-up. Record argues that horizontal escalation invites a dispersion of limited resources, thereby violating the fundamental principle of Frederick the Great, "He who attempts to defend too much, defends nothing."[152] The realists won out. In spite of Weinberger's acceptance of horizontal escalation as a principle, budgetary realities placed it on the backburner.

Other sources of opposition to the moralistic interventionism of the Reagan Doctrine have been international business interests and European allies. For example, the oil companies are not interested in rocking the boat in Libya or Angola as long as a stable business climate can be maintained. Most of Western Europe was unhappy with Reagan's bombing of Libya and has opposed economic sanctions against Libya and Nicaragua. The attacks on Libya have also alienated Arab nations in the Middle East.

The realist limits on the Reagan Doctrine have kept Reagan from implementing his own doctrine to the fullest, and have infuriated the "moralist" right wing. In one country after another, realist considerations—the effect on allies, the effect on American business interests, the possibility of losing American lives—have blunted the right-wing rollback crusade.

While the packaging of the Reagan Doctrine under the slogan of "democracy" did attract many new rollback buyers, especially Democrats, realism has provided a limit to the marketability of the democratically wrapped merchandise. As realist Kennan put it,

> Democracy, as Americans understand it, is not necessarily the future of all mankind, nor is it the duty of the U.S. government to assure that it becomes that.[153]

If any kind of foreign policy consensus emerges from the ashes of Contragate, it will not arise as a moral quest for worldwide democracy. Rather, it will base itself on a calculated estimation of the U.S. national interest, gilded with a democratic veneer.

5

The New Drive for Nuclear Supremacy

An alarming aspect of the rise of the Right was the articulation of nuclear strategies aggressively aimed at the Soviet Union. During the 1970s, the Right trumpeted the need for the United States to regain strategic nuclear dominance over the USSR, and found its program resonating in the corridors of establishment power among some conservative elites who since the dawn of the Atomic Age had pursued such supremacy with vigor.

This quest for military supremacy did not spring from the ideological tracts of the Heritage Foundation or the frightening figures published by the Committee on the Present Danger, but in fact has been a constant theme of post-World War II foreign policy. Only with superior strategic nuclear force could the United States reach the military goal of escalation dominance: the ability to win a war at any level to which that war might escalate. In the 1980s, the right wing launched an unprecedented new drive for nuclear superiority and escalation dominance, but cloaked its campaign in the hopeful rhetoric of an end to nuclear terror.

The Rise and Fall of Nuclear Supremacy

Between 1945 and 1949, only the United States possessed an atomic bomb. During the Berlin blockade of 1948, the Pentagon developed a plan called Broiler to hit twenty-four Soviet cities with thirty-four atomic bombs. The major reason why Broiler was not implemented was Truman's concern that the United States lacked sufficient A-bombs to bring the USSR to a quick surrender; the Soviets might retaliate with a conventional invasion of Europe.[1] While the United States had absolute *nuclear* superiority, it lacked absolute overall *military* superiority.

After the Soviets dropped their first A-bomb in 1949, more discussions took place regarding a "preventive" nuclear attack on the USSR. Doubt persisted that the Soviets could be totally destroyed without retaliating.[2] In 1951, following China's entrance into the Korean War, high-level Pentagon officials again discussed a nuclear attack on China, and on May 20, 1953, the Joint Chiefs of Staff unanimously advocated nuclear strikes against China in order to win the Korean War, with massive bombardment of the USSR if the Soviets intervened. Eisenhower accepted the recommendation provided negotiations to end the war did not bear fruit, which they did.[3] During the Quemoy and Matsu crises of the 1950s, the Joint Chiefs of Staff and Secretary of State Dulles recommended the use of nuclear weapons against China. Eisenhower rejected the plans because public opinion was vehemently opposed to risking World War III over two tiny islands.[4]

In 1954, some Pentagon members recommended preventive war against the Soviets while the United States still held relative nuclear superiority; Eisenhower again rejected the plan because of fear of Soviet retaliation.[5] 1954 was a highly significant year in arms race history; for the first time the United States lost significant ground. In 1953, the Soviets exploded the hydrogen bomb, and by 1954 they had new powerful bombers that could deliver weapons to the United States.[6]

For a brief time the United States regained the edge in the strategic balance through a technological development: the intercontinental ballistic missile (ICBM). Even though Kennedy pledged in the 1960 campaign to close the highly-publicized "missile gap" with the Soviets, in 1961 Kennedy learned the truth: the gap massively favored the United States. The Soviets had a mere four nuclear missiles compared to the United States' forty.[7] This second period of nuclear superiority lasted until 1964.

In August 1961, the Berlin Wall was built, leading to a Kennedy administration top-level contingency plan for a devastating nuclear first strike against the Soviet Union. "If ever in the history of the nuclear arms race, before or since, one side had unquestionable superiority over the other...the autumn of 1961 was that time." Yet Kennedy did not take advantage of U.S. supremacy because even in the most favorable estimates, a few million people in the United States would die.[8] Each time nuclear war against the Soviets was strongly considered, it was rejected because some form of Soviet retaliation might take place.[9]

The Cuban missile crisis was the last occasion on which the United States held clear nuclear supremacy. Whether the United States would have used its weapons will never be known; the crisis was resolved when Khrushchev removed the Cuban missiles. With the subsequent Soviet nuclear buildup, the United States lost its nuclear dominance forever.[10]

Kennedy's Secretary of Defense Robert McNamara is known as the person who rejected the goal of nuclear supremacy in favor of parity with the doctrine of MAD: mutual assured destruction. Yet in 1962, prior to the Cuban missile crisis and during the second era of U.S. nuclear superiority, McNamara had called for the development of a capability to fight and win a nuclear war. This doctrine of "nuclear war-fighting" means that nuclear weapons are developed for the purpose of *winning* a nuclear war; MAD, on the other hand, views nuclear weapons as having the purpose of *preventing or deterring* nuclear war. War-fighting requires superiority whereas MAD needs only parity. McNamara later realized that even with war-winning superiority the United States would sustain millions of casualties. At that point he began to support the MAD approach not as the favored policy but as a pragmatic fallback position.[11] The loss of strategic superiority in the mid-'60s left MAD as the only realistic policy.

During all these years there was a constant push for superiority from the military-industrial complex, the Air Force and later the Navy, the services under which nuclear weapons were placed. By 1970, a new technological breakthrough had taken place: a generation of missiles so accurate that they could hit Soviet missile targets were combined with multiple warheads per missile. The nuclear strategists, centered at the Air Force's Rand think tank, had been developing nuclear warfighting scenarios since the 1950s. Now they had the hardware to make their theories work.[12] The concept of counterforce—striking Soviet military targets rather than Soviet cities—allowed for the possibility of an overwhelming first strike. Counterforce had the potential to bring forth a third period of U.S. nuclear supremacy.

Nixon's Defense Secretary James Schlesinger, himself from Rand, drafted National Security Decision Memorandum 242 calling for an end to the MAD stalemate and the building of counterforce weapons to give the United States nuclear war-fighting capability.[13] Though Nixon signed the memo in 1974, the third era of superiority never arrived. The Soviets soon had their own counterforce weapons. But from 1974 through the 1980s, war-fighting increasingly challenged MAD as fundamental U.S. nuclear doctrine.

What does this brief history tell us? First, the United States would need absolute nuclear superiority in order to attack the USSR with nuclear weapons. Relative superiority is not enough because any retaliation would be disastrous. Even during the two periods of relative supremacy from 1945-54 and from 1961-64, U.S. superiority was considered insufficient to allow an attack on the Soviets. Second, it is possible to regain relative superiority, but only with a technological breakthrough that leaves the other side temporarily far behind. The ICBM was such a breakthrough, and the counterforce weapons could have been such a development had the Soviets been unable to respond quickly. Now a new major technological breakthrough—the Strategic Defense Initiative (SDI or Star Wars)—is in the making.

Third, throughout the nuclear age, supremacy and war-fighting have been preferred—though unstated—U.S. policy. But without absolute superiority, such a policy has not been feasible. MAD served as a realistic fallback. Just as we saw in Chapter One that the United States accepted containment because global rollback was impractical, similarly the United States has accepted MAD because warfighting is impractical.

Finally, MAD or parity—deterring war and maintaining the geopolitical status quo—serves the aims of containment. Nuclear supremacy or war-fighting—victory over the Soviet Union—is the nuclear component of global rollback.

The Purpose of Nuclear Supremacy

Historically, even with relative military superiority the United States has not possessed the power to wage nuclear war against the Soviet Union. Why, then, is nuclear supremacy a practical goal for rollback enthusiasts?

The answer has to do with escalation dominance. Relative superiority does not allow direct rollback of the Soviet Union, but it certainly helps in rolling back Third World governments. A nuclear threat that is credible is an effective war winner. In the words of the American Security Council, "Overall military and technological superiority for the United States would...allow us to control the escalation of war begun at a low level of conflict intensity.... Advantage need not give the United States a first-strike potential, but it should be one that would allow us to control the process of escalation."[14]

Escalation dominance is not simply a theoretical advantage; it has been used many times:

> The public record now reveals more than twenty occasions when U.S. presidents threatened to resort to nuclear war during crises. The pattern began in March 1946 when, according to President Truman, he threatened to drop the 'superbomb' on the Soviet Union if it did not evacuate Kurdistan and Azerbaijan within forty-eight hours...their withdrawal began within twenty-four hours of his threat...the Truman threat was accepted as fact by succeeding presidents and became a model for their foreign and military policies.[15]

Some examples of this "nuclear blackmail" include: 1) Eisenhower threatening China unless it agreed to a settlement of the Korean War on U.S. terms in 1953; 2) Eisenhower sending Strategic Air Command bombers to Nicaragua to back up the CIA-sponsored coup in nearby Guatemala in 1954; 3) Eisenhower offering tactical nuclear weapons to France to break the siege of Dienbienphu in Vietnam in 1954; 4) Eisenhower instructing the Joint Chiefs of Staff to use nuclear bombs if necessary to contain the anti-monarchist revolution in Iraq in 1958; 5) Kennedy in the 1962 Cuban Missile Crisis; 6) Nixon's nuclear threats against North Vietnam in 1969; 7) Nixon threatening the Soviets if Syria intervened in the 1970 Jordanian-PLO civil war; 8) Nixon placing U.S. military forces on nuclear alert to prevent the Soviet Union from intervening in the 1973 Israeli-Egyptian October War. Apparently the Soviets have also threatened the use of nuclear weapons: against Britain and France during the 1956 Suez crisis, and against China on several occasions. Also, there are reports indicating that Britain threatened Argentina with nuclear weapons during the Falklands War of 1982.[16]

The theory of escalation dominance was adapted to the nuclear age during the 1950s at the Air Force's Rand think tank and the Council on Foreign Relations. The typical escalation ladder goes from covert intervention (e.g., Nicaragua) to overt intervention (e.g., Grenada) to limited conventional war (e.g., Korea or Vietnam) to atomic warning shots to theatre nuclear war to protracted nuclear war to a pre-emptive disarming first strike.[17] As the USSR developed nuclear parity with the United States, military strategists faced a major problem: the nuclear threat lost its credibility—it could no longer be used.

Right-wing Goal: Nuclear Superiority

After two decades of consensus on nuclear parity and MAD, the doctrine of nuclear superiority re-emerged as a major contender around 1975. The Coalition For Peace Through Strength, with 191 members of Congress in its ranks, organizationally linked with the Committee on the Present Danger (CPD) and the American Security Council, has gone on record favoring military superiority over the Soviets: the United States should "achieve overall military and technological superiority over the Soviet Union."[18] Eugene Rostow, CPD's chair, made it clear in a July 1978 speech that the CPD's goal is to regain nuclear superiority.[19] Echoing the CPD line, the 1980 Republican Party platform stated, "We will build toward a sustained defense expenditure sufficient to close the gap with the Soviets, and ultimately reach the position of military superiority that the American people demand."

Why the new drive for supremacy? Because a potent right-wing coalition became preoccupied with the erosion of U.S. power abroad, in particular the wave of Third World radical nationalist and socialist revolutions that crested in the 1970s. The Right saw the need to reassert the bedrock foundation of U.S. foreign policy, escalation dominance. As Eugene Rostow said in 1978: "To have the advantage at the utmost level of violence helps at every lesser level." With the decline of nuclear superiority around 1964, the United States lost escalation dominance. Shortly thereafter, the United States lost its first war—Vietnam. For the right wing and for some traditional conservatives, these two losses were inextricably related.

Supremacy Under the Guise of Inferiority

In the 1970s, a powerful coalition was formed between traditional cold war conservative elites (from policymaking organizations such as the Council on Foreign Relations), neoconservative anti-Soviet intellectuals, and members of the traditional and New Right. This coalition, embracing individuals and organizations with ideologies spanning the range of aggressive containment to outright rollback, was led by the CPD, the upcoming Reagan administration defense and foreign policy apparatus in embryonic form.[20] Well-connected to the coffers of the military-industrial complex, the Right/CPD coalition placed responsibility for the Third World defeats of the 1970s squarely on the expanding Soviet empire. But the CPD was too smart to put forth a public advocacy of nuclear superiority. Rather, its analysts created a myth of nuclear inferiority (the "window of vulnerability") and called for the United States to catch up to the Russians.[21]

The right-wing public-relations strategy has been to ignore the underlying nuclear parity and to focus on microinequalities in nuclear strength, thus exaggerating details and obscuring the big picture. One such maneuver to "demonstrate" Soviet superiority has been to utilize figures for missile throwweight and megatonnage (explosive force). Rollnet cadre Gen. Daniel Graham, for example, claimed that the Soviets outnumbered the United States by 5 to 1 in megatonnage. This statement was wrong; the actual Soviet advantage at the time was 3 to 2. But more important, megatonnage has no real military significance. The Defense Department and most nuclear experts agree that the important indicator of strategic strength is total number of deliverable warheads.[22] In fact, the United States has never lost its lead in number and accuracy of warheads. It was to make up for inaccuracy that the Soviets have built heavier warheads with more explosive force. "In megatonnage, the Soviets are way ahead," said Paul Warnke, President Carter's director of the Arms Control and Disarmament Agency, but "it doesn't make a damn bit of difference" because "we have roughly 10,000 strategic nuclear warheads" and "the Soviets have 7,000. We're way ahead."[23]

General Graham also claimed that the Soviets have a "4 to 1 advantage in missile throwweight." In fact the Soviet advantage was 13.2 million pounds vs. 10.4 million pounds for the United States in December 1982, but again, throwweight has little significance except to expose the lower technological development of Soviet missiles.[24]

Another area of right-wing nuclear distortion has been its use of figures for Soviet military spending. In his 1981 inaugural address, Reagan stated that over the previous decade, the USSR had spent $300 billion more on its military than the United States had. In fact, in 1982 the CIA released figures to Congress showing that between 1970 and 1980 the Soviets may have spent $300 billion *less* than the United States.[25] In 1983, the CIA further amended itself by admitting that over the previous seven years, Soviet military spending had increased at a rate of just 2 percent per year, only half the rate the CIA had previously claimed.[26] As with its other comparisons, the right wing had manufactured the myth of Soviet military spending.

Thus the Right established in the public's mind that the Soviet Union had greater nuclear capability than the United States and strongly pushed a policy of U.S. catch-up. In fact, as such rare public statements as that of the Coalition For Peace Through Strength indicate, the "catch-up" policy was a hidden drive for U.S. nuclear superiority.

Where the Right erred in its public relations was to admit on some occasions that it believed nuclear wars could be fought and won. In 1980, Colin Gray, soon to become a Reagan "disarmament" advisor, made this admission in the respectable journal *Foreign Policy:*

> The United States should plan to defeat the Soviet Union and to do so at a cost that would not prohibit U.S. recovery. Washington should identify war aims that in the last resort would contemplate the destruction of Soviet political authority and the emergence of a postwar world order compatible with Western values.[27]

Vice President George Bush has stated: "You have a [nuclear] capability that inflicts more damage on the opposition than it can inflict upon you. That's the way you can have a winner...."[28] That's also a definition of nuclear superiority.

Superiority is also linked with global rollback; CPD member Richard Pipes has stated: "Soviet leaders would have to choose between peacefully changing their Communist system...or going to war."[29]

Winnable Nuclear War and the Reagan Government

With the CPD providing key institutional and ideological weapons, and the New Right adding the grassroots and electoral organizational muscle, the scene was set for a dynamic tranformation of U.S. military and nuclear doctrine and strategy with the election of Ronald Reagan to the presidency in 1980. With his first administration staffed by CPD leaders in key positions of the national security bureaucracy, and supplemented with scores of lower-level New Right politicos, President Reagan was primed for an assault on the Soviet evil empire.

The interrelated right-wing concepts of nuclear superiority, winnable nuclear war, and nuclear war-fighting became the dominant nuclear doctrine in the early Reagan administration. One of the first indications of this new official attitude came with National Security Decision Document 13, signed by President Reagan in 1982, proclaiming that the goal of U.S. policy is to prevail (win) in a protracted nuclear war.[30] In addition, a secret directive (Fiscal Years 1984-88 Defense Guidance) prepared under the supervision of Defense Secretary Caspar Weinberger, states that the United States must have:

plans that assure U.S. strategic nuclear forces can render ineffective the total Soviet military and political power structure... and forces that will maintain, throughout a protracted conflict period and afterward, the capability to inflict very high levels of damage against the industrial/economic base of the Soviet Union...so that they have strong incentive to seek conflict termination short of an all-out attack on our cities and economic assets.[31]

A key component of nuclear superiority is nuclear survivability: the capability to fight a nuclear war and stick around long enough to enjoy the victory. In 1982, in testimony before the Senate Armed Services Committee, the Commander in Chief of the Strategic Air Command, Gen. Bennie Davis, confirmed that U.S. national policy is no longer deterrence, but war-fighting doctrine, which assumes that the United States can survive a nuclear war. The Federal Emergency Management Agency, responsible for civil defense, wrote in January 1981 that "the United States could survive nuclear attack and go on to recovery within a relatively few years."[32]

In a frank answer to traditional conservatives who cite the importance of East-West nuclear stability rather than supremacy, Reagan's Undersecretary of Defense for Policy Fred Iklé pointedly wrote:

> But stability is an idea that has spread beyond its proper habitat, like a fungus infesting most of contemporary discourse on foreign affairs and strategy.[33]

How does the dominance of these doctrines in the Reagan administration differ from previous governments? As we have seen, nuclear war-fighting—which requires nuclear superiority to succeed—has been the preferred nuclear policy since the days when the only war-fighting force on Earth was the Strategic Air Command's fleet of nuclear-laden B-29's. Nevertheless, the strategy articulated in the Defense Guidance marked a significant change, if only for the explicitness of its expression. This was given public testimony by Caspar Weinberger himself, who, facing the outcry, publicly appeared to backtrack by stating that the United States really sought to "survive," not prevail in a nuclear war. However, Weinberger's protestations are belied by more ominous developments in the design of weapons systems that provide the material basis for programs of nuclear war-fighting. What made the Reagan administration more seriously inclined toward nuclear superiority were not its words but its programs and budgets.

In the implementation of nuclear doctrine, the right wing—with considerable influence within the Reagan administration—was unquestionably angling toward nuclear superiority. This was evident through four developments: Star Wars, first-strike offensive weapons, the coordination of Star Wars and offensive weapons in a deliberate war-fighting posture—(Command, Control, Communications and Intelligence, or C3I, and the right-wing arms control position.

Star Wars: New Hope for Supremacy

In the early 1980s the right wing confronted the problem: how to restore a credible escalation dominance. The solution: if you cannot dominate on land, at sea, or in the air, how about outer space? In the words of Undersecretary of the Air Force Edward Aldridge,

> We do not have to stretch our imagination very far to see that the nation that controls space may control the world.[34]

Nowhere has the Right contributed more to the promotion of first-strike and nuclear war-fighting strategies than in the successful lobbying by organizations such as the Heritage Foundation and High Frontier for the Strategic Defense Initiative (SDI), popularly known as Star Wars. President Reagan's famous Star Wars speech of March 1983 may have taken most of the arms control and scientific communities by surprise, but the announcement was the culmination of a three-year plan by the Right to move the United States toward a new era of U.S. nuclear superiority.

SDI was conceived by a group of Rollnet-related scientists, industrialists, military men, and aerospace executives meeting in the offices of the Heritage Foundation in 1981. The planners included right-wing funder Joseph Coors, longtime Reagan confidant Justin Dart, Gen. Daniel Graham, and the Hoover Institution's Karl Bendetsen. Major impetus came from ultraconservative physicist Edward Teller, the "father of the hydrogen bomb" who is also associated with the Hoover Institution. Teller, who as associate director emeritus of the Lawrence Livermore Laboratory is a key member of the military-industrial complex, promoted SDI by reportedly giving misleading and technically inaccurate reports on a key Star Wars weapon in secret letters to Reagan administration officials, charges corroborated by a half dozen eminent scientists long involved with the weapons lab.[35] SDI offered a multi-billion-dollar boon to the large defense contractors at a time when many old space and weapons-related projects were nearing completion, threatening a slowdown in the industry.

Star Wars has been viewed as integral to the global rollback strategies of key individuals who have planned and implemented the Reagan Doctrine. As a prominent example, consider ex-Defense Intelligence Agency chief General Graham, a Board member of CPD and head of the High Frontier organization. As we saw in Chapter Three, Graham has been an important player in the World Anti-Communist League and the Unification Church's CAUSA organization. Graham's own attitude on the nuclear balance—"Do I advocate superiority for the United States? I say yes."—indicates that Star Wars was conceived as the ultimate rollback weapon of the ideological Right.[36]

Chapter Two shows how Star Wars provides the potential for economic rollback of the Soviet Union. In addition, it is the root of future military rollback through the establishment of a technological revolution in weapons that could leave the Soviets crying uncle.

Star Wars is advertised as a defensive rather than an offensive system. However, even the defensive component of Star Wars is aggressive. As originally conceived, it would allow the United States to launch a first strike on the USSR with the very accurate MX and Trident II missiles directed against Soviet missiles, the Pershing II missiles used against Soviet guidance centers, and the defensive shield—even if only partially effective—eliminating a percentage of the Soviet retaliatory strike and thus keeping U.S. casualties down.[37] Dr. Teller, showing how Star Wars might reduce U.S. deaths from 130 million to 30 million in a nuclear war, said,

> I ask you, what is the difference between 30 million people dead and 130 million people dead?...With 30 million dead, the United States can survive....

In the words of Star Wars critic E. P. Thompson, Reagan's fantasy is "of putting a shield over the top of America so it will once again be back in the days of Hiroshima when the United States had the bomb but no one else did, when America could nuke the outside world but no one could nuke it."[38]

Not only is Star Wars destabilizing to the nuclear balance as a defense, it also has awesome offensive capabilities. According to Robert English, a former Reagan administration Defense Department policy analyst:

The development of Star Wars weapon technologies by both sides could result in a world of unimaginable dangers.... The offensive potential of this next generation of kinetic and directed-energy weapons is staggering, with frightening strategic implications. Consider the following possibility: suppose that technological advances in SDI research make it possible to develop space-based weapons capable of the swift and accurate destruction of targets in space *and* on the earth's surface. Such systems might even be able to destroy intercontinental ballistic missiles (ICBMs) in their silos in a matter of moments with minimal 'collateral' damage. Should they prove feasible, there is no doubt that both the U.S. and Soviet military establishments would find suitable rationales for developing such weapons.

The 'surgical' precision of such weapons would make the temptation of a first strike much harder to resist. Even more disconcerting is the extraordinary speed with which space-based weapons could attack...space-based weapons might reduce a half hour of warning to a mere two or three minutes. Of course, the side that felt threatened by such a system might well be compelled to shift from a 'launch-under-attack' or 'launch-on-warning' posture to one of 'launch-under-crisis' for fear of losing the bulk of its retaliatory force before it even knew that it was being attacked. A more hair-trigger world is hard to imagine....

A space-based laser powerful enough to destroy ICBMs in flight could certainly attack satellites and terrestrial targets as well. Separate studies by Argonne National Laboratory and R&D Associates, a private defense research firm, have concluded that space-based lasers could incinerate flammable targets and set numerous fires on the enemy's home soil.... Perhaps most threatening are the various 'kinetic energy' weapons, which range from familiar cannon- and rocket-propelled warheads to sophisticated hypervelocity launchers. These so-called 'rail guns' hurl projectiles at great speed by means of precisely timed boosts of electromagnetic energy....

The kinetic energy weapon most likely to have the capacity to 'bust silos' is the humble rocket. Imagine a fleet of satellites, each bearing a number of small missiles, that passes over the adversary's territory in low earth orbit. Such a system would superficially resemble the one envisioned in the proposals of 'High Frontier,' a pro-Star Wars lobbying group. In this case, the missiles would be aimed at ICBM silos and leadership and command centers.... Hypervelocity missiles launched from altitudes of 100 miles or less could easily complete an attack in several minutes—more than rapid enough to preempt any response....[39]

For military industrialist Simon Ramo, one of the developers of the ICBM, Star Wars has potentially immense offensive power: "Who says that this technique will be used only to knock out missiles in the sky? If it's such a good technique, why not use it to knock out things on the ground?"[40]

Other experts believe that an SDI system could be used in lightning-fast strikes against relatively "soft" ground targets such as airplanes, power plants, and grain fields, causing instantaneous fires that in the words of John Rather, a laser expert and SDI proponent, could "take an industrialized country back to an 18th-century level in 30 minutes." Possibly SDI could ultimately be capable of destroying hard missile silos, thus providing a direct first strike weapon. According to Harvey Lynch, an experimental physicist at the Stanford Linear Accelerator Center, a nation contemplating a first-strike with strategic missiles could fire its space-based laser weapons in a surprise attack to blind enemy satellites and prevent them from performing their vital functions of early warning, reconnaissance, and commanding and controlling enemy weapons, with the enemy's retaliatory capabilities correspondingly severely damaged. In addition, specific targeting of Soviet leadership and command and control centers could be done as part of a first-strike "decapitation" strategy.[41]

An indication of the offensive nature of Star Wars from within the Reagan administration is the statement in the Fiscal 1984-8 Defense Guidance that the Pentagon must be prepared to "wage war effectively from outer space...[and] to project force in and from outer space as needed...." In 1985, the Defense Department was reported to have devised a nuclear war plan and command structure that would integrate offensive nuclear missiles with the projected anti-missile shield embodied in the SDI.[42]

Star Wars can thus be considered a program based on a policy of nuclear dominance rather than deterrence. In line with this perspective, leading members of the Right directly promote the SDI as a necessary tool to move beyond the era of mutually assured destruction (MAD) which they see as having been inimicable to U.S. global interests:

> The balance of terror 'balanced' the Soviet Union...into superpower status. It is precisely the possibility of mutual destruction, combined with the Soviets' reputation for indifference to the suffering of their own people, that has made the USSR the strategic equal of the numerically, geographically, economically, and technologically superior West. It was MAD, largely, that froze the West

into inaction as the Russians expanded into Cuba, Central America, Africa, and the Middle East.[43]

To combat MAD, Star Wars could become the new top rung of the escalation dominance ladder.

President Reagan has issued assurances that "SDI has nothing to do with offensive weapons," that SDI "offered the hope of rendering nuclear missiles impotent and obsolete," and that SDI is a "purely peaceful technology." But in a secret Heritage Foundation document cited in Lt. Col. Robert Bowman's *Star Wars: Defense or Death Star?*, the peaceful nature of SDI rhetoric is exposed. All along, Star Wars advocates planned to provide "political and emotional packaging" to make the program sound like a peace proposal, disarming SDI "opponents by stealing their language and causes," taking over the freeze movement's own advocacy of a nuclear free world.[44]

The peace rhetoric—that Star Wars is purely *defense*—is equivalent to the Reagan Doctrine rhetoric that Third World rollback is nothing more than the global democratic revolution. The relation of the term "defense" to nuclear superiority is the same as the relation of the word "democracy" to rollback—clever public relations.

New Offensive Weaponry

Since SDI would take many years to implement, the right wing and military-industrial complex successfully pushed the Reagan administration and Congress to develop all possible offensive nuclear weapons. In 1982, President Reagan signed a secret authorization calling for the Department of Defense to produce another 16,000 warheads through 1990, adding to or replacing the 26,000 operational warheads already in existence at the time.[45] The Reagan administration's multi-trillion-dollar defense appropriations included the development of weapons systems that, taken together, have provided the United States with a formidable first-strike capability:

- The superaccurate and first-strike-capable MX missile (though a scandal involving Northrop Corp's production of the MX guidance system puts the accuracy in some doubt). At present, fifty are scheduled for deployment, at a cost of $14.8 billion in 1982 dollars;

- The Trident missile, to be deployed on the Trident submarine. With this weapon, the effective retaliatory capability of the submarine arm of the U.S. "strategic triad" has been upgraded to provide a first-strike capability;

- The reversal of President Carter's cancellation of the B-1B bomber program, with the cost of 100 bombers coming to $28 billion;

- The development of the super-secret Stealth bomber, which, by eluding enemy radar, adds to the U.S. first-strike capacity;

- The full-scale development of very accurate cruise missiles, which—though too slow to be first-strike capable *per se*—can be deployed in air, sea, or ground-based modes and thereby add to any protracted nuclear war-fighting scenario;

- The commission of a new set of offensive missiles that complement SDI by zig-zagging or otherwise evading missile defenses that the Soviets may develop in the future.[46]

Developments in nuclear war-fighting doctrine, the expansion of the nuclear arsenal, and the new generation of superaccurate nuclear missiles (for example MX and Trident) cannot be laid at the doorstep of the right wing or the Reagan administration alone. The innovation of the Reagan period consisted of the integration of these weapons into first-strike targeting plans, as revealed by a secret Arms Control and Disarmament Agency (ACDA) document titled "Outcome of Hypothetical U.S. First Strikes, 1993."[47] These costly weapons systems will be locked into production lines over the next decade, comprising an offensive juggernaut impossible to reverse without seriously dislocating an economy primed on such a buildup.

Is there even a remote chance that these first-strike capable weapons would actually be used in a first strike? Asking this question around the Pentagon would bring many affirmative answers; a 1984 *Newsweek* poll (July 9) revealed that 28 percent of senior U.S. military officers believe that there are conditions that would justify a nuclear first strike against the USSR.

C3I: Nuclear Neuraxis

The nuclear war-fighting posture of the United States is more than the sum of the offensive and defensive developments described above and has been given a formidable cohesion by development of the computerized integrated network for controlling and coordinating both these arms of the U.S. threat.

The developments in Command, Control, Communications and Intelligence (C3I) are perhaps the most important for the attainment of nuclear superiority with a "credible" first-strike and nuclear war-fighting position. Since the beginning of the Reagan presidency, a total of $40 billion has been committed to this entire scheme. Plans include:

- A network of covertly deployed, interstate-bound eighteen-wheeler trucks crammed with computers and sophisticated electronic equipment geared towards allowing U.S. generals to conduct protracted nuclear war-fighting, especially if primary U.S. command posts have been destroyed;

- The $10-billion to $20-billion Milstar satellite system, which, according to C3I head Donald C. Latham, would be able to support a "multiple-exchange campaign," in which nuclear weapons would be fired in salvos between adversaries;

- A satellite-based Nuclear Detection System that could report which targets have been destroyed and which need to be hit again.[48]

Interlocked with the above are new developments in Extremely Low Frequency (ELF) communications that are critical for coordinating the activities of the first-strike capable fleet of submarines. This technology, in which the United States has a substantial lead over the USSR, allows submarines to remain submerged for long periods of time, minimizing the periodic resurfacing that is necessary at present, and that poses a danger each time of being spotted and tracked by the Soviets.[49]

Complementing the above are a whole range of nuclear war-fighting plans. For example:

- Former Navy Secretary John Lehman proposed the deployment of nuclear-capable attack subs in the Norwegian fjords for immediate bottling up of ships and subs of the Soviet Baltic fleet, pursuant to the firing of nuclear weapons on the USSR at the early stages of a war.[50]

- The Air Force has been reported to be exploring the possibility of building several hundred small nuclear reactors to generate emergency electrical power for computers, communication lines, and weapon launching sites during a protracted nuclear war. The cost of the plan, which would involve transporting reactors around the country and overseas, is estimated at $20 billion.[51]

- As an example of war-fighting preparations bordering on the surreal, in 1984 the *New York Times* revealed U.S. plans for building a vast underground nuclear missile base, with estimated costs up to $50 billion. The project calls for tunneling missiles of this "Secure Reserve Force" to the earth's surface after the outbreak of a nuclear war to engage in protracted nuclear war-fighting.[52] Perhaps with such a scheme, U.S. nuclear dominance can be maintained once World War III is over, thereby avoiding a dreaded postwar "missile gap."

The Right Wing and Arms Control

The bedrock position of the Right on arms control is to oppose it. Such a position meshes with right-wing views on rollback and nuclear superiority. However, the development of SDI has brought forth a far more sophisticated stance of the Right. After explaining the basic right-wing position, we will analyze an emerging right-wing alternative.

The General Right-wing Attitude

According to William R. Van Cleave, a founding member of the Committee on the Present Danger,

> Arms control has had a depressant effect not only on our military programs but also on our ability to deal with the Soviets. It has thoroughly muddled our thinking.[53]

Richard Pipes, in *Survival is Not Enough,* spends fully 18 pages attacking arms control and disarmament advocates, complaining that "a large part of the population has come to attach an exaggerated, almost manic importance to arms control."[54] On arms control, Jeane

Kirkpatrick has said, "I am willing to be just as generous as we possibly can be, as long as that's consistent with maintaining clear supremacy."[55]

The far Right periodical *Human Events* attacked Paul Nitze (perhaps the leading member of the pro-military Committee on the Present Danger) for being too pro-arms control and for disavowing nuclear superiority.[56] The conservative journal *National Review* has featured one recent article entitled "Why Arms Talks Must Fail," and in another article showed why in general, "summit meetings are a Bad Thing." In a similar vein, the neoconservative magazine *Commentary* ran an article from the right-wing Institute for Contemporary Studies entitled, "Why an American Arms Build-up is Morally Necessary."[57]

As with many other features of rollback, arms control skepticism is also common among center-right Democrats. For example, Zbigniew Brzezinski has stated,

> The time has come to lay to rest the expectation that arms control
> is the secret key to a more amicable American-Soviet relationship
> or even to the enhancement of mutual security.[58]

The most powerful advocate for the anti-arms control view in the Reagan administration was Assistant Secretary of Defense for International Security Affairs Richard Perle, former aide to militarist Democrat "Scoop" Jackson, and a CPD member. Perle testified before the Senate Foreign Affairs Committee on February 25, 1985 that it was a "great mistake" to continue honoring past arms treaties with the Soviet Union. On May 7, 1985, he told the Senate Armed Services Committee that the United States should stop observing SALT I and SALT II. In May 1986, Perle convinced President Reagan to change his policy on SALT II and to cease voluntary compliance with its provisions.[59]

Simultaneously, Perle pressed the right-wing attack on the 1972 Anti-Ballistic Missile (ABM) treaty, which forbids testing and deployment of Star Wars. Though the favored right-wing position has been simply to violate the treaty, strong antagonism of Democrats and European allies to this approach brought about a more diplomatic means for accomplishing the same end: reinterpreting ABM such that it allowed Star Wars testing and deployment. In 1987, Reagan signed a National Security Decision Directive favoring the reinterpretation of the ABM treaty.[60]

The far Right was incensed over the 1986 Reykjavík summit, when Reagan seemed to join Soviet General Secretary Gorbachev in a quest for a nuclear-free world. Burton Pines, senior vice-president of the

Heritage Foundation, admitted, "We were expecting the worst from the Iceland summit."[61] Regarding Reykjavík, Richard Pipes argued that even an arms agreement favorable to the United States would be a mistake because it helps the Soviet economy.[62] Conservative columnist William Safire said that Reagan "walked into an ambush" set by Gorbachev, and Reagan redeemed himself by not agreeing to anything.[63] Following the summit, much of the Right strongly opposed the 1987 intermediate-range nuclear forces (INF) treaty.[64]

The Sophisticated Right-wing Arms Control Posture

The potential for SDI to usher in a new era of nuclear superiority has markedly altered the arms control agenda of a portion of the right wing. SDI is the central military goal of the right-wing movement, as expressed by analysts of the Hoover Institution and the Heritage Foundation, strongly conservative members of congress, and right-wing organizations such as the American Security Council. SDI brings together the sometimes feuding strands of the conservative movement: the traditional right, the New Right, the neoconservatives, and the military Right.[65] The Right appears united on the slogan "Deploy SDI Now."[66] A sigh of right-wing relief could be heard when Reagan stood firm on SDI at the summits in Reykjavík and Washington, D.C.

What has come as a surprise is a more sophisticated right-wing arms control position that not only supports SDI, but also allows for reductions in offensive nuclear weapons, reductions that more "moderate" analysts believe would go too far.

For example, in 1980, the Heritage Foundation in its *Mandate for Leadership* "instructions" for the Reagan administration, did not attack arms control, but admitted that it could play a role in the preservation of U.S. national security. *Mandate* stated that arms reductions, not just limitations should be the goal.[67] In 1984, *Mandate II* continued in the same vein: "The Administration must be willing to negotiate arms reductions with Moscow if such cuts will enhance the chances for superpower strategic stability." At the same time, *Mandate II* stated that the United States should withdraw from the ABM treaty to allow SDI development.[68]

In 1982, Reagan called for START (Strategic Arms *Reduction* Talks) while continuing to attack the previous SALT (Strategic Arms *Limitation* Talks). Though many felt START to be purely a public-relations move to blunt the huge European and U.S. peace movements of the time, Reagan persisted in the arms reduction concept. Following the Geneva summit of 1985, Reagan made proposals for 50 percent cuts in strategic arms.[69] At the famous Reykjavík meeting with General Secretary Gorbachev, Reagan took the unbelievable position that the United States and USSR should eliminate all offensive nuclear missiles—provided that Star Wars could go forward unimpeded. Finally, Reagan negotiated the elimination of intermediate nuclear missiles.[70]

Many center-right figures spoke out against these large offensive arms reductions. Gen. Brent Scowcroft opposed the 50 percent strategic arms reduction and the zero option.[71] Former President Nixon and Henry Kissinger opposed the INF plan. Amazingly, portions of the right wing were pushing for arms control over the objections of former advocates of détente. Why?

One reason is that the Reaganites were working for arms reduction treaties heavily favorable to the United States.[72] The INF agreement, for example, requires the Soviets to destroy over twice the number of missiles the United States has to sacrifice.[73] The reduction of offensive strategic missiles would leave the United States in an advantageous offensive posture because it has far more bombers and cruise missiles (not affected by such an agreement) than the Soviets. But this advantage in the arms reductions balance is not the full answer.

The major reason for right-wing advocacy of offensive arms reductions is to establish U.S. nuclear superiority. Here's how it works: We noted earlier that Star Wars might allow the United States to launch a first strike on the USSR, with the defensive shield—even if only partially effective—eliminating a percentage of the Soviet retaliatory strike and thus keeping U.S. casualties down. The smaller the Soviet retaliatory strike, the more successful the defensive shield would be in protecting the United States. Thus a significant reduction in offensive weapons is of incalculable advantage to the nation that has a missile defense system. Since the United States is far ahead in strategic defense technology, Pentagon planners could look forward to a number of years in which the United States would have a defensive system and the Soviets would not. During those years, *given a reduction in offensive missiles,* the United States would have clear nuclear superiority.

Leading right-wing nuclear strategist Fred Iklé, a member of the CPD and Undersecretary of Defense for Policy in the Reagan administration, also points out how offensive weapons reductions would bolster SDI: "The more the offensive armaments can be reduced by agreement, the easier and cheaper the job of providing effective defenses."[74]

A Senate report on SDI demonstrates identical logic: "it is generally agreed within SDI that a U.S. defensive deployment would have to proceed hand-in-hand with deep reductions in Soviet offensive nuclear forces for the defense to be truly effective."[75] An SDI report by James Fletcher states, "If the Soviet Union agreed to reduce its force of intercontinental ballistic missiles, then an effective missile defense would be less expensive and would pose fewer technical challenges."[76]

SDI critic Noam Chomsky similarly remarks: "Take the case of SDI, once again. Whatever slight prospects such a system might offer for defense of the national territory depend crucially on general reductions of offensive forces, to prevent the adversary from overwhelming the system with new offensive weapons."[77] Another SDI critic, the Union of Concerned Scientists, agrees, arguing that the Reagan administration's offensive weapons reductions are for the purpose of allowing SDI to become effective.[78]

Another aspect of right-wing pro-"arms control" thinking is that U.S. superiority in technology may allow for a new generation of offensive weapons, making the current weapons obsolete over the next decades. It is to the advantage of the United States to reduce current weaponry such that both sides will have to start their arms buildup anew, a situation greatly favoring the nation with better technology. Fred Iklé suggests this mode of thinking in this statement, "The United States is now pursuing new technologies that hold promise for success.... Our thinking on nuclear strategy must reach far into the future. It is not enough that our strategy serve to prevent nuclear attack in this decade or the next. Nuclear armaments and defensive systems take ten years or more to design, develop and build."[79] Arms control agreements also take many years to design, negotiate, and sign. By the time an offensive weapons reduction agreement is in place, the weapons to be eliminated might already be obsolete for the United States.

To summarize, the sophisticated right-wing position favoring offensive nuclear arms reductions in conjunction with Star Wars is a posture designed to achieve nuclear superiority.

The Limits of Right-wing Nuclearism

Why is the right-wing position on Star Wars and offensive arms reductions so controversial? Would not all nuclear thinkers look forward to a new era of nuclear superiority based on these two developments?

In fact, the nuclear "establishment" is not united on nuclear superiority. Superiority is principally a rollback goal. For many traditional conservatives, East-West stability is more important. Business cannot make profits in a postnuclear wasteland. And the U.S. budget deficit, fueled by military spending, is creating major problems for the U.S. economy. Arms control could help to create reductions not only in weapons but in the deficit as well.

Star Wars remains a bitter and divisive issue. Perhaps the major debate has centered on the impact of SDI—with its undefined but certainly gargantuan costs—on the domestic U.S. economy. The military-industrial corporations favor SDI because of the direct benefits of more than $26 billion in contracts awarded through 1987, more than 90 percent of which were garnered by the largest ten such corporations. Other business leaders less tied into this sector are worried about SDI's worsening effect on the already massive budget deficit. Though some accede to the possibility of positive SDI spin-off effects on the domestic economy, many feel that the monies would be better used for direct investment in modernizing civilian sectors. The domestic electronics industry mirrors this division, with those directly benefiting from Pentagon contracts going along with SDI in opposition to those in the industry that foresee a further reduction in competitiveness *vis-à-vis* the Japanese.

Similar splits are seen within the scientific community. By 1987, half the science and engineering faculty in each of more than 100 research departments pledged to accept no more SDI money. In the twenty top-ranked departments, more than 50 percent of the combined faculties, including fifteen Nobel laureates, asserted that they would not participate in the program. A poll of National Academy of Sciences members whose disciplines are related to SDI found that 70 percent of respondents opposed or strongly opposed SDI, while 9.8 percent supported or strongly supported it.[80]

One powerful argument of numerous authoritative individuals and professional organizations opposed to SDI is that the system as a nuclear defense is unworkable. For example, it has been deemed impossible to develop sufficiently error-free computer software to coordinate all the components of the defense. Even top weapons experts at Lawrence Livermore Laboratories, the leading Star Wars research facility, doubt the system can work as a nuclear defense.[81] These fears have been underscored by recent revelations of the destructive effects of computer "viruses"—glitches in the software that could wreak havoc in any computerized missile defense system.[82]

Leaders in the national security and foreign policy establishments are also divided over the impact of SDI on the strategic relation with the USSR, reminiscent of the debates that took place during the time of the ABM Treaty in the early 1970s. The central issue has always been the destabilizing nature of defensive systems on the "stability" of MAD. Even some who favor nuclear superiority are skeptical that SDI is the way to go, because (as argued by the 1985 Congressional Office of Technology Assessment report) the Soviets could decide to preemptively shoot down the system before it becomes fully deployable as a first-strike threat.[83] Another worry is that the Soviet Union would proliferate offensive weaponry in order to overload the defensive capabilities of any SDI system. The Soviets could also enter into an SDI-related anti-satellite arms race that would threaten the U.S. "early-warning" system and other U.S. war-fighting capabilities.[84]

Offensive arms reductions *without* SDI is not destabilizing on a global scale; it is the reductions coupled with SDI that creates strategic instability. Thus the traditional conservatives (for example George Shultz and Senate Armed Services Committee Chairman Sam Nunn) generally oppose the right-wing position of scrapping the ABM treaty and rapidly deploying SDI. Liberals on Capitol Hill would allow SDI to go forward as a research project, but not yet as deployment.[85]

While the conservative elites with the backing of many scientists have put a crimp in right-wing plans for SDI-based nuclear superiority, the Right has achieved a victory in getting SDI locked into the system. The more than $26 billion in outstanding contracts and the integration of NATO, Japanese, and Israeli allies into the plan have brought SDI to a "critical mass." The plan has developed and sustained a political/bureaucratic vested interest, making it increasingly difficult to derail. To underscore this point, many influentials who were initially highly skeptical of SDI because of its cost and destabilizing nature have now embraced the gradual introduction of SDI technologies.

The 1987 Summit and the Response from the Right

The limits of right-wing nuclearism were all too evident at the December 1987 Reagan-Gorbachev summit in Washington, D.C. The intermediate-range nuclear forces (INF) treaty signed at that historic meeting caused serious rifts within and between the traditional conservatives and the right wing. Although a small number on the sophisticated Right recognized the opportunities afforded by arms reductions integrated with a viable SDI, much of the Right fervently opposed the treaty. While the treaty's missile reductions were highly favorable to the United States, the Right saw the momentum of summitry undercutting the "Evil Empire" logic that had been the center of gravity of the Reagan foreign policy. The Right's concern escalated to the point when Conservative Caucus leader Howard Phillips accused "the Gipper" of being "a useful idiot" for the Soviets.

In its attack on the INF, the Right resurrected the fear of U.S.-Western European "decoupling" in the face of Soviet aggression that would supposedly result from U.S. missiles no longer physically stationed in Europe. Although such decoupling is extremely unlikely given the robust U.S. nuclear presence on bombers and submarines in or near Europe, this "fear" has formed the basis of a tactical alliance between the Right and a number of Atlanticist-oriented conservatives. The latter included such notables as Henry Kissinger, who are attuned to the political necessities of a conservative NATO defense establishment that has sustained itself on the Soviet "threat" since the dawn of the Cold War.[86]

In early 1988, the Right, led by Sen. Jesse Helms, attempted to attach a number of "killer amendments" aimed at forestalling the adoption of the treaty by, at a minimum, causing it to be renegotiated with the USSR. In addition, plans were made to attach amendments that would make it more difficult to subsequently negotiate a reduction in long-range, strategic weapons. The campaign against INF was waged by a number of the organizations that were effective in derailing the SALT II Treaty in the late 1970s, such as the American Security Council and the Conservative Caucus.[87] While failing to stop the treaty, the Right did delay its passage for four months, thus lessening the prospects for further Reagan-Gorbachev arms control agreements.

Hand in hand with the attack on the INF Treaty was a renewed push for SDI and for the weakening of the 1972 ABM Treaty. At the Washington summit, Reagan and Gorbachev scrupulously avoided raising differences over SDI that would prejudice future talks. However, within a week after the talks, Reagan falsely asserted that the understandings reached with Gorbachev set no limits on the testing, development, and deployment of space-based systems.[88] Just before the summit, the Moonie-associated American Freedom Council sponsored a letter-writing campaign to push for SDI, concurrent with High Frontier's continued grassroots lobbying efforts aimed at pushing Congress to adopt short-term deployment of Star Wars. In early January 1988, the military began top-secret ground tests of the anti-missile laser that the Reagan administration wanted to launch into space in the early 1990s as part of such early deployment, tests that themselves were interpreted by SDI critics as calculated to violate the ABM Treaty.[89] Even Sen. Sam Nunn, who had criticized the Reagan administration plan to undermine the interpretation of the ABM Treaty, stated his support of a limited land-based anti-missile defense system, a stand applauded by the Hoover Institution's Star Wars advocate Gregory Fossedal as keeping SDI alive.[90]

But this concerted attack by the Right met substantial opposition from traditional conservatives who, in a period of increasing economic crisis signified by the 1987 stock market crash, desired to build a more stable relationship with the Soviet Union under Gorbachev. By the early part of 1988, many of the hardline elements in the Reagan administration had either resigned or were forced out of office, including Richard Perle, Fred Iklé, Kenneth Adelman, and Frank Gaffney. Most notable was the resignation of Casper Weinberger, who until leaving office reportedly for personal reasons was the leading administration adherent of the short-term deployment of SDI. According to conservative columnist William Safire, Weinberger actually quit because Reagan capitulated to Congress in allowing the traditional interpretation of the ABM Treaty (prohibiting Star Wars deployment) to stand at least through October 1988.[91]

At the time of this writing, arms control policy remains in flux. Most traditional conservatives will likely press for further understandings with Gorbachev. But their moves will be predicated on a position of strength fortified by the continued development and deployment of new offensive weapons integrated with some version of the SDI to pressure the USSR to "behave." Fred Iklé underscored how SDI had become fundamental to U.S. strategic thinking: "In the 1970s, it was inconceivable that the country would make a major effort to build ballistic missile defenses. Now it is inconceivable that we would not at least continue research and development of antiballistic missile defenses."[92]

SDI may become central to the strategies of traditional conservatives striving to build a lean and powerful conventional force based on Star Wars technologies. Hence the findings of the January 1988 Report of the Commission on Integrated Long-Term Strategy, co-chaired by Fred Iklé and Albert Wohlstetter, with members including Zbigniew

Brzezinski and Henry Kissinger. This milestone report called for the production of new powerful non-nuclear as well as nuclear munitions that could be delivered with pinpoint accuracy by such space-age technologies.[93] This new generation of weaponry would blur the distinction between conventional and nuclear warfare and could erase the recent gains in arms control verification procedures, thereby contributing to a new level of East-West instability.

In conclusion, during the 1980s, a decade of great flux, the Right became a potent force in setting the agenda of nuclear policy. On SALT II, Reagan succeeded in scuttling the treaty. On the ABM Treaty, its defenders are on the defensive. Star Wars remains the most prominent legacy of the Right's nuclear program, as exemplified by the Reagan administration's absolute insistence on its non-negotiability with the Soviets, and the failure of Star Wars critics to kill the SDI program. Since the deployment of SDI is equally non-negotiable for the Soviets, this issue may deadlock major strategic arms control progress.[94]

The stern Soviet attitude toward offensive arms reductions without limits on SDI, and the opposition of traditional conservatives to rapid SDI deployment and to destabilization of the nuclear balance, will likely derail the right-wing drive toward nuclear superiority. The right wing set the nuclear agenda for much of the Reagan administration, and will continue to have an influential voice in the debates over that agenda. The Right will have a difficult time winning those debates. However, with the training of its cadres in arms control issues and with greater penetration of the arms control bureaucracy, the Right will likely continue to vex efforts at true disarmament for years to come.

6

Economic Decline: Fertile Soil for Right-wing Growth

Why Did Rollback Make a Comeback?

Why did right-wing foreign policy gain such influence in the late 1970s and 1980s? Why was détente scrapped? And for what reason did the United States reassert a new wave of global interventionism?

The conventional wisdom holds that the right-wing resurgence was a response to a major upturn in Soviet aggressiveness around the world, and to the fourteen Third World revolutions of the 1974-80 period. That interpretation may have some truth to it, but it also has some serious problems.

Compared with the 1970s, the Soviets were equally or more aggressive during the Cuban missile crisis, the Berlin crises, and the interventions in Hungary and Czechoslovakia. Yet the United States did not respond to these events with a major long-term hardening of foreign policy. The increased rate of Soviet military expenditures widely broadcast by the Committee on the Present Danger (CPD) in the late 1970s actually took place in the 1960s, bringing in its wake détente rather than a renewed cold war.[1] Reagan's own Scowcroft Commission rejected the right-wing view that the United States was vulnerable to Soviet nuclear attack and without adequate deterrent capability. The estimates cited by anti-détente forces that Soviet military spending grew 3 percent to 4 percent during the late 1970s were shown to be wrong by the CIA.[2] Soviet conventional power in Europe did not change in the 1970s. While the Soviets made some gains in the Third World during détente, especially in Southeast Asia and Africa, they also suffered compensating losses in influence, for example in Egypt and India.[3] The Iranian Revolution had nothing to do with the Soviets at all. And by the time of the 1979 Soviet intervention in Afghanistan, CPD already had spent five years successfully tearing down détente. In sum, changes in Soviet behavior are inadequate to explain the right-wing comeback and the U.S. military buildup. Perhaps the Soviet Union was more the excuse and less the cause of the rightward foreign policy shift.

In fact, a more fundamental reality explains the rejuvenation of the right wing in the 1970s. That reality is economic crisis. Understanding the crisis is crucial to grasping the economic causes of the right-wing resurgence and the rejuvenation of rollback policy.

To start with, there are actually two economic crises, not just one. First is the world economic crisis and second is the decline in U.S. economic power relative to other nations. When the nation that has been undisputed number one sees itself slipping, the response is to fight back, to reconquer the number one slot. That is what global rollback symbolizes: putting the United States on top again.

There are serious inconsistencies in the right-wing approach. For instance, it is not the USSR that provides the direct economic challenge to the United States; this comes mainly from Japan, the newly industrializing nations of Asia, and from Western Europe. With unemployment and inflation high in the 1970s, it was important to redirect popular discontent against an external enemy. One quick grab into the Cold War bag of tricks would suffice. The evil empire was the obvious choice.

Prosperity Capitalism

The years following World War II brought world economic expansion. While the world population increased by 46 percent from 1950 to 1970, total production increased by 170 percent, and world trade expanded by 285 percent.[4] Because the United States held unquestioned economic and political hegemony, it gained most of the benefits of this postwar boom. Unemployment and inflation in the United States were relatively low and corporate profits high. The dollar served as the undisputed medium for international trade.

Because so much of the world's expanding wealth flowed to the United States, two major developments became possible domestically. First, big business could respond to postwar labor militancy by granting portions of the U.S. working population rising wages and substantial benefits. Second, the government could afford to placate demands of the elderly, minorities and the poor by constructing a large welfare state. This period of U.S. history, roughly from 1945 to 1970, was the era of prosperity capitalism. Under prosperity capitalism, utilizing the theories of British economist John Maynard Keynes, the higher wages and governmental benefits stimulated the economy by increasing consumer demand for products. Since things were going well for the United States, the goal of foreign policy was to maintain the status quo—the doctrine of containment.

During the era of prosperity capitalism, mechanisms were employed to increase consumer demand in order to prolong the good times. The government initiated a period of planned (Keynesian) federal budget deficits which through increased spending stimulated the economy. Federal domestic spending increased from 8.6 percent to 19.9 percent of GNP between 1955 and 1975, and military spending rose dramatically during the Korean war and remained at high levels thereafter. In addition, sales were fueled by increases in consumer and government borrowing.[5]

However, during the 1960s, the very mechanisms that had stimulated the U.S. economy, allowing for the prolonged economic prosperity, began to create severe problems for U.S. corporations. The creation of consumer demand by excess government spending kept unemployment low enough to allow workers to gain the bargaining power to demand higher wages and benefits, thereby causing a corporate profit squeeze. From 1965 to 1970, the ratio of profits to wages was cut in half.[6] As the conditions of the world and the U.S. economies were changing, Keynesian policies were becoming unprofitable.

The World Economic Crisis

In the 1970s, the capitalist world entered its most serious postwar recession. Production showed declines of up to 10 or 15 percent.[7] The average annual growth rate of gross domestic investment in the industrialized countries dropped from 5.6 percent in the 1960s to 1.5 percent from 1970-78.[8] Inflation-adjusted after-tax rates of profit for all nonfinancial U.S. corporations fell from 15.5 percent (1963-66) to 9.7 percent (1975-78). Similar trends took place in Britain, France, and West Germany.[9] To make matters worse there was an unprecedented creation of paper money and other forms of credit which created inflationary pressures.[10]

According to economic expert Andre Gunder Frank, the decline starting in the 1970s was

> analogous to the great crisis of 1873 to 1895 and the long crisis from 1913 to the 1940s, which included the Great Depression of the 1930s, fascism, revolution and two world wars.... Major investment in technological innovations and new leading industries cannot take place again until the profit rate is raised again through political action. Recessions in 1967, 1969 to 1971, 1973 to 1975, and since 1979-80 have become more frequent, deeper, and increasingly coordinated throughout the industrial capitalist countries. Unemployment in these countries has risen from 5 million in the first of these recessions to 10 million in the second and 15 million in the third recession.[11]

In the words of Henry Kaufman, partner in one of New York's most prestigious money market firms,

> How close we came to disaster in 1970, and then again in 1974 and early 1975, no one will ever accurately record. It was a frightening period with rapidly rising interest rates, some spectacular business failures, spiralling preferences for high credit quality and liquidity, and doubts about the strength of some of the largest and most prominent financial institutions.[12]

The start of the 1980s saw a recession even greater than those of the '70s, with unemployment in the United States rising to the highest level since the 1930s, and unemployment in the industrialized nations going up from 15 million to 20 million.[13] Even after the 1983-85 U.S. recovery, unemployment was the highest it had been in decades at a comparable stage of the business cycle.[14] Growth in the European Common Market countries has averaged less than 1 percent per year since 1980, compared with 3.1 percent per year between 1976 and 1980 and 4.6 percent during the 1960s.[15] Unemployment in Europe rose from 9 percent to 11 percent between 1982-84.[16] Furthermore, the situation of the non-oil-producing Third World is catastrophic, with growth rates less than 2.2 percent per year compared to 6.1 percent between 1961 and 1980.[17] Although the oil price drop moderated the problem temporarily, the rebound in world economic growth rates was far less than expected.[18]

The supply of many products in the world market far exceeds the ability of people to buy these products. Thus we have a global glut of autos, computer chips, petrochemicals, steel, and many other commodities. Nearly every major industry and sector of the world economy has excess production capacity; factories can produce 21 percent more autos and steel than can be sold worldwide. For petrochemicals this overcapacity figure is 20 percent to 30 percent, and for semiconductors 23 percent. The United States has the worst overcapacity problem, 31 percent, but Japan is not far behind at 25 percent. In September 1986, U.S. manufacturers were operating at 79.8 percent of capacity compared with 86.5 percent in the late 1970s. "Those are terrible numbers, and they are not going away," said Joseph Bower, senior associate dean of Harvard Business School. By 1990, U.S. steel companies will have to close a fifth of their mills and permanently lay off more than 40,000 steel workers. The glut could produce a deflationary spiral in the world economy caused by wholesale dumping of products on the market, a wave of bankruptcies, greatly increased unemployment, and a decline in world trade.[19]

Adding to the overall global recession is the explosive problem of Third World debt, a phenomenon described in detail in Michael Moffitt's book *The World's Money*. This debt of $800 billion, much of it concentrated in Latin America, has the potential to destabilize the entire world financial structure.[20] Already the debt-related economic crisis is having major effects on the U.S. economy; between 1982 and 1984 U.S. exports to Latin America dropped by 42 percent.[21] Latin America traditionally buys almost a quarter of U.S. exports.[22]

In spite of one bailout measure after another concocted by the private banks and governments, many observers are convinced that the debt is unpayable. Mexico, Brazil, Peru, and other countries are still in danger of defaulting.[23] Even if the debt problem stops short of actual default, the consequences of Third World nations tightening their belts to pay off the interest makes their populations less and less able to buy products, thus compounding the world recession. For example, in Mexico real wages have declined 50 percent since 1983; and the $100-billion debt required $10 billion in interest payments in 1986, accounting for fully 70 percent of Mexican federal revenues.[24]

Charles Cerami of the Atlantic Council of the United States recently summarized the world economic situation:

Unless we start now to create new jobs by the millions in scores of countries, some of the most difficult years that man has ever known may be facing us.... The underlying global trend is for more and more persons to compete for a scanty supply of jobs...the jobless hordes are building to a 'critical mass' that could be harder to control than any nuclear arsenal.[25]

The United States Falls from Hegemony

At the same time the world was beginning its major economic downturn, the United States was falling from the pinnacle of economic power. The 1970s was the decade of a war lost in Southeast Asia and a system of international finance beneficial to the United States lost with the collapse of the Bretton Woods accords. The post-Vietnam War period signalled the new era of an empire in decline.

In the words of Nixon's Treasury Secretary John Connally: "No longer does the U.S. economy dominate the free world."[26] According to the House Banking Committee, "The United States once dominated the world economy with virtually effortless superiority. Those days are gone forever."

Many indicators show that the proportion of the world's wealth benefiting the United States has dropped. The U.S. share of world industrial production fell from 60 percent in 1950 to 30 percent in 1980.[27] U.S. per capita income fell below that of Switzerland, Sweden, Denmark, West Germany, and other Western European countries by the end of the 1970s.[28] The U.S. balance of trade has deteriorated disastrously, from a trade surplus ten years ago to an annual trade deficit of more than $150 billion in 1986 and 1987.[29] That represents $400 million leaving the country each day. Since 1980, the volume of U.S.-manufactured exports has remained flat while imports have risen more than 70 percent.[30] The share of the U.S. domestic market held by foreign televisions and radios went up from 59 percent to 66 percent between 1981 and 1986; for shoes the increase was from 33 percent to 63 percent, for machine tools 27 percent to 45 percent, and for computers 7 percent to 25 percent. Japan's international banks now have more total assets than their U.S. counterparts.[31] Only one U.S. bank is among the top ten largest banks, and it ranks ninth.

Central to the economic decline is the loss in productivity of U.S. manufacturing. In 1958, it took 9 hours to make a ton of hot rolled sheet steel in the United States and 27 hours in Japan. By 1980, it took

5.3 hours to make the same ton of steel in the United States but only 4.4 hours in Japan. For televisions, it took 7.6 work hours to make a set in the United States in 1965 compared with 9 hours in Japan; by 1980, it took 2.6 hours in the United States but only 0.8 hours in Japan. In the auto sector, it took about 210 hours to make a car in the United States in 1970 compared with about 260 hours in Japan; by 1981, it still took 210 hours in the United States compared with 140 hours in Japan. Worse yet, in such new high tech sectors as semiconductor memory chips formerly monopolized by the United States, Japanese producers now control 60 percent of the market for 64K RAM chips and 85 percent of the market for the new 256K RAM chips.[32] More than 70 percent of the components as measured by their value in an IBM computer are made in Japan and Singapore.[33] From 1961-65, the average annual growth in U.S. productivity (output per hour of all workers) was 3.86 percent; from 1976-80 it had plummeted to 0.33 percent.[34] Not only is U.S. productivity failing to keep up, the quality is also falling. U.S. cars require 3.5 repairs a year compared with 1.1 for Japanese cars; U.S. semiconductors have had a significantly higher defect rate than those made in Japan.[35]

With these marked reversals in the U.S. world market share, profits for U.S. corporations have tended to fall.[36] Between 1950 and 1974, the share of profits in the U.S. gross corporate product (nonfinancial corporations) dropped from 22 percent to 11 percent.[37] The rate of after-tax profit for U.S. corporations in the 1970s was 25 percent below the rate in the 1960s. Business failures, as measured by liabilities, more than doubled in the 1970s compared with the 1960s. Since 1979, an estimated 250,000 farmers have gone bankrupt.[38] In 1984, 76 savings and loans collapsed, the largest number since 1938.[39] If trends set in the first half of the 1980s continue, profits in the '80s will be substantially below those earned in the 1970s.[40] The result of reduced profits is that investors do not put their money into those economic sectors that need revitalization most, thus ensuring continued U.S. economic decline.

An exception to companies feeling the profit squeeze can be found in the military sector. Over the period of many years, the profits on military contracts have averaged 56 percent of invested capital, 300 percent higher than the average return on civilian work. In fact, the savior of the near-bankrupt Chrysler Corporation was neither the heavily debated federal loan guarantee nor the organizational genius of Lee Iacocca; it was the U.S. Army. In the mid-1970s Chrysler received a massive contract ($19 billion) to build the XM-1 tank, which brought a bonanza profit margin of 78 percent.[41]

The Impact on the People of the United States: Austerity Capitalism

The people of the United States are beginning to feel the effects of the economic crisis, both as a result of the structural economic changes and from the actions of business to shift the crisis to the working population. These actions, which are beyond the scope of this book, have been well publicized and include tax reductions primarily for business and upper income individuals, an anti-union offensive designed to reduce wage levels, and major cutbacks of New Deal governmental transfer payments that formerly redistributed income toward lower economic groups. This domestic program is the antithesis to New Deal Keynesianism which attempted to stimulate demand by keeping wages up and by increasing consumer buying power through welfare-type payments. Since we have characterized the New Deal business strategy as prosperity capitalism, it is logical to call the current corporate program "austerity capitalism."

The economic crisis and the corporate policy of austerity capitalism have already had major effects on the working population. The trade deficit indicates that more and more goods bought in the United States are produced overseas, thereby increasing U.S. unemployment. The four years of record trade deficits have cost as many as 2.3 million manufacturing jobs.[42] Between 1900 and 1970, except for the Depression of the 1930s, the United States suffered an unemployment rate of over 7 percent in only four years: 1908, 1914, 1915, and 1921. From 1975 to 1986, the unemployment rate topped 7 percent every year except in 1978 and 1979. Unemployment averaged 8.1 percent during most of the 1980s. The dip below 7 percent in 1987 is probably temporary, based on the flow of foreign investment into the United States and the continued federal budget deficit that stimulates the economy.[43] Since 1950, there has been a long-term increase in the unemployment rate, and since 1970, there has been a 300 percent increase in the number of workers so discouraged that they have ceased looking for work and are not included in the unemployment statistics.[44] Counting discouraged workers and those forced into part-time work because of lack of full-time jobs, the true rate of joblessness might be twice as high as the official rate.[45]

Related to the growth of unemployment is the fall in wages. The average U.S. weekly earnings have declined 14.3 percent since 1973, taking inflation into account. In 1973, family income stopped rising and started to fall.[46] Because of the level of unemployment, "Unions are fearful of seeking wage increases and instead bargain over the size of pay cuts."[47] And the manufacturing jobs lost because of poor industrial productivity tend to be the higher paying jobs, while many of the new service industry jobs offer low wages. According to the Congressional Joint Economic Committee, of the eight million jobs created between 1979 and 1984, nearly 60 percent pay less than $7,000 a year, compared with fewer than 20 percent in that category in the previous six years.[48]

The rate of unemployment and the increase in low-wage jobs caused the percentage of people living in poverty to rise from 11.7 percent in 1979 to 13.6 percent in 1986.[49] Since 1978, the number of persons with full-time work who are below the poverty level has grown by 66 percent.[50] A pastoral letter issued by the National Conference of Catholic Bishops called the current levels of poverty in the United States a "social and moral scandal."[51] Related to economic hardships, social problems have grown. The number of people without homes is somewhere between 250,000 and three million.[52] Families, making up 28 percent of the urban homeless, have become the fastest-growing group without a regular place to live.[53] Thirty-seven million people lack health insurance, an increase of 40 percent from 1980.[54] According to the National Urban League, the economic and social gap between blacks and whites has widened; by 1985, the median income of blacks had declined to 56 percent of whites' median income (from 62 percent in 1975). Unemployment among black youths increased from 24.4 percent in 1960 to nearly 40 percent by 1985.[55]

Some frightening, but not unreasonable, predictions have been made about the end result of these trends. In *Prisoners of the American Dream,* Mike Davis warns of

> three distinct societies, as segregated from one another as if apartheid were economic common law in the United States. At one pole will be the sumptuary suburbs and gentrified neighborhoods occupied by the middle classes, the rich and elements of the skilled white working class.... Outside, in the first circle of the damned, will be the ghettoes and barrios, now joined by declassé and deindustrialized layers of the white working class...there will also be a large outer perimeter of U.S. society composed of workers without citizen rights or access to the political system at all: an U.S. West Bank of terrorized illegal laborers...this third tier could be a social layer of twenty to thirty million people, a poor Latin American society thrust into the domestic economy.[56]

In a Crisis, Solutions Create New Problems

The current dilemma for the U.S. economy is that solutions to the problems are creating new problems of their own. The federal budget deficit has been a major method for stimulating the economy, with the deficit running about $5 billion per year in the 1960s. But the Reagan-generated deficit, an amazing $221 billion in fiscal year 1986 bringing the national debt to $2 trillion, is worsening the other deficit, the trade deficit. The towering federal deficit keeps interest rates high relative to inflation, and pushes up the value of the dollar which in turn makes it harder to export U.S. goods.[57] The Committee for Economic Development, a prestigious business group, warns that the federal deficits "pose calamitous risks for domestic and international financial markets and for interest rates.... Future deficits will ultimately threaten the basic standard of living and national security of our own and future generations." But if the budget deficit were rapidly reduced, a recession could ensue; that is the economic bind of the United States.[58]

Another historic economic stimulant has been the growth of private debt created by excessive consumer spending. Consumer installment credit rose from $314.3 billion to $585 billion from the end of 1981 to September 1986; it has more than tripled since 1976. Almost one-third of average monthly household income is allocated to debt payments.[59] In the words of Alan Binder, Princeton economics professor,

> spending expanded at a 3.4 percent annual rate while GNP grew at a 2.4 percent rate.... Unproductive America went on a spending spree financed by foreign borrowing. But no binge lasts forever. The drunk eventually sobers up. Sooner or later America will awaken to the hangover of Reaganomics. No nation can long consume more than it produces. Since our spending now greatly exceeds our output, and since we are piling up international debt on which interest must be paid, America is headed for a painful adjustment period during which spending will grow more slowly than GNP.[60]

Not only consumer debt, but also corporate debt represents a great danger. The borrowing of U.S. corporations has caused a steep rise in debt-equity ratios. If a recession takes place and corporate debt payments are defaulted, a wave of major bankruptcies could occur. To make matters worse, corporate borrowing is directed toward takeovers and mergers rather than the building of new, productive plants.[61]

Another effect of the burgeoning private and public debt (which doubled over six years to hit $8.2 trillion in 1985—over $30,000 for each man, woman, and child in the United States) is the instability of the dollar internationally. The dollar rose dramatically from 1980 to 1985 because federal and private borrowing attracted capital into the United States, increasing the price of the dollar. The overvalued dollar makes U.S. goods expensive to other nations and reduces U.S. exports; it also makes foreign goods cheaper for the United States and increases imports. To correct the trade deficit, the Reagan administration in 1985 took measures to lower the value of the dollar, which fell 50 percent from 1985 to 1987. But the trade deficit has responded only slightly to this move because the more fundamental cause of the trade deficit, the decline in U.S. productivity, has not been addressed.[62] Since less productive U.S. companies take more time and therefore more money to produce their goods, domestic goods are often more expensive and unable to compete with foreign goods in both U.S. and foreign markets, thereby causing a decrease in exports and an increase in imports.

The sharp slide of the dollar has its own negative consequences. If it continues, the devaluation could cause inflation, higher interest rates, and possible recession without solving the trade situation. In the long run, the fall of the dollar allows foreign investers to

> buy into America at bargain-basement prices. Fewer and fewer yens and marks are buying more stocks, bonds, real estate, and factories.... If the United States gets caught in this trap, we will be selling off a growing share of America at lower and lower prices.[63]

At the same time, the dollar plunge strains relations with Europe. West German Bundesbank President Karl Otto Pohl warned that the United States is "playing with fire" in knocking down the dollar, and European Economic Community President Jacques Delors said that "this blackmail inherent in the fall of the dollar" was threatening the global monetary system. French Foreign Trade Minister Michel Noir charged that the U.S. monetary policy uses "Rambo-like methods" to whip dissenters into line.[64]

The stock market fall of October 1987 was the most dramatic indication that the U.S. economy is living on borrowed time. According to *Business Week,* "the 508-point market crash on October 19 was a reluctant admission that there are no tricks left in the 'voodoonomics' bone bag."

Bloody Monday was the signal that the world of finance had finally lost patience with a nation that had failed to come to grips with its double debt problems.... America's foreign debt is already enormous, and even if the United States cuts its trade deficit in half, a huge jump in interest paid abroad will help double the foreign debt by 1990.[65]

According to the *New York Times,*

The economy will never be the same. No matter where the stock market heads in coming months, the whole process of doing business, making a living, choosing investments...even buying a house...has been radically transformed. Last Monday's market collapse was one of those pivotal events that shape everything that comes afterward.[66]

Economic Decline and U.S. Foreign Policy

Many commentators on the causes of U.S. economic decline pay insufficient attention to U.S. foreign policy. Probably the most important factor contributing to postwar U.S. economic hegemony was U.S. control over the world economy and political system. This allowed for vast expansion of sales and investments overseas, thereby increasing total demand for U.S. products. Yet this very control was a key contributor to the subsequent economic decline. Domination of the entire capitalist world entailed numerous expenditures which have been called "the costs of empire." By "costs of empire" we mean the economic burdens of maintaining the global political and military dominance that provides a favorable environment for the overseas operations of U.S. business. It is these costs that paradoxically are undoing the very empire they were intended to construct.

To simplify this discussion of costs of empire, we will divide it into three interrelated parts: 1) the dollar drain, 2) the internationalization of capital, and 3) the looting of the United States.

The Dollar Drain

The initial postwar cost of empire was the rebuilding of Europe, accomplished to both reconstruct a vital consumerist economy that could buy U.S. goods and to contain the expansion of influence of the USSR. This feat was performed with the Marshall Plan, which was extremely successful but very costly. In addition, the U.S. postwar occupation of Japan was one of the features allowing for the economic modernization of that nation's industry.[67] The U.S. policy of rebuilding Western Europe and Japan eventually allowed these competitors to surpass U.S. industry and to erode markets previously controlled by the United States, including within the United States itself.

The military expenses of maintaining the worldwide empire, based on containment of the Soviet Union, caused a vast outflow of dollars from the United States. Beginning as a steady trickle to pay for the building and operating of military bases abroad, the outflow greatly accelerated with the war in Vietnam. The total cost of that war was more than $150 billion, a significant part of which was spent overseas.[68]

In the late 1980s we read each day about the trade deficit, but in the late '60s the economic headline was the dollar drain. Before this dollar drain, which represented part of the cost of maintaining an empire, everyone in every country wanted dollars. But after billions of dollars had been spent overseas, so many individuals and governments had so many dollars that the green paper became worth less and less. The dollar holdings of foreign governments doubled to over $50 billion in just one year, from 1970-71. These governments began to cash their mountains of dollars in for gold, utilizing the promise the United States had made at the Bretton Woods financial understandings in 1944.[69]

The international dollar glut led the Nixon administration in 1971 to abandon the gold standard and the Bretton Woods system of government-dominated fixed exchange rates so favorable to the United States. A new era of worldwide financial instability began, with fluctuating exchange rates subject to monetary speculation.[70] It appears that the dollar is first too high, then it drops too low. First U.S. goods are too expensive and U.S. exports drop, then foreign investors come in and buy up U.S. companies. Whether the dollar is high or low, whichever is the case, new problems are created for the United States and the world economy.[71] That is the legacy of the dollar drain, one of the costs of empire.

The Internationalization of Capital

The second cost of empire is even more serious; U.S. capital, which built the great productive machine that gave the United States world hegemony from 1945 to 1970, is abandoning the United States to invest in the very areas that the containment doctrine "saved from communism." Between 1950 and 1980, direct foreign investment by U.S. business increased sixteenfold, from about $12 billion to $192 billion.[72] Between 1970 and 1981, the ratio of foreign to total earnings of the ten largest U.S. banks rose from 17.5 percent to 48 percent.[73] In 1977, Citicorp earned 83 percent of its banking profits outside the United States.[74]

Twenty-nine percent of the "foreign imports" that are wrecking the trade balance came from plants owned by U.S. corporations. For every $1 billion in direct private U.S. foreign investment, about 26,500 domestic jobs are eliminated.[75] The existence of the world empire has allowed U.S. corporations to accumulate capital on an international rather than on a national scale, a trend that is creating major problems for the domestic economy.

Huge transnational corporations no longer see themselves as purely U.S. companies, but feel at home anywhere in the world. As U.S. industrial productivity falls, corporations invest in low-wage, non-unionized Latin American or Asian countries rather than modernize their U.S. plants. Jobs formerly held by U.S. workers are shifted overseas. During the 1970s, General Electric added 30,000 foreign jobs and reduced its U.S. payroll by 25,000. Ford recently reported that 40 percent of its capital budget will be spent outside the United States.[76] The total job loss from domestic capital disinvestment during the 1970s may have reached 38 million jobs.[77] Markets lost to the United States by Western European competition may actually benefit U.S.-based transnational corporations that have invested in Western Europe; in 1970, fifty percent of U.S. foreign investment went to Europe.[78] The U.S. government is unable to tax most of the overseas profits of U.S. corporations and banks, which is one reason why some of the largest companies have paid no federal taxes at all.[79] And with one flip of the telex machine, transnational corporations can switch billions from dollars into marks or yens, thereby destabilizing monetary exchange rates.[80] In addition to military expenditures abroad, it was transfers of private capital outside the United States that made the dollar drain a full-fledged hemorrhage.[81]

Giant transnational corporations have become world powers in their own right, often with interests separate from, and even in conflict with, those of the U.S. economy. Yet the U.S. government has spent billions in taxpayers' money to support foreign governments friendly to those very transnationals that are exporting U.S. jobs and evading

U.S. taxes. It is with U.S. military and economic aid that many governments—for example South Korea, Taiwan, and the Philippines under Marcos—institute repressive policies to keep wages down. (Interestingly, the slightest lifting of repression in South Korea and the Philippines was accompanied by major labor unrest.) These cheap labor havens are the recipients of the U.S. runaway shops that have caused so much domestic unemployment.

The ultimate irony is that war-torn economies that were rebuilt with U.S. capital to provide markets for U.S. goods have become strong enough to compete with U.S. businesses not only for a market share in their countries but for a share in the U.S. market as well. South Korea, for example, which the United States spent billions to defend and to build, has helped to kill the U.S. domestic textile industry. The United States made South Korea safe for capitalism, and South Korea is now beating the United States at its own game.

The Looting of the United States

Among all the causes of the U.S. economic decline the primary problem is the failure of productive manufacturing. If U.S. companies making autos, textiles, and computers could compete in the domestic and world market, many of the other economic problems would be manageable. Why, then, is U.S. industry so unproductive? One important reason is the military budget. As a cost of empire, military spending has brought disaster in its wake. It has virtually looted the U.S. domestic economy.

For each $100 of capital available for modernizing steel, auto, and other domestic industries, the United States spends $46 for the military. In Japan, for each $100 of civilian capital a mere $3.70 goes to the military.[82] In the United States, fully 70 percent of federal research and development funds go to the military. This compares with 10 percent to 15 percent in West Germany and 5 percent in Japan.[83] The United States spends few R&D dollars to improve the technology of the faltering steel, auto, and machine-tool industries. Skilled engineers and scientists are also diverted from improving civilian technology to the military.

In a study of investment vs. military spending that compared the performance of 17 nations between 1960 and 1980, investment as a percent of GNP was inversely proportional to military spending as a percent of GNP. Among the 17 countries, Japan had the lowest military spending and the highest rate of investment while the United States and the United Kingdom had the highest rates of military spending and the lowest level of investment.[84] In addition, between 1960 and 1978, countries that spent a far lower percentage of GNP on the military (i.e., Japan, Canada, Sweden, West Germany) far surpassed the United States in their rate of growth in manufacturing productivity.[85]

The military build-up has seriously undermined the strength of the entire U.S. economy and its ability to compete in the domestic and world markets. Ronald Reagan has congratulated himself for building a "strong America." But is a country that doubles its military budget in five short years getting stronger or weaker?

Economic Decline Brings Political Isolation

Related to its economic decline, the United States has experienced a serious diminution in its world political/diplomatic influence. Following World War II, with the U.S. role in the defeat of the fascists, and Roosevelt's vision of permanent world peace through the United Nations, many nations looked up to the United States as the world champion of peace, freedom, and democracy. By the end of the Vietnam War in 1975, however, the U.S. image in many parts of the world was that of a brutal imperialist power. Already the United States had overthrown governments and established repressive regimes in Iran, Guatemala, the Dominican Republic and elsewhere. The Vietnam War, including indiscriminate bombing of civilians by the United States, resulted in two million deaths[86] and was protested throughout the world. The CIA-engineered overthrow of the elected Allende government in Chile in 1973 added to the world's condemnation.

The failure of the dollar as stable international currency and the loss of U.S. markets to Europe and Japan were associated with a corresponding weakening in the necessity for nations to do whatever the United States desired. The United States became less able to persuade other nations to follow its policies. In the Dominican Republic in 1965, for example, the Organization of American States supported and participated in the U.S. military intervention. Now, the OAS is no longer willing to rubber-stamp U.S. actions in Nicaragua, and OAS members have issued declarations condemning the U.S. role in the Latin debt crisis. The United States has been unable to get rid of a thorn in its side, General Noriega of Panama. In Western Europe, the United States was unable to persuade its Western European allies to cancel or boycott their participation in the Soviet natural-gas pipeline. In Africa, 51 states have deplored the U.S. government's support of South Africa. In the Middle East, the United States was forced out of Lebanon and has diminished influence over events in that region.

Another important signpost of U.S. political decline has been the increased strength of resistance movements in the Third World, often as direct reactions to U.S. imperial policy. The revolution in Nicaragua was an outgrowth of the U.S.-installed and supported Somoza dictatorship. The 30-year guerrilla insurgency in Guatemala has been directed against a series of military rulers brought into power by the U.S. intervention of 1954. The strong leftist movement in the Philippines derives popularity from its opposition to inequitable land ownership patterns related to the penetration of U.S. agribusiness and the U.S. government's support of the armed forces, which protects that inequality.

Many U.S. political/diplomatic reversals can also be viewed as costs of empire, as reactions to postwar U.S. efforts to dominate the international landscape. Yet combined with economic troubles, it was this growing political isolation that planted the seeds for a militaristic foreign policy that "goes it alone" rather than establishing influence through negotiation, diplomacy, and the building of alliances.

In this chapter we have tried to explain the decline of U.S. economic hegemony and the associated loss of world political leadership. But what does this have to do with the right wing, with rollback foreign policy, with the Reagan Doctrine? As we will argue in the next chapter, sectors of the business community attempted to solve the economic crisis through increased military power abroad (to allow multinational businesses to penetrate more vigorously into the Third World) and increased military spending at home (to stimulate the economy). This renewed determination to reassert U.S. world economic power led to a coalition of traditional conservative and right-wing business interests. In the era of prosperity capitalism when business was booming, containment—preservation of the status quo—was the logical foreign policy doctrine. In the 1970s and 1980s, decades of transition from prosperity to austerity capitalism, when business was less booming, global rollback—a return to the past—became a more attractive foreign policy goal.

7

Ruling Elites Move to the Right

According to a foremost expert on U.S. political parties, Walter Dean Burnham:

> ...as is well known, in the United States the making of foreign policy and military decisions is the province of a bipartisan elite drawn from the executive establishment and from private industry. It is not the province of the political parties, and it is not normally capable of being structured into a cluster of issues on which the parties are opposed and between which the voters can choose. Since these decisions involve the expenditure of between three-fifths and three-quarters of the current federal administrative budget, depending upon which items are included, it is not inaccurate to say that most of the present-day activities of the federal government lie quite outside of areas in which parties can make any positive contribution to the political system.[1]

Two Strands Within the Ruling Elites

Many authors have demonstrated at least two currents among ruling elites in postwar foreign policy. These sometimes interwoven strands have been given such colorful names as Yankees vs. Cowboys, Industrial Belt vs. Southern Rim, Frostbelt vs. Sunbelt, Eastern Establishment vs. Right Wing, Traders vs. Prussians, Internationalists vs. Nationalists, Containment vs. Rollback, Atlanticists vs. Pacific Rimmers, and Trilateralists vs. Militarists.[2] Each of these formulations contains an element of truth and an element of oversimplification. But the categories are helpful in explaining those struggles, delays and compromises over foreign policy issues that reflect disagreements within the power elite.[3] While the arguments between elite groupings may be heated, it is important to remember that on many foreign policy issues there is a narrow range of disagreement, with basic underlying assumptions being undisputed.

For our particular brand of oversimplification, we are using the terms right-wing (i.e., reactionary) vs. traditional conservative. Reactionary implies global rollback, returning to the status quo prior to the Russian Revolution; whereas conservative has generally indicated containment, preserving the world balance of power with the United States as the world's most powerful nation.

We saw in Chapter One that traditional conservative business is the Eastern Establishment of large multinational industries and banks. Corporations within this grouping provided business support for the New Deal. Being capital rather than labor intensive, they had lower relative labor costs and could live with unions (though many had no unions), and because they were multinational they gained from free trade and opposed protectionism. In the 1930s this bloc, with such companies as Chase Manhattan Bank, Standard Oil, General Electric, IBM, and many others, supported internationalism rather than isolationism abroad. It was through its most important foreign policy organ, the Council on Foreign Relations, that conservative business planned the entire postwar conception of a U.S.-dominated world order, bringing us the Bretton Woods system of international finance, the Truman Doctrine of containment, the Kennedy corporate tax cuts and tariff reductions, and the Johnson Great Society welfare programs.[4] Traditional conservative business has operated within both the Democratic and Republican Parties.

Right-wing business has included national industries and smaller businesses with little interest in international trade, for example pro-protectionist textiles and steel; labor-intensive companies with strong anti-union and anti-welfare-state sentiments; military contractors for whom international tension is a profit maximizer; and a mix of raw materials producers, national oil companies, and agribusinesses. This grouping, located more in the South and West, grew more rapidly within the United States during the 1960s than did traditionally conservative business and thus increased its relative political power.[5] National oil companies, military contractors, agribusiness corporations, and southern textile manufacturers are longtime funders of the right wing. It is this grouping that provides the U.S. economic base and part of the funding for the global rollback network.

In this chapter, we will attempt to demonstrate a general right-wing shift in foreign policy attitudes of the ruling elites, related to the economic crisis described in Chapter Six. Between 1975 and 1980, two important developments took place: an increase in the power of right-wing business, and a marked rightward shift in the views of conservative business. During most of the 1980s, the range of foreign policy options moved considerably to the right compared with the 1970s détente era.

The Ruling Elites from 1975 to 1980

The Nixon administration was a mix of influence by traditional conservative multinational business and right-wing business interests such as textiles, steel, and independent oil. Foreign policy, dominated by Henry Kissinger, was the province of the Eastern Establishment. The dollar drain panicked both business groups, and many corporate leaders began to oppose the war in Vietnam, a major contributor to domestic economic problems. The watershed was the severe 1973-75 recession, which ended the long period of postwar growth and changed the U.S. role in the world economy.[6]

These economic events, along with the first U.S. military defeat in modern history, led to a crisis in the 1945-1970 postwar foreign policy consensus. For one business grouping led by Chase Manhattan Bank Chair David Rockefeller, the economic crisis required the opening of large new international markets, specifically in the socialist world of China and the Soviet Union. This proposal brought about the Kissinger-Nixon policies of détente with the Soviets and rapprochement with China.[7] In 1973, Rockefeller brought this grouping together into the Trilateral Commission. The "Trilats" consolidated their power by inviting onto the Commission Georgia Governor Jimmy Carter and successfully promoting Carter's presidential candidacy in 1976. The Trilats thereupon gained 25 high-level positions in Carter's administration.

The Carter administration featured a tug of war between the more right-leaning Trilaterals, who in spite of détente viewed most world events in the context of U.S.-USSR rivalry, and the more liberal Trilats in the State Department and the UN who saw the world in more complex terms. Regarding the USSR, the basic Trilat position was to preserve the military balance, ratify SALT II-like arms agreements, support peaceful conflict resolution in the Third World, and keep the Trilateral (U.S.-Atlantic-Japanese) alliance strong as the best defense against the Soviets.[8] In the Third World, Trilat strategy was to shore up shaky regimes while installing new ones if needed, attempting to keep Third World governments as conservative and pro-U.S. as possible. Although military force would be utilized in situations like the Shaba rebellion in Zaire, the Trilats preferred to seek compromise solutions such as that negotiated in Zimbabwe. As an example, the Carter policy toward Nicaragua was to work for a non-Somocista, non-Sandinista solution; when that failed, the Carter administration tried to co-opt the Sandinistas away from the socialist bloc. This type of diplomatic maneuvering was the Trilat *modus operandi*.[9]

With the recession of the 1970s, doubts about the entire New Deal spread through the business community including its multinational wing, formerly New Deal's business backbone. The switch from prosperity to austerity capitalism began to take hold, setting the stage for Reagan's domestic policies of corporate tax cuts, reduced wages and social spending, and military budget hikes to stimulate the economy. In foreign policy, a battle emerged between the Trilateralist position favoring trade and diplomatic maneuvering vs. an emerging right-wing view that détente must be ended and the military geared up for increased involvement in the Third World. The Republican Party, with far less of a constituency for social programs and labor benefits than the Democrats, was the obvious institution for implementing the domestic program of austerity, and in 1980 virtually the entire business community threw its funds to the Reagan candidacy.[10]

At the same time, the rise in oil prices of the 1970s strengthened the economy of the South and West. Independent oil provided the funds by which the New Right gained major influence in the Republican Party. Also, right-wing Western mining interests and such conservative backers as Joseph Coors, opposed to environmental controls, strengthened the Right and the Republicans.[11] The weapons manufacturers, angered by the relatively anemic military budget rises of the 1970s, became militant supporters of ultraconservative causes. Thus right-wing business gained in economic power *vis-à-vis* the traditional conservative multinationals during the course of the 1970s.

The revival of lobbying activity by such old Cold War groups as the American Security Council (representing the military-industrial complex) was a pressure for greater hawkishness among such multinationally-oriented organizations as the Trilateral Commission, the Council on Foreign Relations and the U.S. Atlantic Council.[12] Right-wing publishing companies, think tanks, religious groups, and anti-détente crusaders received millions of dollars from both right-wing-oriented businesses (for example, independent oil companies, protectionist textile producers represented by Jesse Helms, and raw materials producers) and from rightward moving multinationals.[13] While these two rival business groups still disagreed on free trade vs. protectionism, their agreements far outweighed these differences.

In foreign policy, right-wing business joined with right-leaning multinationals in the Committee on the Present Danger (CPD). A cross-section of businessmen and onetime military figures, CPD received its start-up grant from David Packard, a major military contractor. The CPD strongly attacked liberal Trilat positions; for example, CPDers mounted a campaign against the nomination of Trilateralist Paul Warnke to be Carter's chief arms control negotiator.[14] While a few business leaders worried about the economic consequences of the CPD-led defense build-up, (e.g., Donald Kendall, Chairman of Pepsi, which had a major contract with the Soviets, and boardmember of the pro-détente Committee on East-West Accord) they were in the small minority.[15] The CPD was so successful that it turned Carter's foreign and military policies around: détente had its demise during the second half of Carter's term.[16] The most liberal Trilats in the administration, Cyrus Vance and Andrew Young, resigned.

A helpful paradigm of ruling elite foreign policy attitudes was developed by Professor Richard Falk and amended by a leading scholar on right-wing foreign policy, Jerry Sanders. The Vietnam defeat generated a splintering of the postwar foreign policy consensus, with a continuum of views from right to left including unilateralists, imperialists, managers, and transformers. The unilateralists are the extreme Right who prefer to go it alone without relying on allies. The imperialists (including CPD) ultimately use military power to keep the United States empire intact. The managers are the pragmatic Trilats who emphasize economic rather than military power. And the transformers are liberals who desire a new system of world order. By the late '70s, this continuum had polarized into two camps, the unilateralist-imperialist hardliners of the CPD, and the managerialist center-left wing of the Trilats. The transformers virtually disappeared from ruling elite circles.[17]

In this polarization, the Trilateral détente consensus was fractured; even Trilat founder David Rockfeller admitted in 1980 that we cannot count on an alliance of angels to defend the free world.[18] The Trilats themselves split apart, with some, like David Packard and conservative labor leader Lane Kirkland, joining the CPD. When the dust cleared, some Trilateralists—George Bush, David Abshire, Henry Kissinger, Caspar Weinberger—were with Reagan while others—Alan Cranston, Sol Linowitz, Gerard Smith, Cyrus Vance, Paul Warnke—strongly opposed Reagan's foreign policy.[19]

Why was the right wing so successful in destroying the Trilateral policy that dominated elite thinking in the 1970s? The major reason, returning to Chapter Six, was the economic crisis and decline of U.S. economic hegemony, which became severe and permanent in the 1970s. The domestic response to this crisis was a rightward move as austerity capitalism replaced prosperity capitalism. Another domestic response was the increased subsidization of business through the federal military budget. The overseas response to the crisis involved the shifting of manufacturing and banking processes to low wage areas in the Third World. This renewed business drive into the Third World required a more interventionist foreign policy to protect U.S. investments, especially since the Trilateral diplomatic tactics appeared to have failed, with fourteen revolutions taking place in the Third World between 1974 and 1980. The desire for a greater military interventionist capacity fit perfectly with the policy of stimulating the domestic economy via the military budget.

How about the Soviet Union? Were not increased Soviet aggressiveness and its rapid military buildup responsible for a right-wing reaction in the United States? As we argued at the beginning of Chapter Six, the facts show otherwise. Soviet behavior of the 1970s was not the direct cause of détente's collapse.

Why, then, was détente scrapped as a policy of traditional conservative ruling elites? The whipping up of a new Soviet threat was extremely useful for both the military budget buildup and the increase in Third World military interventionism. The history of high-level committees peddling the Soviet threat is an old one (see the military-industrial complex section later in this chapter), and is most useful to justify military spending increases. The revving up of the Soviet threat also helps to gain public support for military exploits in the Third World by mislabeling Third World social movements as "Soviet expansionism." And finally, the ruling elites were united in believing that the global balance of power had shifted toward the Soviet Union during the 1970s and that the United States needed to reverse this trend. Thus the traditional conservatives allied themselves with the ExSET advocates of the Right; in the late 1970s, especially in the wake of the Soviet intervention in Afghanistan and the Iranian revolution, the two tendencies in the ruling elite had convergent interests.

In addition, the right-wing business groupings generally opposed to détente were increasing their political clout: 1) older labor-intensive industries that were against trade in general (the protectionist industries), 2) raw materials producers, chemicals, natural gas concerns, and others who could not land contracts with the USSR because the Soviets had a comparative advantage in those areas, and 3) the weapons industry. Many détente supporters became disillusioned when U.S.-Soviet trade failed to develop rapidly.[20]

By 1980, splits within the Trilateral Commission had progressed so far that the CPD-oriented members actively supported the Reagan-Bush ticket while the Trilats who promoted a more peacefully managed world order were out of power. East-West and military policy became dominated by the tenuous coalition of hardline conservatives and the Right. This coalition was embodied in a major conservative think tank, the Georgetown Center for Strategic and International Studies, where Trilats such as David Abshire and Henry Kissinger worked with prominent right-wing figures such as Jeane Kirkpatrick and Ray Cline. Hence, major Trilateralists maintained a locus of power and influence within the Reagan administration that would emerge during the tumultuous events winding up the second Reagan term.

The Ruling Elites from 1980 to 1986

Ronald Reagan was originally supported by right-wing entrepreneurs in California and elsewhere, including some protectionist textile industrialists, independent oilmen, arms producers, and small business owners. In his quest to unseat Gerald Ford from the presidency in 1976, Reagan failed to gain the blessing of other top business figures mainly because of his protectionist views. But by 1980, two developments had taken place: as we have seen, business had become more conservative in the areas of taxes, military spending, labor, and the environment; and Reagan himself, in order to gain conservative multinational business support, made some concessions. He backed away from defense of Taiwan toward the Trilateral China policy, he stopped his attacks on the Trilateral Commission, and he became a free trader. These adjustments in Reagan's positions opened the way for virtually all of U.S. business to support him. As a sign of this unified support, the media gave Reagan a positive image, ignoring the unreality and illogic of his program, which promised to cut taxes, increase military spending, preserve essential social spending, and balance the budget—all at the same time.[21]

Reagan succeeded in bridging the polarization between right-wing and traditional conservative business by emphasizing what for the elites were less "contentious" domestic policies during his first year. The Trilats had always called for a limitation of economic aspirations of the population, higher unemployment, and less social spending; on these issues, Reaganism fit the Trilats fine.[22] While it is difficult to unify protectionists and free traders, it is easy to gain agreement from business on corporate tax cuts and social spending reductions. Indeed, business made billions from the 1981 tax bill. Potentially divisive foreign policy and trade initiatives were placed lower on the agenda at the start of the Reagan administration.[23] However, not all foreign policy issues were divisive; the great majority of ruling elites believed that a more aggressive international posture was needed to reverse the perceived Soviet advantage. Pro-détente business forces had been decisively beaten with the coalition of the CPD and the conservative Trilats; there was little elite opposition to Reaganism. The enormous increase in military spending found few dissenters.

In less than two years, the Reagan consensus cracked. The two main currents of Reagan's business support had ultimately incompatible goals. In the late 1970s, the Business Roundtable (including virtually all sectors of big business) conducted a major lobby for lower corporate taxes; at the same time the CPD mobilized for unprecedented peacetime military budget increases. The only way to reconcile these currents would be a large reduction in social spending, including the universally popular Social Security, which even Republicans could not touch for fear of losing public support.[24] The result was that Reagan implemented the programs of both the Business Roundtable and the CPD, creating an unheard-of federal budget deficit. As we saw in Chapter Six, this deficit has worsened the economic problems of the United States.

The budget deficit combined with the scary escalation of anti-Soviet rhetoric and behavior—including the administration's goal of winnable nuclear war, uncovered by the press in 1982—began to sour some multinational business leaders on the Reagan program. While business supported Reagan's attempt to ensure U.S. domination in East-West matters, such domination had to stop short of destabilizing the Cold War into a great power-shooting match. An excess of military zeal on the part of the Reaganites might strengthen more hawkish elements in the USSR, resulting in an uncontrollable escalation of East-West hostility. Thus the attempt to re-establish dominance over the U.S.-Soviet competition had to be approached with some caution.

By 1982, the perceived lack of such caution on Reagan's part re-created dissension within the ruling elite. Averill Harriman, Thomas Watson of IBM, and others sharply attacked Reagan for neglect of arms control and downplaying relations with U.S. allies. The elite Arms Control Association (including Robert McNamara and many business leaders) reemerged as a strong and vocal critic of Reagan's arms control policies. The Rockefeller Foundation, Ford and Carnegie became actively involved in the arms control field, and there was a spectacular rise in foundation funding for arms control issues, including the nuclear freeze movement. Sol Linowitz of Xerox initiated meetings between the elites of the United States and Latin America. Financed by Ford, Rockefeller, and IBM, this Inter-American Dialogue was critical of Reagan's Central America policy. The Council on Foreign Relations, in its annual report for 1982-83, distanced itself from Reagan in Central America. These critiques had the purpose not only of moderating foreign policy but of slowing down the military-generated rise in the budget deficit.[25] In May 1984, an open letter to Reagan appeared in the *New York Times* warning him that the federal deficit must be controlled, in part by reducing military spending increases. It was signed by five former Treasury Secretaries, both Democrat and Republican, and many corporate executives with the notable absence of military contractors.[26] In order to win a second term, Reagan did moderate his foreign policy and military spending to a slight degree, thereby retaining most of his business support in the 1984 election.

However, the mid-'80s moderation of Reagan's militarist foreign policy had its limits. The limits were set by the growing power of the military-industrial complex.

The Military-Industrial Complex

While significant elements of the conservative elite have questioned the trillion-dollar Reagan military budget increase, a growing number of corporations rely on the continuation of that same budget. Those corporations plus the Pentagon (which together make up the military-industrial complex) became stronger than ever as a result of the Reagan military buildup. Increasing numbers of companies and communities throughout the country are dependent on the military sector, giving the military-industrial complex a major voice in formulation of foreign policy. Although the military budget has long-term adverse consequences on the economy, in the short run significant reductions in military spending have harmful effects on the employment picture. Since the Cold War is needed to justify a giant military budget, strong economic pressures exist in support of an aggressive foreign policy.

During the past three decades the military has been the largest single source of demand in the economy.[27] One job out of every ten depends directly or indirectly on the military. In 1983 alone, the increase in military procurement expenditures created 420,000 new jobs.[28] In 1981, the Defense Department directly employed more than three million people, with two million more employed by military contractors. Through indirect employment near weapons factories and military bases, military spending benefits at least 12 million people and probably many more.[29]

Arms sales to foreign countries create close to one million jobs.[30] Arms sales are an important tool for improving the deteriorating U.S. trade balance; these sales also stabilize employment in the military sector of the economy, cushioning the up and down fortunes of military contractors' employees as Pentagon contracts ebb and flow.[31]

The military buildup was a key factor in the 1983-84 economic recovery; for example in March 1984, U.S. factory orders rose by the largest amount in six months; 99 percent of that gain was from military orders.[32] In the 1985-86 period, it was military spending that bolstered the GNP and prevented an economic contraction.[33] The more the economy is geared to military spending, the greater are the dislocations if that spending is reduced.

The military boom also revived the industrial core of U.S. industry, which was dying in the late 1970s. Chrysler received a $19-billion tank contract to revive its flagging fortunes. The declining metal manufacturing sector (autos, steel, aluminum, and machine tools) received a major boost from the Reagan program of constructing a 600-ship navy.[34] General Motors had $1.6 billion in prime military contracts in 1985, Ford Motor Co. boasted more than $1 billion, and Goodyear Tire and Rubber over $500 million.[35]

Just as military spending helped out the old "rustbelt" industries in the 1970s, so a new generation of military weapons is designed to revive the high-tech boom battered by the Japanese computer industry in the 1980s. The prototype of this new weapons generation is Star Wars.[36] While most of the SDI and anti-satellite contracts in 1983 and

1984 went to the usual military-industrial corporations, "these giants subcontract much work to the minnows of the trade, and to computer and electronics companies, some of whom hope to grow into whales...An investors newsletter called SDI 'money from Heaven,' and another commentator likened the excitement among high-tech operators to 'a fish-feeding frenzy.' "[37]

The entire concept of an arms sector of the U.S. economy is a great oversimplification. Though the top ten contractors contain the familiar names of General Dynamics, Boeing, and Lockheed, fully two-thirds of military contract funds go to corporations outside these big ten, many of which are not primarily military oriented. In 1985, General Electric, best known as a domestic producer, was the fourth largest Pentagon contractor.[38] Several oil companies are on the list of the Pentagon's top 100 contractors, among them Atlantic Richfield, Chevron, Exxon, Mobil, and Texaco. Other well-known names in the top 100 are AT&T, DuPont, Eastman Kodak, IBM, ITT, Motorola, Pan American World Airways, Penn Central, RCA, and Westinghouse.[39] The profitability of military contracts makes many companies seek military work to help underwrite losses or lower profits in domestic production. According to a 1984 study, military contracts yielded a 25 percent return on equity, double the profit for manufacturing corporations in general.[40] Thus a large military budget is extremely desirable not just for the military sector, but for any corporation that can get a piece of that budget.

The firms specializing in military output also have close links with the non-military economy. Directors of banking, oil, communications, electric power, steel, and chemical companies can be found on the boards of the military industry. This practice of having the same people sit on different corporate boards is called "interlocking." All the largest banks lend to military contractors and therefore have a stake in a high military budget.[41]

The universities are another important source of support for the military; at least 30 percent of all research and development performed in universities and university-administered research facilities is military related. University faculty and students are thus attracted to research on military problems, thereby increasing influential civilian support for the military.[42] Some corporate directors of military contractors have also served as university officials; for example, those at Grumman have been involved with Harvard, Lockheed with University of Southern California, McDonnell Douglas with both University of California at Berkeley and Washington University in St. Louis.[43] Johns Hopkins University and the Massachusetts Institute of Technology are on the 1985 listing of 100 largest Pentagon contractors.[44]

To further spread their web of influence, military contractors have corporate board interlocks with the press and the publishing industry including Time, Inc., the Tribune Co., American Broadcasting Corp., and Doubleday. In addition, numerous board members of military firms sit on such policymaking bodies as the Trilateral Commission, Council on Foreign Relations, Brookings Institution, and the Business Council.[45]

Pentagon contracts are purposely distributed to many states and Congressional districts in order to discourage senators and representatives from voting against military expenditures. In 1981, the Pentagon planned for the many components of the B-1 bomber to be produced in 48 of the 50 states, thereby ensuring the votes of such liberals as Sens. Alan Cranston (California) and Howard Metzenbaum (Ohio).[46] Employees are a major political asset for military contractors, often organized to lobby in support of new contracts for their firms. In its major campaign to land the B-1 bomber contract, Rockwell—through its employees—generated 80,000 letters to Congress. This practice of "grassroots" lobbying has become standard fare in the military business.[47]

Military contractors have enormous influence over Congress, not simply by virtue of the employment they create in many Congressional districts, which translates into votes at election time, but also through their heavy doses of campaign contributions. They are among the largest corporate campaign donors through Political Action Committees (PACs); General Dynamics alone raised $300,000 in 1981-82.[48] Defense industry PACs tend to concentrate their contributions in the Armed Services and Defense Appropriations committees of the House and Senate.[49] PAC contributions from military contractors doubled between 1980 and 1984.[50]

The particular types of military expenditures in the Reagan period make it inevitable that military spending will continue at high levels for years to come. The uncontrollable share of Pentagon outlays (money firmly tied to already existing weapons contracts) increased from 27 percent of the military budget in 1980 to 38 percent in 1986.[51] Because the Reagan budget tended to invest in expensive weapons systems rather than personnel or maintenance functions, and since weapons systems take years to develop, many billions of Pentagon dollars are virtually impossible to cut without scrapping major weapons investments.[52] Historically, once a weapons system is underway, it is almost never canceled.[53] The events following Carter's cancellation of the B-1 bomber are recounted by Jerome Weisner, president emeritus of the Massachusetts Institute of Technology and advisor to Presidents Eisenhower and Kennedy:

> After the project was shut off by the Carter Administration, funds from the space shuttle and other government projects were fraudulently diverted to keep the B-1 alive...the manufacturer then scattered contracts so widely that almost every state and hamlet in the country had a stake in the B-1's future. Even though it is generally agreed that the B-1 is unnecessary, the campaign succeeded...labor unions and chambers of commerce lobbied vigorously for this marginally useful aircraft at a time when budget deficits were destroying the U.S. economy and the infrastructure of American society.... It is no longer a question of controlling a military-industrial complex, but rather, of keeping the United States from becoming a totally military culture.[54]

High levels of military spending will continue to have a major impact on the economy and thus upon U.S. politics for years to come. The larger the military budget, the greater the impact of its economic stimulus, and the greater the voice of its beneficiaries.

What does the size and power of the military-industrial complex have to do with foreign policy? Clearly, world tensions provide the political environment in which military contractors thrive. Widespread support for a continued military buildup cannot exist in a peaceful international environment; the expenditures have no purpose and can be more easily reduced by those sectors of the economy less dependent on the military. In addition, military contractors welcome shooting wars as a way to test their new equipment; defense stocks shot up immediately after the 1986 bombing of Libya when high-tech weapons systems were given their first trial by fire. In contrast, when Reagan began his November 1985 Geneva summit, the defense industry became anxious; one weapons consultant worried that an arms control agreement could soften public perceptions of the Soviet threat and squeeze defense spending. "Détente is bad for defense budgets," said the consultant.[55]

Because of its anti-détente preoccupation, there is a natural alliance between the military-industrial complex and the right wing in the United States. Mainly located in the South and West, high tech military industries supply large sums for right-wing political forces in the United States. Through such organizations as the Committee on the Present Danger, American Security Council, and the Coalition for Peace Through Strength, the military contractors have mobilized many politicians behind right-wing foreign policy causes. In the late 1970s, members of the Trilateral Commission with ties to the military sector had no trouble agreeing with the CPD on the need to raise the military budget.[56] We have seen in Chapter Three the linkages between the military-industrial complex and the global rollback network.

The military-industrial complex—both the Pentagon and the contractors—plays a major role in fueling the periodic rises in anti-Soviet sentiment in the United States. Three times since World War II a heightened perception of the Soviet threat has been generated by elites in government and industry. These peaks in anti-Soviet rhetoric and actions, as analyzed by Alan Wolfe in *The Rise and Fall of the Soviet Threat,* include the late 1940s, the early 1960s, and the late 1970s-early 1980s periods. In each case, the rise in perception of the Soviet threat was not a response to increased Soviet aggressiveness, but rather was generated to justify more interventionist foreign policy actions and increased military budgets in the United States. Also in each case, key documents produced by ruling elites supported the proposed foreign policy changes in light of the resurrected Soviet threat: NSC-68 in 1950, the Gaither Commission in 1957, and the Team B report of 1976.[57]

The military-industrial complex played no small role in the preparation of these three Cold War reports. NSC-68 (see Chapter One) was written by Paul Nitze, an investment banker with business ties to military contractors.[58] The Gaither Commission, whose findings formed the basis for the great increase in military expenditures and foreign interventionism of the Kennedy-Johnson years, was dominated by the Rand Corp., an air force-funded think tank. Rowan Gaither was chairman of Rand's board, and Rand weapons analysts provided much of the committee's staff work.[59] Team B, authorized by President Ford under pressure from air force Gens. George Keegan and Daniel Graham, among others, painted a frightening picture of Soviet military superiority; their report kicked off the campaign of the Committee on the Present Danger leading to the massive military budget growth of the 1980s. Team B was heavily loaded with air force and Rand representatives, and the campaign to publicize its report was strongly supported by the military industry.[60]

All three of the crisis-creating reports came after economic recessions and post-recession moves to stimulate economic growth through government (including military) spending.[61] In this way, the military sector of the economy has traditionally used the exaggeration of the Soviet threat to increase its profits through growing military budgets.

A birds-eye view of how it all works is provided by President Eisenhower and Soviet Premier Khrushchev in a 1959 conversation:

> *Eisenhower:* Tell me, Mr. Khruschev, how do you decide the question of funds for military expenses? Perhaps first I should tell you how it is with us. *Khrushchev:* Well, how is it with you? *Eisenhower:* It's like this. My military leaders come to me and say, 'Mr. President, we need such and such a sum for such and such a program.' I say, 'Sorry, we don't have the funds.' They say, 'We have reliable information that the Soviet Union has already allocated funds for their own such program. Therefore if we don't get the funds we need, we'll fall behind the Soviet Union.' So I give in. That's how they wring money out of me. They keep grabbing for more and I keep giving it to them. Now tell me, how is it with you? *Khrushchev:* It's just the same. Some people from our military department come and say, 'Comrade Khrushchev, look at this! The Americans are developing such and such a system. We could develop the same system, but it would cost such and such.' I tell them there's no money; it's all been allocated already. So they say, 'If we don't get the money we need and if there's a war, then the enemy will have superiority over us.' So we discuss it some more, and I end up giving them the money they ask for. *Eisenhower:* Yes, that's what I thought.[62]

The Realignment of 1987

In this chapter, we have attempted to show that ruling elites, who have frequently split into right-wing and traditional conservative groupings, unified behind the early Reagan administration, in part due to its domestic program and in part because of a desire to solve the economic crisis through increased military power abroad and military spending at home. The ruling elites moved toward the right in two respects: 1) right-wing business interests became stronger, and 2) traditional conservative business came closer to the right wing in its goals. These developments were both related to the economic decline of the United States. The military budget was seen as a method for stimulating the economy to help solve the economic decline. And as multinational business—searching for a way out of the unproductive U.S. economy—attempted to move more vigorously into the Third World, it required a stronger interventionary policy to protect its interests.

However, some of Reagan's foreign and military policies recreated divisions within the generally rightward-moving consensus. A portion of conservative business came to feel that relations with the Soviets should be stabilized, with the United States dominant but not so dominant as to risk direct East-West confrontation. This fraction of business—because of the budget deficit—also wanted a slower rate of growth in military spending. In early 1987, Peter Peterson, Chairman of the Council on Foreign Relations, wrote a column in the *New York Times* warning of the economic effects of the budget deficit.[63] Yet until the latter part of 1987, those businesses profiting from military spending, which requires anti-Sovietism as justification, succeeded in keeping the Cold War relatively hot. The military-dependent sectors have grown along with the military budget and have become increasingly interlinked with traditional conservative business.

In late 1987, one event appears to have critically changed the balance between conservative and right-wing business in favor of the traditional conservatives: the stock market crash of October 19. The loss of $1 trillion in investors' wealth between August and October sent a powerful message to Washington: economic problems—including the budget and trade deficits—must become a national priority and the United States must "rethink its long-standing role as military hegemon of the non-communist world."[64] Three weeks after the stock market's Bloody Monday, a two-page advertisement appeared in the *New York Times,* signed by more one hundred of the nation's most powerful corporate and media executives, bankers, lawyers, and former public officials from both political parties. The warning: cut the federal budget deficit, including the military budget.[65] Less than one month later, Defense Secretary Frank Carlucci announced $33 billion in military budget cuts.[66] Seven weeks following the stock market debacle, President Reagan and Soviet General Secretary Gorbachev met in a political atmosphere reminiscent of 1970s détente.

In the late 1980s, traditional conservative business appears to have realized that the right-wing solution to the declining economy has only worsened the economic crisis, and is moving toward a posture of restrained military spending and the expansion of East-West trade to stimulate U.S. exports.

The implications of this development—which was taking place as we were in the final stages of writing this book—are the subject of Chapter Nine. To set the context for that chapter, Chapter Eight will demonstrate that right-wing power is far greater than it was before the détente of the 1970s. In the mid-1970s, the attempt of the Trilateralists to drastically change U.S. Cold War posture alienated the military-industrial complex and provoked a counteroffensive led by the CPD.[67] In the late 1980s, the traditional conservatives will probably not make the same mistake, but will doubtless compromise with, rather than confront, the military contractors, who in some cases are themselves. In the cheery glow of the post-summit period, we must not forget that the right wing will do all possible to undermine a permanent East-West thaw.

8

The Breadth of Right-wing Influence

From Think Tanks to Democrats

From the vantage point of mid-1988, it appears that extreme versions of right-wing foreign policy are on the wane. However, we must not underestimate the continued strength of the Right. During the 1980s, the overall conceptions of the Right—rollback, military rather than negotiated solutions, the Expanding Soviet Empire Theory, and America as Number One—have burrowed into the councils of the ruling elites, into the Republican and Democratic Parties, and into the writings of influential foreign affairs experts.

Before presenting evidence on the breadth of right-wing influence, we should ask: how is U.S. foreign policy formulated? In Chapter Seven we cited Walter Dean Burnham on the critical role of a bipartisan elite in making foreign policy. Sociology Professor William Domhoff spells out the policy formation process. According to Domhoff, the ruling elite supplies money to foundations, think tanks and universities who fund and undertake foreign policy studies; in addition, the ruling elite provides money and members to consensus-seeking groups (for example, the Council on Foreign Relations) in which the corporate elites and the experts they have funded discuss foreign policy problems. The solutions reached are proposed to the government, where members of the consensus-seeking groups are often key policymakers. Once policy is agreed upon at the top levels of government, it must be implemented by the foreign policy bureaucracies.[1] We

179

are not able to review the entire literature on how foreign policy is formulated. Suffice it to say that we agree with Burnham, Domhoff, and many other commentators: foreign policy is made by elites, not by the general public.

Chapter Seven discussed the foreign policy views of the ruling elite, and their move to the right in an initial period of economic decline. We will now turn to a discussion of right-wing influence on the other actors in the policy-setting process: the foreign policy intellectuals, the two major political parties, and the government bureaucracy that implements the policy once it is decided.

The Neo-Intellectuals

The 1980s, with its new and confusing labels, might be termed the "neo" era of foreign policy. Reading the foreign policy journals, one finds that the neoconservatives are actually neo-internationalists and the neoliberals are neo-realists. The real liberals are the neo-isolationists, who always fight the neo-interventionists. Whatever the words may be, expert thinking on foreign affairs moved considerably to the right following the period of détente.

After Vietnam, the Democratic Party split into a majority grouping opposed to the war and a minority pro-war faction, heir to the Cold War liberalism of Truman and Kennedy, led by military-industrial-complex-linked Sen. Henry Jackson. The military industrial complex shaped Carter's foreign policy while the Jackson wing founded the Coalition for a Democratic Majority (CDM), helped create the Committee on the Present Danger (CPD), and in some cases worked for the election of Ronald Reagan and served in his administration.[2]

The CDM/CPD Democrats were the nucleus of the intellectual movement of neoconservatism, which believed that the greatest evil on earth was communism, and that the United States had a *moral* obligation to wipe out communism and foster worldwide democracy. In Chapter Three we saw the links between the neoconservatives and the global rollback network, particularly through the CIA. Leading neoconservative Irving Kristol was founding editor of the 1950s journal *Encounter,* financed by the CIA.[3] The "neocons" joined with the right wing to re-invigorate rollback foreign policy, eventually producing the Reagan Doctrine of overthrowing the "peripheral outposts" of the Soviet empire.

Because democracy became the stated objective of the neoconservative rollback philosophy, this movement attracted certain sectors of formerly anti-war Democrats. Prominent among such neoconservative allies is the magazine *The New Republic,* a symbol of the 1980s move by foreign policy intellectuals to the right. *The New Republic* was a strong opponent of the war in Vietnam, and has a long New Deal history.[4] Now this journal's foreign policy coverage strongly advocates the Reagan Doctrine. Most prominent in this regard is CDM-linked senior editor Charles Krauthammer.[5] Krauthammer's writings are persuasive to liberals because they emphasize the obligation of the United States to act as a force for democracy in the world. Only when one looks at the actual "democrats" Krauthammer supports (i.e., the contras in Nicaragua) does his argument unravel.

Krauthammer supported Oliver North's goals in the Iran-contra operation, criticizing only North's methods. Krauthammer wonders why people are so aghast when the CIA interferes with a foreign government. After all, isn't that precisely the CIA's business?[6] Krauthammer's article "The Poverty of Realism" categorizes the views of U.S. policy-oriented intellectuals.[7] The post-Vietnam Democratic split was between the pro-human rights anti-interventionists and the pro-interventionists. The latter, to which Krauthammer belongs, contend that the standard by which foreign policy is judged is an active defense of democracy anywhere in the world, using unilateral military action if needed.

However, the debate is not two-sided. The realists (sometimes called neorealists) include such authors as Robert W. Tucker, George Kennan, Alan Tonelson, and Christopher Layne. They generally reflect the views of the traditional conservative elite. The realists challenge both the liberal non-interventionists and the right-wing interventionists, arguing that these schools are wrongly based on morality. (Non-intervention is based on the moral right to sovereignty by other nations; intervention is based on the moral crusade for "democracy.") In contrast, the realists have limited interest in morality. They claim to be concerned with only one thing: the U.S. national interest.[8]

For the realists, the Reagan Doctrine, as an ideological crusade, universally commits the United States to defend freedom everywhere; it fails to set priorities, inviting overextension and disaster. Realists apply the yardstick: is a particular intervention in the national interest?

But, Krauthammer argues in return, who defines the national interest? For Kennan, the United States should mind "our own business wherever there is not some overwhelming reason for minding the business of others."[9] Krauthammer finds this simply a noninterventionist position without the moral arguments. For other realists, the United States should intervene wherever needed to preserve a favorable world balance of power. This reduces to an interventionist position without the moral dimension. Thus, according to Krauthammer, realism divides into the other two camps; as a system of thought it fails to tell policymakers whether to intervene or not. What divides the realists from the other schools is not policy implications but the mode of reasoning: power considerations vs. moral values.

In the late 1980s, a challenge to neoconservative prominence in foreign policy is coming from the grouping labeled neoliberals. Domestically, most neoliberals are anti-union and prefer a scaled down but not dismantled welfare state. Neolibs share with neocons a belief in U.S. military power and a desire to spread U.S. influence abroad. They criticize right-wing excesses but not the basic policy. While they do defend arms control, they see the world as essentially a conflict between superpowers. They support military spending but want to make it more effective. They are pragmatists rather than crusaders, realists rather than moralists. They believe in intervening for the national interest, however that is defined.

In posing the question, Where are foreign policy intellectuals moving?, Krauthammer happily and accurately responds: the noninterventionists have virtually died out. During the 1970s the debates raged between those favoring intervention and those opposed. In the 1980s the debate is confined to those who favor intervention on moral grounds vs. those who favor intervention on power considerations. Since the 1970s, a major change has taken place in the limits of acceptable foreign policy debate: the right (or duty) to intervene is unquestioned. The only issues on the table are why to intervene, where to intervene, and how to intervene.

Think Tanks and Consensus Councils

"Think tanks" and "consensus councils" are critical institutions to the foreign policymaking process. Since many are funded by the ruling elite, they provide a transmission belt for elite foreign policy goals to be translated into government policy.

The traditional conservative think tanks and consensus councils (TTCCs) include the Brookings Institution and the Council on Foreign Relations (CFR), in addition to departments in elite universities. The détente-oriented Trilateral Commission, derived from the CFR, was founded in the early 1970s. Also in the 1970s, the growth of right-wing business allowed for the funding of a new generation of right-wing or right-leaning think tanks including the American Enterprise Institute, the Heritage Foundation, and the Georgetown Center for Strategic and International Studies. The rightist Hoover Institution received increased funding and took on a new importance. As traditional conservative business moved rightward, it joined in the financing of this new generation of think tanks. Not surprisingly, the TTCCs mirrored the political changes of the ruling elites: the right-wing think tanks grew in importance and the more moderate TTCCs moved to the right.

The American Enterprise Institute produces a continuous flow of editorial page articles for 100 daily newspapers in the United States, writes a vast array of books and monographs, and testifies at Congressional hearings. Irving Kristol of AEI is considered the "father of neoconservatism," AEI's Ben Wattenberg cofounded the Coalition for a Democratic Majority. From 1970 to 1980, AEI funds increased from $880,000 to $10.4 million, coming from such diverse sources as Ford Motor Co. and the ultraconservative John M. Olin Foundation. An AEI Development Committee includes representatives from General Electric, General Motors, Citibank, and Chase Manhattan.[10]

The Heritage Foundation was formed by right-wing businessman Joseph Coors and New Right strategist Paul Weyrich in 1973. It quickly grew to have an annual budget of $10 million. Heritage has in many ways been the brains of the Reagan administration, supplying detailed policy directions through its *Mandate for Leadership* volumes compiled for the first and second Reagan terms. Heritage also performs such favors as a briefing book for the 1985 Gorbachev summit, designed to train the president how best to stand up to the Soviets. Fourteen Heritage members served on the Reagan transition team in 1980. Heritage's journal *Policy Review* features New Right activists and neoconservative intellectuals. Heritage has received funding from Chase Manhattan Bank, Mobil Oil, Gulf Oil, and the Olin Foundation; it received more than $3 million from ultraconservative Mellon family heir Richard Scaife, who has also funded the Hoover Institution, Committee on the Present Danger and the Georgetown Center for Strategic and International Studies.[11]

The Hoover Institution had in its 1982 annual report an acknowledgement from Reagan stating that "with hard work and diligence, you built the knowledge base that made the changes now taking place in Washington possible."[12]

The Center for Strategic and International Studies (CSIS), formerly based at Georgetown University in Washington, appears to be the
leading contender for the super-think tank of the post-Reagan period.
CSIS is a prime link between Rollnet operatives, neoconservative
policymakers, and conservative realists. Most of CSIS's initial money
came from such right-wing funders as Richard Scaife and Justin Dart.[13]
Former CIA officer and Rollnet activist Ray Cline resides at CSIS.[14] Rollnet
and Contragate actor Michael Ledeen also works there. More recently,
CSIS has attracted more prominent foreign policy experts, including
neoconservative Jeane Kirkpatrick and hardline "realists" Henry Kissinger, Zbigniew Brzezinski, and ex-Rand analyst James Schlesinger.
CSIS sponsors hundreds of seminars and congressional study groups
for administration and congressional staffers, and had 4,100 contacts
with the press in 1985. CSIS publishes *The Washington Quarterly,* which
has gained significant influence in foreign policy circles. CSIS mixes
right-wing and traditional conservative funds, getting its $8.7 million
budget both from Richard Scaife and from the Rockefeller, Ford and
Carnegie foundations.[15]

While the right-wing tanks grew, the liberal TTCCs became more
conservative and less influential. From 1945 to 1970, CFR was without
question the hegemonic TTCC, run directly by the corporate conservative elite.[16] Attacked by the left for Vietnam and by the right as being
part of the communist conspiracy, CFR's influence in Washington was
being supplanted by a cadre of foreign policy professionals. These full-
time experts wrote constantly in influential journals and the press, and
worked in the backrooms of Washington as governmental advisors or
in the government itself as policymakers. They crowded out the establishment elite of businessmen or lawyers doing their stint in
Washington. These emerging experts were ambitious individuals, not
used to the collegial climate of the CFR. Some, such as Richard Perle,
Fred Iklé, and Michael Ledeen, were linked to Rollnet. In one analysis
by Professor James Petras, the substitution of this new breed of self-ag-
grandizing foreign policy "intellectuals" for elite CFR Ivy League "Wise
Men" is a mirror of the decline of productive industry and its replacement by Ivan Boesky-type financial managers and speculators.[17]

In the late 1970s the CFR held serious discussions on East-West
relations, in which the ExSET view made strong inroads into the early
1970s CFR détente position. A major CFR report viewed the Soviets as
relentlessly hostile and called for a major military buildup.[18] The New
Deal-oriented Brookings Institution, a designer of programs during
Democratic administrations, appointed a moderate Republican, Bruce

MacLaury, as its president in 1977, with the aim to dilute the liberal image of the institution.[19] One commentator noted in 1984 that Brookings "is sounding more like Ronald Reagan every day." The Trilateral Commission also moved to the right, as discussed in Chapter Seven. It is clear that foreign policy intellectuals, including those in TTCCs, moved rightward in their views, reflecting the overall shift of the ruling elites who finance these intellectuals.

The Democrats

The Democratic Party is no stranger to rollback. It was the Democrats who crafted NSC-68, the policy document with strong hints of rollback (see Chapter One). The Democrats brought the United States into its two major "postwar" wars, Korea and Vietnam; it took Republicans to get out of these wars. The Democrats were responsible for several of the rollback actions undertaken since World War II.

The CPD of the 1970s was led not by Republicans but by neoconservative Democrats. CPD started out of an exchange between Democrat Eugene Rostow and Republican Henry Kissinger, with the Democrat the hardliner and the Republican the wizard of détente. The CPD Democrats were strong advocates of rollback and favored nuclear superiority and the economic isolation of the USSR.

Related to the neoconservative Democrats were the military-oriented Democrats led by Sen. Henry Jackson, a longtime advocate of Boeing military contracts for his state of Washington. A chief aide to Jackson was Reagan's Assistant Defense Secretary Richard Perle, noted for his anti-arms control stand. Another strand among the rollback Democrats was big labor, including AFL-CIO President Lane Kirkland (who was on CPD), Jay Lovestone, and Albert Shanker.[20]

After Vietnam, the rollback Democrats were eclipsed by the détente advocates and the anti-interventionists. The 1976 Democratic platform concentrated on reduction of East-West tensions rather than military might. In the 1980 platform, anti-Soviet rhetoric was relatively muted. The 1984 platform, while more concerned with the Soviet threat than the previous two documents, concentrated on attacking Reagan for his war-mongering.

The 1980s: The Democrats Move to the Right

On April 18, 1986, a remarkable document emanated from the Democratic Party. Entitled "New Choices in a Changing America," the manifesto's foreign policy contains significant contributions from the right wing, particularly on East-West relations.

> We understand that the Soviet Union poses the greatest threat to world peace and freedom.... [The Republicans] have spent more than one trillion dollars on defense. Most Americans don't quarrel with this, in and of itself. After the brutal Soviet invasion of Afghanistan, the Iranian hostage crisis, and signs of unrest in Central America, they knew America's defenses had to be repaired. And they supported the build up.... The expansion of Soviet influence continues to pose the major threat to American interests and world peace. We must not and cannot relax our vigilance against Soviet imperialism.... The United States can neither police the world nor retreat from it. Neither unilateralism nor isolationism is consistent with our global interests, but the United States must not be afraid to act alone when there is no alternative...there are times when the threat or use of force is necessary to preserve our vital interests.[21]

While Harry Truman might have felt perfectly at home with this statement, it marked a major change from the post-1968 Democratic Party. Why did the Democrats move so sharply rightward? One reason is the declining importance of the low-income voter. In *The New Politics of Inequality,* Thomas Edsall analyzes the reduction in voter turnout among lower income groups, the increased dependence of Democratic members of Congress on a more conservative middle-class constituency, the relative decline of labor's influence within the Democratic Party, and the great increase in business domination of the party.[22] The Democrats have become more and more dependent on large contributions from wealthy individuals and corporations.[23]

Democratic business backers also moved right as part of the conservative trend described in Chapter Seven. In 1980, virtually all of business backed Ronald Reagan. In 1984, the Democrats badly wanted to recapture some of that business support. To do so, they moved toward more acceptable pro-business policies. When Reagan again dominated corporate campaign contributions in 1984, the pressure became even stronger for the Democrats to move rightward. The economy, relations with Europe, and trade policy continued to make some business leaders unhappy with Reagan; they came to check out the Democrats. For example, some Atlanticist-oriented businesses (those trading with and investing in Europe) moved back toward the Democrats along with companies interested in trading with the Soviets. The first-strike character of the nuclear buildup, the evil empire rhetoric, and Reagan's efforts to limit Europe's trade with the East—all these were problems for trans-Atlantic business.[24] The more unhappy the elites were with Reagan, the more the Democrats molded themselves into "reasonable Reagans" to accommodate those elites. The process has not simply been a mutual attraction between business and the Democrats; active campaigns were also waged to conservatize the Democratic party by such groups as the American Enterprise Institute, the Trilateral Commission, and the Coalition for a Democratic Majority.[25] In addition, the Democratic Business Council, requiring members to contribute $10,000 per year, discusses and influences party policies.

The Democrats' pro-business positions have included domestic spending cuts and strong support for military spending.[26] The importance of business-dominated Political Action Committees (PACs) for campaign funding is a major factor in the Democrats' political stances. As one member of Congress explained, "These PACs are influencing a lot of Democrats. You're seeing people from mainstream Democratic districts, elected with labor support, who are now voting with business." PACs related to military contractors gave half their money to Republicans and half to Democrats.[27]

Another reason for the Democrats' right turn is the demographic shift toward the more conservative South and West. The Democrats cannot win a presidential election without carrying the South, the West, or both. The Northeast and Midwest states have lost 21 electoral votes to the Sunbelt since 1968, and after 1990 they will lose 20 more.[28] One development that makes the South and West more conservative is the dramatic shift in military spending to those regions. The Northeast Midwest share of military prime contract dollars dropped from 72 percent in 1951 to 37 percent in 1983, while the South and West's share increased from 28 percent to 63 percent.[29]

As a result of these factors, major developments have taken place in the Democratic Party. The Sunbelt strategy is reflected in the development of the Democratic Leadership Council (DLC). Formed in 1985, the DLC's goal is to move the Party toward the right. Its organizers are predominantly from the South and West, including such leaders as Richard Gephardt of Missouri, Chuck Robb of Virginia, Bruce Babbitt of Arizona, and Sam Nunn of Georgia.[30] Democratic National Committee Chair Paul Kirk has sharply reduced the role of minority caucuses in the party and has increased the power of elected officials. He has been supported by business groupings that wished to dilute the influence of blacks, women, and grassroots organizations.[31] More Democratic House members are from middle-class districts than previously, spreading Democratic conservatism from its initial base in the South to other regions and leading to a more conservative Democratic congressional delegation.[32] In the 1987-88 Senate, fully half of the Democratic committee chairs have had pro-Reagan records, backing Reagan 58 percent to 73 percent of the time.[33]

The Democrats' Foreign Policy Positions

The Military Budget

Former Democratic National Committee chair Robert Strauss has unhappily said that Democrats are perceived as unwilling to project our nation's military power. Even liberal Tip O'Neill has stated that Democrats must shed the image of being weak on defense.[34] Neoliberals Gary Hart and House Armed Services Committee Chairman Les Aspin, and conservative Senate Armed Services Committee Chairman Sam Nunn want the Democrats to be the party of lean hawks. They prefer less Defense Department waste, but more military power.

Aspin provides a prime example of the Democrats' shift to the right. In 1970, he was a leading dove. In the late 1970s, he opposed Carter's military budget increases. But by 1983, he supported the MX missile, and in 1985 he took a pro-military position on Pentagon funding. Aspin does not oppose SDI. He recently appointed Coalition for a Democratic Majority (CDM) director Jay Winnick as his top aide.[35] In 1986, he supported contra funding in Nicaragua. Aspin and Sam Nunn are firmly established as the party's defense spokesmen. While Aspin hails from the party's peace wing, Nunn comes from the military strength wing. Their collaboration symbolizes a partial bridging of the post-Vietnam party schism.[36]

In 1986, Aspin and Nunn were drafting the defense and foreign policy position papers for the Democratic National Committee Policy Council and for the conservative Democratic Leadership Council.[37] Their influence gives CDM substantial power in setting foreign and military policy.

But the military budget issue is not an easy problem for the Democrats, as it is for the Republicans. Military-industrial supporters conflict with bankers' worries about the federal deficit and with multinational businesses unhappiness with East-West nuclear instability.

Recently, the Democrats have come up with an answer trying to please all three of these business interests: high-tech conventional weapons. This solution allows for a reduction in nuclear capacity, a disarmament program for intermediate range missiles in Europe, and military budget reductions in some high-cost offensive nuclear weaponry. At the same time it emphasizes a strong conventional military with a potential for new 21st century weapons contracts for the computerized battlefield.[38] Gary Hart's book *America Can Win* provides the rationale for this new Democratic direction. One difficulty is that high-tech conventional military reforms may cost more than the buildup of the Reagan years.[39]

East-West Relations

Prior to the 1987 East-West thaw, the issue of U.S.-Soviet relations produced less intra-Democratic conflict than the topic of Third World interventionism. Strong anti-Soviet sentiment prevailed from Charles Robb to Stephen Solarz.[40] In "New Choices for a Changing America" the traditional Democratic support for arms control was packaged with the warning label: "Democrats harbor no illusions about arms control."[41] Even Democratic liberals were toughening their language on the Soviet threat.[42] Regarding SDI, many Democrats have favored a limited program, but few have wanted to scrap it altogether. The advent of Gorbachev in the Soviet Union has softened the Democrats' anti-Soviet posture as it has with many Republicans; the depth of this change remains to be seen.

Third World Interventions

Few Democrats flatly oppose the Reagan Doctrine of Third World rollback. Even Rep. Stephen Solarz, on the liberal end of the Democratic spectrum, believes that Democrats should "steer a middle course between rampant interventionism and total isolationism." He feels that rollback should be employed on a case-by-case basis. While Solarz comes down against contra aid in Nicaragua, he supports such aid to insurgencies in Cambodia and Afghanistan.[43] Sen. Joseph Biden appears to speak for a majority of Democrats in his statements that Democrats must be willing to use military force in addition to diplomatic and economic power.[44]

Nicaragua has provided the most significant debate on interventionism. The Democrats' response to the Reagan war was initially mixed but increasingly supportive. By March 1986, Sen. Jim Sasser, replying to a Reagan nationwide address on Nicaragua, did not oppose aid to the Nicaraguan contras but simply suggested placing the contra aid money in escrow for six months during which time negotiations would be given a chance. The importance of this response is that Sasser (himself previously opposed to contra aid) had met with dozens of Democrats before making his reply to Reagan and was taking a pro-contra consensus position on behalf of Congressional Democrats.[45]

Democrats concerned with getting elected in 1988 have tended to oppose contra aid because it is unpopular. Democratic leadership figures, on the other hand, have been reluctant to challenge Reagan on this issue. Governor Charles Robb, a leader of the powerful conservative Democratic Leadership Council, has called for military aid to the contras. The Coalition for a Democratic Majority has blocked any anti-contra positions in party policy documents. Thus on both the military budget and on Third World interventionism, the CDM plays a central role.[46]

The matter of Nicaragua is highly significant: it is the first time an overt rollback issue has been publicly debated at some length in the United States. Previous selective rollback actions—for example Iran, Guatemala, the Bay of Pigs, Brazil, Indonesia, Dominican Republic, Chile, and Grenada—were done so secretly or rapidly that no debate took place until the event was completed. The Democratic Party's inability to draw the line and reject Nicaraguan rollback as a policy is a stark reminder of the continued strength of interventionism in U.S. foreign policy.

Dukakis and Foreign Policy

Right-wing foreign policy faces an uncertain future in the event of a Dukakis presidency. Michael Dukakis is a foreign policy liberal by temperament, opposed to the Nicaraguan contras, a critic of the Grenada invasion, and—like the 1970s Trilats—a believer that economic rather than military strength should be the basis of U.S. foreign policy. However, he has moved in a conservative direction on some foreign/military issues. He became less opposed to new strategic nuclear weapons programs and has become a supporter of conventional military buildup. His chief foreign policy advisors include a former aide to conservative Zbigniew Brzezinski and several analysts previously with the Pentagon. In any Democratic administration, Sen. Sam Nunn, who helped kill the SALT II treaty and who has supported large military budget increases, would have a powerful voice in foreign and military policymaking. Dukakis is on the defensive as a supposed

"Carter foreign policy liberal," and would likely respond to Republican and conservative Democratic attacks by moving toward the right.[47]

The Republicans

Just as the Democrats moved toward the right in the Reagan era to look more like Republicans, the Republicans in the post-Reagan era may move slightly toward the center to look more like Democrats. The right wing took over the Republican Party in 1964 with Goldwater, lost it after his defeat, and shared it with the traditional conservatives in the Nixon years. After Nixon's resignation in 1974, President Ford picked Nelson Rockefeller to be his vice-president, a Trilateral choice that enraged a right wing that had bitterly fought the "Rockefeller Wing" for control of the Republican Party for so many years. The 1976 Republican primary featured a battle between the right-wing Reaganites and the traditional conservatives who stuck with Ford; but in the election the traditional conservatives tended to support Trilat Democrat Jimmy Carter, leaving the defeated Republicans to the right wing.

As the 1980 Reagan candidacy became invincible, traditional conservative business came to his support with the *quid pro quo* that Reagan abandon protectionism. Reagan's vice-presidential partner, George Bush, was the perfect mix of independent Texas oilman with an Eastern elite background. By the time Reagan hit the White House, he already had many debts to the Eastern Establishment, as shown by such key appointments as James Baker as Chief of Staff, former Kissinger aide Alexander Haig as Secretary of State, Malcolm Baldridge as Secretary of Commerce, and William Brock as U.S. trade representative. But the hoped-for-Bush-like peaceful blend of Wall Street and Texas oil did not materialize, and constant battle raged between the right-wing and traditional conservative elites in the administration. The struggle came to a head with Contragate, which featured the right wing's attempt to circumvent the established foreign policy channels. In the waning months of the Reagan administration, traditional conservative Republicans held the upper hand.

More important in its policy implications than Contragate has been the running battle among Republicans over the mounting problem of the military budget vs. the federal deficit. The re-establishment of traditional conservative power in the party led the administration to the Reagan-Gorbachev summits and to the cutting of the military budget.

But on the Central America issue, the Right (generally supported by the traditional conservatives) continued to dominate Reagan administration thinking. If the views of Reagan's Secretary of State George Shultz, a traditional conservative, are any model, selective rollback policy in the Third World will continue as Republican policy, but with the abandonment of global rollback and the partial relaxation of tensions with the USSR.

As the battle for the 1988 Republican presidential nomination showed, the Right and traditional conservatives are contending for control of the post-Reagan Republican Party. In order to win this fight, the more moderate Republican presidential candidates, George Bush and Robert Dole, have consistently courted the Right. Dole, a traditional conservative, who is strongly for the contras in Nicaragua, played a key role in arranging covert military aid to the Angolan rollback effort, and attempted to add Mozambique to the rollback list.[48]

Bush, as CIA director under President Ford, ordered the right-wing-dominated "Team B" to study Soviet military power; this study became the basis for the Committee on the Present Danger's attack on détente in the 1970s. As cited in Chapter Five, Bush has taken the extreme position that nuclear war can be fought and won by the United States. Bush was closely involved with the Nicaraguan contra operation and stated during the 1988 presidential campaign that he supports the Reagan Doctrine. He also pledged to rescind the Anti-Ballistic Missile (ABM) Treaty so that Star Wars testing could move forward unimpeded; this is an important position promoted by the right wing. Bush appears to be a political opportunist rather than an idealogue; he courted the right wing during his quest for the Republican presidential nomination, but publicly distanced himself from the far Right after winning, thereby trying to position himself as a centrist in his campaign against the Democrats. Any Republican president in the foreseeable future will have to balance the concerns of the Right and the traditional conservatives.[49]

The Relation between Democrats and Republicans

According to Thomas Edsall, writing in March 1987, the United States is witnessing a remarkable equilibrium between the two parties; the Republican rise has come to a halt, but the Democrats are unable to increase their long-term share of the vote.[50] While the Republicans stand to gain from the electoral vote shift toward the Sunbelt, the Democrats remain strong in their ability to elect members of Congress. In state legislatures, which will redraw congressional districts after 1990, the Democrats control both houses in twenty-nine states compared with Republican bicameral control in only nine smaller states.[51]

In spite of the fact that the three Republican national campaign committees have had a 5 to 1 fundraising advantage over the Democratic committees, there is no evidence that the "emerging Republican majority" is actually taking place. On the other hand, the Democrats are shaky in their successes; in the 1986 Democratic U.S. Senate takeover, a change of 26,000 votes would have kept the Senate Republican.[52]

If Contragate helps the Democrats, it will be a temporary rather than a major political trend; Watergate only delayed, but did not halt, the 1970s Democratic decline. From 1976 to 1984, the biggest single reduction in Democratic voting was among lower- and middle-class white voters below the age of forty. The only chance for the Democrats to regain their role as a majority party is to re-attract these voter as well as to increase voter turnout among their traditional constituencies, in particular the black population. Otherwise we can expect a back and forth contest between elites.[53]

Yet the Democrats have apparently rejected a strategy to mobilize the many working-class and lower-middle-class whites who do not vote or have voted Republican. Thus it is likely that a back and forth contest between elites will characterize the coming foreign policy era as one of hotly debated specifics and agreed-upon general principles, the latter including a hard line against challenges emanating from the Third World. If any consensus takes hold, it would be a consensus born of the 1970s drop-out of eighteen million former voters, most of them lower income; a consensus based in the ascent of the middle class with its two political poles, neoliberalism and neoconservatism.[54]

In this back and forth contest that takes place within the broad consensus, barring a major war, the actual party and individuals in power will be decided far more by the state of the economy than by foreign policy considerations. Elections rarely hinge on international issues.[55] That is one reason why Dean Burnham was accurate when he stated that elites, not voters, determine foreign policy. Another factor that moves foreign affairs far from the electoral arena is the power of the foreign policy bureaucracy.

The Foreign Policy Bureaucracy

When a new administration takes office, foreign policy rarely takes a radical turn. A certain continuity carries through Democrat and Republican administrations alike, a continuity that holds firm even in the absence of a bipartisan policy consensus. This continuity is rooted in the powerful foreign policy bureaucracy. The bureaucracy can change slowly as new people with different ideas join its ranks. The right wing understands clearly that without getting its cadres into the bureaucracy, it will not be able to effect a change in U.S. foreign policy.

The role of the bureaucracy is analyzed by Franz Schurmann in *The Logic of World Power*. Schurmann describes

> the dual nature of the state—as a realm of ideology and a realm of interests. The realm of ideology centers on the chief executive of the state, and the realm of interests centers on the state's bureaucracies. The realm of interests tends to remain fairly stable over time, while the realm of ideology changes constantly.... As the realm of ideology changes, it inflicts or tries to inflict those changes on the realm of interests, which naturally tends toward inertia. The agencies of change which the realm of ideology creates over time in turn transform themselves into interests and, thus, gradually join the realm of interests.
>
> The realm of interests within the state, whatever its particular origins, usually meshes with the realm of interests within society. In other words, bureaucracies eventually come to develop a mutually satisfactory accommodation with corporate and other interests, usually marked by the back-and-forth transfers of key personnel from bureaucracy to corporation and *vice versa.* The realm of ideology, on the other hand...generates agencies of the state that are instruments of power, the capacity to mobilize men and resources for the achievement of goals. Ideological power is directed toward change, whereas interest power is directed toward maintenance or incremental expansion. Thus, although a new ideologically motivated state agency will seek to change interests both within and outside the state, over time the process of accommodation will set in.
>
> Revolution is an extreme form of the remaking of the state where an entirely new realm of ideology is created which then destroys or significantly rearranges the realm of interests of both the state and society.... The chief executive always seeks to expand his power *vis-à-vis* the interests...any chief executive who fails to fight the interests soon finds himself at their mercy....[56]

Though Schurmann wrote these passages in 1974, they precisely describe the situation of the right-wing rollbackers at the accession of Ronald Reagan to the presidency. The rollbackers wanted to institute the "Reagan Revolution," which required rearranging or destroying the realm of interests (in particular the State Department bureaucracy). Failing to do so, the right wing relied on its own private apparatus to go around the foreign policy bureaucracy. When Schurmann says, "The realm of ideology...generates agencies of the state that are instruments of power, the capacity to mobilize men and resources for the achievement of goals," the function William Casey and Oliver North played by mobilizing men and resources (Secord, Singlaub, money, arms) to achieve a goal (overthrowing the government of Nicaragua) provides an uncanny example.

In his later work, *The Foreign Politics of Richard Nixon,* Schurmann uses the term "political class" to describe that group of people which operates full-time in the political arena: professional politicians, professional bureaucrats, and professional journalists. Conflicts within the political class can rock the government, as they did during the time of Joseph McCarthy, Watergate, and Contragate. McCarthy represented the right wing attempting but failing to dislodge the traditional conservatives from control of the political class. Nixon was also determined to break the Eastern Establishment's hold on the federal government, and undertook some major purges (especially in the intelligence community) of "old boys' networks" that failed to cooperate with his major new thrusts in foreign affairs such as the rapprochement with China. Unlike McCarthy and Reagan, Nixon was not looking for right-wing ideologues to staff the foreign policy agencies; he wanted "apolitical" technical-professionals who could give good advice but not meddle in the policy aspects. With the Watergate break-in and its cover-up as the mistake that could be pounced on, Nixon met the fate of most who shake up the political class: banishment.[57]

In 1980, the right wing understood the problem of the bureaucracy. The Heritage Foundation's *Mandate for Leadership* warned that "the single most important sign of the advent of a conservative administration would be a thorough 'housecleaning' of existing political and other non-career appointments who can be removed at the discretion of the president." According to Heritage, for the Right to take full control would require the purge of the traditional conservative bureaucrats.[58]

In its assessment of Reagan's first year, the Heritage Foundation admitted failure in cracking the foreign policy bureaucracy:

> The principal reason for the Administration's failure to accomplish more in the first year is surprisingly consistent from department to department and from agency to agency—personnel. Possibly the greatest problem has been the absence of a sufficient number of key leaders at all levels of the State Department devoted to the Reagan philosophy of foreign policy.... A thorough housecleaning was recommended in *Mandate* and continues to be a major priority.[59]

In the words of neoconservative Irving Kristol: "Our State Department, however, is not interested in foreign policy, only in its own version of diplomacy. And it just does not seem to matter who is president or who is secretary of state. The department, in the end, always manages to prevail."[60]

According to *Mandate for Leadership II* (1984), it appeared that Kristol was accurate; the Heritage Foundation was so distressed by the bureaucracy that it devoted 100 pages to the problem.

> Over the years, foreign policy-making has been abdicated generally to liberal, internationalist academics, lawyers and foreign policy 'experts.' They have run American foreign policy, regardless of whether a Democrat or Republican occupied the White House.... With such a large number of career officers in top-level positions, the foreign service bureaucracy exerts a powerful influence on... foreign policy recommendations (liberal and cautious), and implementation of the Administration's foreign policy directives (slowly).... Since the bureaucracy supports the status quo...they are particularly opposed to the policy agenda of a conservative administration.... [They will] ally with Congress to defeat the positive policy changes proposed by the President and his political executives.[61]

Mandate II cites Reagan's first Secretary of State, Alexander Haig, as saying, "I found no great enthusiasm in the Department of State for the Reagan Administration," and then laments that Haig failed to do much about this situation.[62]

The Right has tended to be overly concerned with the State Department, the foreign policy agency with the least power. Richard Barnet, whose analysis of the national security apparatus is extremely perceptive, wrote in the early 1970s that the military and intelligence agencies had taken over foreign policy from the State Department.[63] Thomas Etzold agrees, citing general acceptance of the Munich Syndrome as instrumental in increasing the military's role in the conduct of foreign affairs. Etzold describes the

State Department building lying like a great gray whale on the riverbanks in Washington away from the center of town—and of power....[64]

But State was not the only problem for the Right; the CIA was also seen as harboring a hostile bureaucracy. *Mandate for Leadership* noted that in the 1970s, more than 800 senior clandestine data collectors were terminated from the agency. According to Heritage, CIA data analysis, on Soviet military strength and other areas, had been politicized by leadership that did not realize the international danger the United States faced. Thus the job in 1981 was to "rebuild the cadre of experts in covert action," i.e., to bring Rollnet operatives into power in the agency.[65] Alas, four years later the situation had not improved sufficiently. "At least part of the reason for this is that the Administration made only a handful of political appointments to the CIA, not nearly enough to re-invigorate or re-orient the agency."[66]

What does all of this have to do with the prospects for global rollback? Certainly, if the right wing succeeded in placing hundreds of loyalists into the foreign policy bureaucracy, the Right would have far greater strength in determining long-term foreign policy. Aside from the complaining of the Heritage Foundation, what are the facts? Has the right wing successfully infiltrated the bureaucracy, thereby guaranteeing influence regardless of who occupies the White House?

Some observers feel that Reagan did a great deal to bring right-wing people into the State Department. Reagan filled 40 percent of ambassadorships with political loyalists rather than career diplomats. In 1981, 75 percent of ambassadors were career diplomats; by 1986 the number had fallen to 60 percent, a low point for the past four decades. Far Right Sen. Jesse Helms and the Heritage Foundation waged a campaign to get their people into State Department slots. Senior officials in the Reagan government acknowledge that in Central American positions, their aim was to get rid of everyone who could not be entrusted to implement the president's policy. Some compared it with McCarthy's attempt to blame professional diplomats with treason for the gains made by communists in Eastern Europe and Asia.[67] But Reagan appointments could be wiped out when he left the White House; more important were deeper levels of the bureaucracy.

Sidney Blumenthal, a leading scholar of the right wing, has analyzed this question. The Right has understood for over ten years that to prevail, the "liberal establishment" had to be shattered.

Nixon tried, but the events surrounding Watergate shattered him. Gerald Ford dealt with the liberal establishment by containment, but

Reagan's strategy was rollback. To do this, the right wing needed a strong counterintelligentsia to define a framework for lasting change—by staffing the new institutes, writing policy papers and newspaper editorials, or serving as political advisors.[68] Such groups as the Institute for Educational Affairs and the Heritage Foundation carried these tasks out and were instrumental in developing people to become right-wing cadres.

Following the 1984 election, "The cadres of the Counter-Establishment were burrowing into every agency and department, in the West Wing of the White House and the Old Executive Office Building. They comprised an informal but tightly knit network.... But difficulties remained. First, there was a sheer scarcity of qualified right-wing job-holders." The Heritage Foundation intensified its recruitment of likely candidates for government slots. Virtually the entire leadership of Heritage was deeply involved in the job hunt. Some gains were made in foreign policy and in controlling the judiciary.[69] However, no observers believe that committed right-wing cadres have wrested control over the foreign affairs bureaucracy.

In the short term, the Right failed. Yet in the long haul, the Reagan years were extremely significant in building a conservative "counter-establishment." As Heritage Foundation director Edwin Feulner explains it,

> Not only do you have conservative cadres coming into entry-level jobs, but once out of office they will serve as consultants. Come ten years from now, you'll have them ready to go, two or three notches higher, even at the cabinet level. Our infrastructure was never built up in the Nixon administration. By and large Reagan relied on the Establishment to staff his administration. Our bright young people hadn't had the on-the-job training to be really credible. Ten years from now it will be very different. Next time around, there might be fifty percent conservatives—an order of magnitude larger.[70]

Other authors have emphasized the long-range strategy of the Right: to infiltrate all institutions of society with their people. The Heritage Foundation acted as the personnel office for the Reagan administration, while the American Legislative Exchange Council has recruited rightists for state government. A conservative elite is slowly establishing itself in the executive branch and in Congress, in universities and research institutes, and in the press.[71] Morton Blackwell, a special assistant to President Reagan, recruits and trains conservatives for the State Department through the Leadership Institute. While the old Rollnet cadres were primarily operatives, the new generation include intellectuals and policymakers. According to Blumenthal, the pool of newly trained right-wing foreign policy experts may not influence the next administration, but will be ready for the one after that.

While the Right may not have placed a sufficient number of its cadres into the national security apparatus, that bureaucracy is still strongly influenced by the military-industrial complex, which itself generates right-wing views within the bureaucracy. The current composition of the bureaucracy—perhaps more pragmatic and less ideological than the perfect Heritage recruit—assures that it will strongly support selective rollback as it has done for many years.

Contragate can be viewed as the classic battle between the realm of ideology and the realm of interests, between the ideological right wing and the traditional pragmatic foreign policy bureaucracy. In the short term the right wing lost the battle, though the defeat was only partial because of agreement between the two tendencies on Third World rollback as exemplified by Nicaragua. The setback of the Right could be shortlived and minimal compared with McCarthy's and Nixon's drubbings. A key difference is that the Right of the 1980s has what it lacked in the 1950s and 1970s: a growing cadre of committed, trained, increasingly experienced people who—over the long haul—will likely exert great influence on the conduct of U.S. foreign policy.

The Rightward Shift of Foreign Policy Views

Viewed from the perspective of early 1987, it appeared that the non-interventionist school that flourished after Vietnam had been decisively defeated among foreign policy elites. Holly Sklar, in her 1986 book *Reagan, Trilateralism and the Neoliberals* discusses shifts in the range of views on foreign policy. In Sklar's analysis, the politically relevant spectrum during the Carter years went from UN Ambassador Andrew Young on the left to Secretary of State Cyrus Vance in the center, National Security Advisor Brzezinski on the right, and out to the neoconservatives on the far Right.

In the Reagan period, the spectrum shifted rightward: Andrew Young went off the chart; Vance, Sen. Edward Kennedy and former House Speaker Tip O'Neill made up the left, the Neoliberals (represented by Rep. Stephen Solarz and Gary Hart) occupied the center-left,

Brzezinski was a centrist, the realist conservatives (Henry Kissinger, Senate Minority Leader Robert Dole, Secretary of State George Shultz, and Vice President George Bush) were at the center-right, Defense Secretary Caspar Weinberger was a "center-right megamilitarist who likes piling up weapons more than using them"; the right included President Reagan, Rep. Jack Kemp, former UN Ambassador Jeane Kirkpatrick, and farther out Sen. Jesse Helms and Jerry Falwell (who were previously considered extremists but became respectable).[72]

Even the least interventionist members of this spectrum supported selective rollback. An example is the InterAmerican Dialogue, featuring Sol Linowitz, Cyrus Vance, Robert McNamara, McGeorge Bundy, Elliot Richardson and the Rockefeller Foundation. This grouping backed military aid to the rebels in Afghanistan, and did not oppose rollback in Nicaragua. In July 1987, Sol Linowitz advocated aid to the Nicaraguan contras.[73] The most liberal edge of the politically relevant spectrum was not opposed to rollback.

During the 1980s, a traditional conservative-Right coalition, using the Right as the shock troops, successfully pushed the non-interventionists off the relevant political spectrum. One of the few remaining influential non-interventionists, Thomas Hughes of the Carnegie Endowment for International Peace, decried this development, describing how "internationalism"—belief in international cooperation, consultation and conciliation, international law, and negotiation rather than use of force—has been attacked:

> Today these internationalist impulses have pretty well exhausted themselves in mainstream American political life. Traditional internationalist themes…are the objects of derision and contempt…. Today the rule of law is scoffed at in the current American national climate and lampooned by the president…. When ranking neoconservative denizens in America hear the word 'internationalism' these days, they rush to murder it in yet one more panegyric to rampant patriotism and 'manly honor' in *Commentary*, the *Washington Times, Human Events,* or the *National Interest*. Such views have moved from the bleachers to the playing field, from the wings to center stage.[74]

Conclusion: What Next?

Given the formidable power of the Right in every aspect of foreign policy making, a series of events in 1987 came as a surprise to many observers: 1) The ever deepening revelations related to Contragate; 2) Serious negotiation on nuclear arms reduction; 3) A major peace initiative in Central America; 4) Serious steps toward an end to the Afghan war; 5) The defeat of Robert Bork's Supreme Court nomination, marking a major setback in the right-wing attempt to gain long-term control of one of the branches of government; 6) A disaster on Wall Street that scared the daylights out of the ruling elites; 7) The 1987 summit in which Ronald "Evil Empire" Reagan welcomed the Soviet General Secretary to the White House like a long-lost friend.

What is happening? Are the non-interventionists making a comeback? Will right-wing views move back to the bleachers? The next chapter moves into the treacherous waters of analyzing future trends.

9

The Prospects for Future Right-wing Power

No one can reliably predict the future. The temptation is great but the perils are greater. This chapter partially succumbs to the temptation while trying to heed the perils.

The question addressed in this chapter is: what will be the influence of the right wing on U.S. foreign policy in the years to come? We think it will be significant. The Right suffered many setbacks in 1987, and no one can say how long these setbacks might last or to what extent the Right will make a comeback in the future. We anticipate that bitter foreign policy battles will take place between the Right and traditional conservatives, and that the pre-Vietnam foreign policy consensus will not be revived.

The Current Conjuncture

As the 1980s progressed, traditional conservatives, who had joined with the Right in support of the Reagan presidency, increasingly had their doubts about the right-wing solution to the economic crisis and the aggressiveness of Reagan's foreign policy goals. These doubts progressed as the trade and budget deficits deepened, and conservative elite uneasiness with the economy no doubt contributed to the debunking of the Reagan administration through the Contragate revelations.

The loss of faith in the Reagan government came to a head with the Wall Street crash of October 1987. But the crisis of confidence went far deeper. The entire 1980s right-wing-conservative theory that the United States' economic decline required a reassertion of the United States as number one in the world was called into question. As stated in *Business Week*, the United States must "rethink its long-standing role as military hegemon of the non-communist world."[1] The re-establishment of U.S. global power via global rollback was not working.

As the decade of the 1980s draws to a close, a major realignment of the ruling elites is taking place. The right-wing-conservative alliance appears to be ended for the proximate future. The realist school of foreign policy is reasserting its dominance over the ideological wing. According to the realists, not only must the United States recognize its limitations in military and political power, but it must adjust to its new role as an economy with serious problems. In the 1970s and 1980s, the economic decline was indeed fertile soil for right-wing growth. But right-wing growth did not bring in its wake national economic growth. Thus at the current conjuncture, continued economic decline has led to right-wing decline.

Yet the Right is in no mood to give up. After all, Truman had shaken up the right wing when he fired General MacArthur, and the Right turned the defeat into a major campaign for rollback. The Right took a licking during Watergate, but elected Ronald Reagan a short six years later. One cannot underestimate the capacity of the Right to regroup.

In this chapter we will look at the impact of three major foreign policy developments of 1987—Contragate, the intermediate-range nuclear forces (INF) treaty, and the Central American peace process—and then attempt some generalizations about right-wing power in U.S. foreign policy.

The Effect of Contragate

When the Contragate affair broke in late 1986, some observers felt that the Right had sustained a fatal blow. There is no question that the Reagan government was severely injured. But right-wing causes suffered far less than Reagan as a political figure. Almost no one during Contragate challenged the policy of overthrowing the Sandinista government in Nicaragua; the debate remained a narrow one concerned with the legality and wisdom of the methods used. In the middle of Contragate the Congress failed to cut off $40 million for the contras, which it had the power to do. During the Contragate hearings, Reagan provided $15 million in new military assistance to the insurgent forces in Angola.[2] Most importantly, the right wing effectively utilized the public hearings as a major platform to espouse its view of Nicaragua as a battle between freedom fighters and communist devils.

One interpretation of Contragate holds that it will help rather than hurt the cause of foreign interventionism in the long run by reducing Congressional power over foreign affairs. Zbigniew Brzezinski has said that Congress' push into foreign affairs has reached "absurd proportions."[3] In December 1986, Lawrence Eagleburger, president of Kissinger Associates and an influential figure in the national security apparatus, wrote an article entitled "Now that Reagan's Ship of State Has Joined the Titanic...." Eagleburger, like Oliver North, cites the responsibility of Congress for Contragate because its excessive oversight makes impossible the conduct of any covert policies.

> In order to support an insurgency in Angola or Nicaragua, we must first go through a public debate in Congress that only emphasizes to the potential recipients of our aid the tenuousness of our support.[4]

Many witnesses at the Iran-Contra hearings expressed exactly that view, condemning Congress' on-again off-again funding of the contras. In the long run, Contragate could create a a backlash against Congress and a strengthening of presidential powers which would make foreign interventions easier to accomplish. The fact that the Tower Commission recommended reducing covert operations oversight by concentrating it in one committee shows that such a trend is not unlikely.[5] The traditional conservatives, with their liking for covert operations, were probably not unhappy when Oliver North told Congress:

> Plain and simple, you are to blame because of the fickle, vacillating, unpredictable, on-again, off-again policy toward the Nicaraguan democratic resistance—the Contras.

A radical version of this view finds the constitutional separation of powers to be obsolete. According to conservative analyst Kevin Phillips, Watergate revealed the dysfunctional nature of the separation of powers. The process of passing a federal budget reminds us of this problem each year.[6] Contragate could be used as another example to argue that foreign policymaking under the separation of powers does not work. If we add to these views the 1970s Trilateral Commission study claiming that the United States suffers from too much democracy, an anti-democratic movement might develop to centralize and stream-line government policymaking. Such a development would reduce cur-rent restraints on military adventures abroad.

While the outcome of the executive-congressional struggle could proceed in an anti-Congress direction, the opposite is also possible, with Congress strengthening its foreign policy role. It is historically too close to the Contragate developments to predict their final legacy. The most reasonable observation is that Contragate itself will not be the main determinant of future trends. According to political analyst Thomas Edsall,

> What makes analysis of the consequences of the Iran-contra scan-dal particularly tentative, however, is the fact that the country ap-pears to be at an unsettled political stage. The rightward drive has lost much of its momentum, but there is no resurgence of the left or of liberalism.... The short-term prospect appears to be a kind of trench warfare between the two parties and their candidates, in which the Iran-contra scandal is part of the struggle, but, for the moment, not decisive.[7]

The Reagan-Gorbachev Summits

While Contragate represented a setback of uncertain proportions for the Right, the December 1987 Reagan-Gorbachev summit was a momentous right-wing disaster. The entire Expanding Soviet Empire Theory (ExSET) with its "evil empire" popular ideology was buried in the public eye, as *Time, Newsweek* and TV network news heralded the new détente led by the United States' new-found friend, Mikhail Gor-bachev.

While the Right seethed, Gorbachev waged an ideological offen-sive, cultivating contacts with major U.S. business and cultural leaders, many of whom came away impressed with the Soviet leader as "some-one we could deal with." "Deals" that were particularly attractive to the traditional conservative elites included opportunities for U.S. companies to form joint ventures and market their products in the USSR.[8] One U.S. business leader favoring increased Soviet trade expressed "When you look at the trade deficit that was announced today, it's really outrageous that we are excluding ourselves from this market."[9] Gorbachev's entice-ments to U.S. business increased right-wing ire against such figures as Commerce Secretary Verity, a recent Reagan appointee, regarded as someone who would sell the Soviets the rope to hang the capitalists.[10]

The desire to deal with the USSR even spread to involve the writ-ings published by the Heritage Foundation. In the Winter 1988 *Policy Review,* the lead article suggested a unique strategy aimed at moving the Gorbachev-type reformers to support a transition from the present "Marxist-Leninist totalitarianism" to the formation of a non-socialist Rus-sian nationalist authoritarian state that could be a potential future ally. To facilitate this, the author proposed a "Grand Bargain" that would in-volve the United States and its allies providing large-scale economic and technical assistance to the USSR—a "Marshall Plan for Post-Soviet Russia."[11]

These developments, together with the fact that Gorbachev be-came one of the ten men most admired by citizens of the United States in 1987 (just behind Oliver North)[12] threw most of the Right into a fren-zy. Seeking to reverse the momentum posed by the "current resurgence of détentist policy toward Moscow,"[13] the Right actively mobilized against the INF Treaty signed by Reagan at the summit. Immediately after the summit, Caspar Weinberger broke the rosy spell, calling the Soviet Union by its familiar name, the "evil empire."[14] Rollback Democrat Eugene Rostow of the Committee on the Present Danger (CPD) warned that the INF treaty is a new Munich, a U.S. retreat in the East-West conflict.[15] After branding Reagan a "useful idiot" of the USSR, Howard Phillips of the Conservative Caucus took out a full-page ad in *Human Events,* extending the Munich appeasement analogy to the Reagan presidency in graphic terms. In the ad titled "Appeasement is as Unwise in 1988 as in 1938," Reagan and Gorbachev are respective-ly pictured below photos of Neville Chamberlain and Adolph Hitler.[16] In a *New York Times* column, Phillips added, "If this [INF] treaty is ratified by the Senate, a major battle of World War III will have been lost by default, without a shot having been fired.... We must defeat the Reagachev Doctrine."[17]

Reagan further alienated the Right during the Moscow summit of May 1988 when he stated that his characterization of the Soviet Union as an evil empire was no longer valid. The Right also squirmed when the president attributed human rights violations to the Soviet bureaucracy rather than being a fundamental feature of socialism in the USSR.

Caution against succumbing to "Gorby fever" was not confined to the Right. The Brookings Institution's moderate Sovietologist Jerry Hough characterized Gorbachev as "a dictator consolidating his power."[18] Soviet specialists from the liberal Carnegie Endowment for International Peace warned against wishful thinking about Gorbachev, pointing out that the USSR still works indefatigably to undermine U.S. international interests.[19] In a pre-Washington summit column, center-right Democrat Zbigniew Brzezinski feared the creation of a public-relations atmosphere that assumes an end to U.S.-Soviet conflict.[20] *New York Times* columnist A.M. Rosenthal wrote that agreements which dictator Gorbachev makes today he can take away tomorrow.[21] George Bush put forth a harsher view of the Soviets than Reagan, during the 1988 campaign.[22]

However, "Gorby fever" has put an end to the 1980s anti-détente coalition between the Right and traditional conservatives. Now the battle lines are drawn, with the conservative elite ushering in a new period of cautious East-West rapprochement while the Right, on the defensive, tries to hang onto global rollback.

Rollback and the Central American Peace Process

On August 7, 1987, the five Central American presidents signed an agreement authored by Costa Rican President Oscar Arias in consultation with U.S. Democrats.[23] The agreement called for an end to all support for rebel groups from outside the region, the prohibition of any nation's territory being used by rebel groups seeking to overthrow governments in the region, and a commitment to democratization within each country.[24] These peace accords were an outright repudiation of Reagan Doctrine rollback and the Reagan administration subverted the plan in every possible way. Requiring of the Nicaraguan government a series of democratization demands while asking nothing of the military-controlled regimes in Guatemala, El Salvador, and Honduras, Reagan pressed for more and more aid to the contras, which is expressly forbidden by the Arias Plan.

The peace plan was a direct challenge to rollback Democrats and traditional conservatives, who now had an alternative that was neither the terrorist contras nor the "totalitarian" Sandinistas. The traditional conservative reaction was to waffle, mouthing support for Arias but not wanting to cut off the contras. The traditional conservatives' problem with the Arias Plan was simple: it left the Sandinistas in power.

House Speaker Jim Wright led the traditional conservative response to the Arias Plan. In December 1987, while strongly accusing the Reagan administration of sabotaging the plan, he allowed the House to cave into the administration's wishes and provide the contras with $14.4 million.[25] One factor in this Reagan victory, showing the fickleness of the anti-contra sentiment, was the Reagan-orchestrated testimony of Nicaraguan defector Major Roger Miranda who trotted out a Sandinista "worst case" military planning document and falsely accused the Nicaraguans of preparing a definite increase in its military strength in presumed violation of the Central American peace accords.[26] Even though a Pentagon official later admitted that many of Miranda's statements were speculative, and even though Oscar Arias—on the eve of receiving the Nobel Peace Prize—urged the Congress to deny all funds to the contras, the Miranda incident was sufficient to turn wishy-washy Democrats back into contra supporters.[27] The traditionally conservative *New York Times* also took the self-contradictory position that the United States should support the Arias Plan and also give aid to the contras.[28]

On February 3, 1988, a more definitive contra aid vote came before Congress, which Reagan lost in the House by a narrow 219-211 vote. Prior to this vote, Arias himself remarked that the future of the contras would be determined by whether or not Nicaragua democratizes. He thus retreated from his previous position calling for an end to contra aid on the grounds that Nicaragua could not be expected to democratize while it was under military attack.[29] Arias and other Central American presidents had been threatened by the Reagan administration with a loss of economic assistance if they failed to join the United States in ganging up on Nicaragua.[30]

The reaction to the Arias Plan and to the February 3 contra aid vote makes it clear that many traditional conservatives, including ostensibly anti-contra Democrats, continue to support rollback in Nicaragua. Following Reagan's contra aid defeat, Jim Wright again compromised, promising to formulate a "humanitarian" aid package to keep the contras in business.[31] The Council on Foreign Relations' (CFR) Director of the Latin American Program, Susan Purcell, argued in late 1987 that the Sandinistas cannot be trusted and the contras must be supported.[32]

Whatever the outcome of the March 1988 Sapoa agreements between the contras and the Nicaraguan government, the contras have the potential to continue as a major military and/or electoral force in

Nicaragua. Though weakened by internal power struggles[33] they could receive funds and arms as a smaller sabotage team either through U.S. government funding or with support from other Rollnet nations and organizations. For example, in early 1988, the Council for Inter-American Security planned to sell millions of dollars of private "Nicaraguan freedom bonds" to arm the contras.[34] Even if the contras disappear as a military force, they will re-emerge as an electoral opposition within Nicaragua still dedicated to the government's overthrow. Such "new contras" are already closely associated with Nicaraguan private business, and will conduct economic sabotage less through military raids and more by the hoarding and black marketeering of essential goods.

In the post-Reagan period, traditional conservative policy toward Nicaragua will probably be a combination of economic destabilization and electoral rollback, using the "new contras" as an economic and electoral rather than as a primarily military opposition. The United States will continue to provide trade embargos and deny credit, with the threat of a naval quarantine and ultimately of direct military action. The goal will remain to overthrow the Nicaraguan government or to transform it into a pro-U.S. regime. The new contra electoral force in Nicaragua, whose beginnings are already financed from the United States, will play upon discontent created by the economic difficulties to destabilize the Nicaraguan government. Whether or not the Sandinistas are eventually overthrown, the positive achievements of the Nicaraguan revolution could slowly be eaten away.

Will a New Consensus Emerge?

Many foreign policy influentials expect a new consensus to emerge, ending the divisions of the post-Vietnam period. This implies that, following Vietnam, the foreign policy elite—which had been unified on selective rollback policy from 1947 through 1968—split into an interventionist vs. anti-interventionist rivalry, and that this split is beginning to heal into a new bipartisan policy.

The analysis of a post-Vietnam split does have its critics. International law professor Richard Falk, for example, argued in 1983 that the bipartisan consensus did not break down:

> American foreign policy remains compulsively bipartisan on the most basic issues of principle and practice. Whether the issue is the controversial deployment of Pershing II and cruise missiles in

Europe, the application of the War Powers Act to American military operations in Lebanon, the exclusion of the PLO from the Mideast peace process, or even the costly pursuit of interventionary goals in Central America, disputes between leading Democrats and Republicans are generally restricted to tactics and nuances. Underlying assumptions are rarely questioned.[35]

For Falk, genuine alternatives would include renouncing the nuclear and the interventionary options in U.S. foreign policy.

Within the gross consensus, three currents were vying for power during the 1970s: the détente/internationalist/Trilateralist, the right-wing/CPD, the Coalition for a Democratic Majority (CDM), the global rollbackers, and the traditional conservatives who were caught in the middle of those two poles. Because more traditional conservatives leaned toward the Trilateralists, détente became the policy for a few years. But those traditional conservatives who rejected détente allied with the Right to defeat détente in the late 1970s. After using the Right to depose the détente internationalists, the traditional conservatives could not control the Right, which was far stronger than in the 1950s. Thus in the early 1980s, global rollback strongly challenged selective rollback as the basis for U.S. foreign policy.

By 1982, the traditional conservatives no longer needed the Right to combat détente; the non-interventionists had been pushed out. Thus the traditional conservatives could safely turn against their recent allies on the Right. From 1982 through 1986, the conflict raged, with Contragate perhaps the final battle. By 1987, the traditional conservatives had successfully substituted realist (selective) rollback for the crusading global rollback of the Right. Just as a "no rollback" position has been an accepted belief among elites, so is global rollback a waning view among all but the pure right wing.

Even during the most heated battles of the 1970s between the CPD and the Trilats, Falk is accurate in saying that broad consensus existed; U.S. power in the world—rather than a world order based on peace, national sovereignty and respect for international law—was the main goal of both groups. However, since Vietnam there has not been a *practical* consensus, i.e., a degree of agreement that prevents political battles from erupting over most foreign policy decisions. While most actors in the political class agree on the need for the United States to intervene in the world (overall consensus), significant disagreements exist on major political questions such as where to intervene (Nicaragua, Persian Gulf, Angola), and how to interevene (alone or with allies, militarily or through diplomacy). In the 1980s, almost every foreign policy initiative has encountered substantial resistance, whether East-West trade, arms control, El Salvador, Nicaragua, the Persian Gulf, arms to Saudi Arabia, South Africa, or relations with Japan. The question remains: while selective rollback may have reasserted itself as the *overall* consensus, will a *practical* consensus exist or will battles continue over each and every foreign policy issue?

We think that practical consensus may not develop. Before Vietnam, U.S. power was great but the right wing was weak. Thus the traditional conservatives could compromise with the Right and keep it under control by engaging in successful selective rollback actions. Now, the right wing is stronger and wants to expand U.S. interventionary activity to bring the United States to its former position as the Number One power. At the same time, the political realists are increasingly wary of such activity precisely because the United States has lost a great deal of power and is too weak to carry off successful interventions easily. While the Right has been temporarily set back, it is still a strong contender for power.

Analyst Sidney Blumenthal, looking forward to the next White House occupants, wrote in late 1987 that any new Republican president

> immediately would confront a crisis of governance. Right wingers would demand important cabinet and subcabinet positions, particularly in foreign policy, where they feel they have been denied under Reagan. They would...carry their struggle into the Republican primaries of 1992. In that arena the influence of the conservative movement should not be discounted. Another conservative figure may have emerged by then.... But no moderate Republican can govern coherently if he grants significant footholds within his administration to the right wing. And perhaps no Republican president can survive politically if he does not.

> If a Democrat is elected president, the right-wing assault on his foreign policy will quickly reach a fever pitch.... The Reagan administration's conservatives will then be distinguished "formers," whose credentials will give them public credibility in their harsh criticisms. The conservative columnists and polemicists will grind away. If the Democratic president does not have a clear sense of his own policy, his confusion will be highlighted and exploited to the fullest.... A future technocratic president, like Carter, who fails to appreciate the political importance of ideology, will be vulnerable to its [the Right's] thrusts. Without a sense of ideology, a Democrat ultimately will fail to control the intellectual and political atmosphere.[36]

Whether or not a practical consensus develops, certain attitudes are widespread regarding East-West relations and Third World interventions. On the East-West axis, most of the political spectrum now accepts the need for U.S.-Soviet trade. The destabilization of the USSR through a heightened arms race is seen as a problem since the arms race is economically damaging to the United States as well. Quiet attempts to create instability within the Soviet Union and Eastern Europe will probably continue. While many are attracted by Gorbachev, the realist streak looks at Gorbachev as a potential long-term danger, since he could strengthen the Soviet Union. In the words of William Hyland, editor of the Council on Foreign Relations journal *Foreign Affairs*,

> For American policy, Gorbachev is a complicating factor. There is a strong temptation in the United States to 'help' him because he presents himself as a liberal reformer—which in fact he may well be…[But] we should help Gorbachev only if we thereby help ourselves…. The first objective for America is to create the circumstances that will make it difficult for the Soviet Union to resume the offensive if and when Gorbachev or his successors have rebuilt Soviet power. In the near term, this approach rests on the assumption that Gorbachev still wants a 'breather' in world affairs. But the United States has to be clear about Gorbachev's purposes; he wants to gain time to 'reconstruct' Soviet power in all of its dimensions.[37]

Concerning the Third World, traditional conservative realists are acutely aware of the limits of U.S. power. Their motto continues to be: intervene if you can get away with it. But the United States can get away with far less than before. As realist James Schlesinger has put it, the gap between too many commitments and reduced U.S. power means a foreign policy of "bluff backed by inadequate forces."[38]

One realist scholar, Robert W. Tucker, felt by some to be a bellwether of elite views, proposes that the United States intervene where it needs to, but not when it simply wants to. The degree of risk is also at issue, thus the appellation "cost-benefit containment" or "cost-benefit rollback."[39] But the question still remains, what is a "want" vs. a "need" (a vital interest)? There may be agreement that the Persian Gulf is a "need." But while Henry Kissinger feels that Central America is also a "need," others—assuming the Soviets are not really major players there—consider it a "want."

To worsen the discord of the "wants vs. needs" debate is another problem: what to do if U.S. power is insufficient to intervene successfully? The heated opposition to the 1987 entrance of the U.S. military into the Persian Gulf—an area agreed by most to be "need"—was based on the fear that the United States could lose in the treacherous Gulf. Similarly, the growing tendency for traditional conservatives to seek a negotiated settlement in Nicaragua is nothing but a realist recognition that the contras are losers and are a U.S. liability besides. In the present situation of limited U.S. power, the realists think twice or three times before intervening.

Yet the realists have to share power with the Right, making likely the continuation of military confrontation in the Third World. The January 10, 1988 report of the bipartisan Commission on Integrated Long-Term Strategy, reflecting the thinking of both the right-wing and conservative elite (through such notables as Fred Iklé, Henry Kissinger and Zbigniew Brzezinski), calls for a shift in military resources from Europe to the Third World through a buildup of high-tech conventional weaponry and an increased capacity to wage "low intensity" warfare.[40] This Commission also reflects the needs of the military-industrial complex, whose profits are endangered to some extent by military budget reductions and arms control measures. Military contractors will be pushing strongly for new high-tech conventional weaponry.[41] Financial analysts predict that arms control will not have a serious effect on military industry, but will mainly shift spending from the nuclear to the more costly conventional side.[42] As *Business Week* explains, "missile treaties are good news for contractors that build tanks, rifles and other basic weapons." Most military industry executives expect tight budgets to last only a few years, with the 1990s bringing a host of new programs.[43]

If Paul Kennedy's sweeping historical analysis of the rise and fall of empires is accurate,

> Past experience shows that even as the relative economic strength of number-one countries has ebbed, the growing foreign challenges to their position have compelled them to allocate more and more of their resources to the military sector, which in turn has squeezed out productive investment and, over time, led to a downward spiral of slower growth, heavier taxes, deepening domestic splits over spending priorities, and a weakening capacity to bear the burdens of defense.[44]

Some Conclusions and Predictions

1. Selective rollback is the basis of current U.S. foreign policy. Where and how to intervene is a topic of sharp debate.

2. Business is stronger than ideology. The extreme shift to the right under Reagan was supported by conservative business for domestic economic more than foreign policy considerations (reduced social spending, reduced taxes, higher military budgets, breaking of labor). In 1987, with the economy in serious difficulty, the traditional conservative elite is limiting the move to the right, especially in the foreign policy arena.

3. To the extent that the traditional conservatives wanted a stronger stand against the Soviets, the right-wing arguments for global rollback were convenient; when the right-wing stance became counterproductive, the conservatives separated themselves from the Right. The 1987 elite realignment represented a significant challenge to the extreme right-wing foreign policy. On the other hand, it was not a reversal to the less interventionist approach of the immediate post-Vietnam period. The conservative elite would like to undermine the Vietnam Syndrome which is still prevalent in the U.S. electorate.

4. Until 1987, the leadership of the Democratic Party had moved to the right with more hardline views toward the Soviet Union and a more interventionist approach to the Third World. The electoral base of the party, however, never shared these views. The effect of the 1987 events, in particular Gorbachev's détentist policies, may move the leadership closer to the base, though some CDM Democrats will be extremely resistant to Gorbachev's initiatives. The Republican Party is currently seeing a revival of traditional conservative power and is thus a divided party. The Republican traditional conservatives will attempt to make the party abandon global rollback in favor of a hardline realist approach to both the Soviet Union and the Third World. Practical implementation of the Reagan Doctrine and nuclear superiority through SDI have not been rejected as Republican goals. The spread between the two parties may narrow on foreign policy issues, with the main battles featuring the Republican Right vs. the Democratic/Republican traditional conservatives.

5. There will be more accommodation with the USSR; the Third World will be the main battleground. Control over the Third World is key to solving the crisis of the U.S. economy, while anti-Sovietism hurts the U.S. economy (except for the military-industrial complex) because it is too expensive and reduces East-West trade. If Gorbachev pulls back

from the Third World, there may temporarily be less conflict in that area to the limited extent that the Soviets influence developments there.

6. The ExSET view that the expanding Soviet empire is responsible for Third World unrest will persist as a right-wing legacy, but in a less dogmatic form, and with the understanding that local factors also play a role in Third World conflicts. The threat of Soviet expansion will continue to provide justification for Third World interventions.

7. The military-industrial complex and the web of interests surrounding it will continue to play a major role in formulating U.S. foreign policy. Thus even the reduction in East-West tensions will face limits. While a new era of détente could come about, it would be relentlessly opposed by the military-industrial complex and the Right.

8. Well-trained, competent right-wing cadres could move into the foreign policy bureaucracy, thereby keeping up the pressure for more rollback actions. The number of Rollnet members may grow due to the contra wars and the many covert actions of the 1980s, also providing pressure for rollback.

9. Interventions may continue to be justified by the perception that the United States must spread freedom and democracy to the peoples of the world. On the other hand, whether or not to intervene in specific cases will be decided on realist grounds rather than as a crusade for democracy.

10. Sharp foreign policy debate will continue. The situation of the United States in the world as described in Chapter Six calls for a return to the more favorable world of the past, which implies rollback. However, the same economic weakness makes such rollback less and less possible to achieve. This conflict could bring about a widening schism over whether and how to intervene. In such an unstable situation, the right wing could play an unpredictable and dangerous role.

10

Rollback Doctrine: Undermining the United States

Rollback as a foreign policy is dangerous. Foreign intervention has a way of erupting into local war and local war may spread to become regional war. A likely spark to ignite nuclear war is a local war that takes on the character of an East-West conflict, which modern local wars often do.[1]

Rollback policy also undermines the very goal its adherents wish to achieve: U.S. global predominance. For the millions of U.S. citizens who consider themselves patriots, rollback is a prescription for disaster. Rollback policy leaves the domestic economy and social fabric in turmoil, causes untold devastation and misery for millions overseas, and hinders any potential positive U.S. influence in world affairs.

To the extent the U.S. public backs rollback, this support is rooted in a misguided sense of patriotism. Patriotism in itself—love of one's country and one's people—is a natural and reasonable human feeling. But patriotism which measures one's country by military superiority over all rivals regardless of consequence is irrational, particularly in the nuclear age. The ultimate logical consequence of such patriotism is the willingness—if the nation is challenged as during the Cuban missile crisis of 1962—to fire a nuclear first strike even though such an action would destroy the very country being defended.[2] There is surely a more rational form of patriotism that searches for excellence in social, economic, and moral spheres rather than in weapon systems.

Rollback and the Looting of the United States

In Chapter Six we discussed the foremost economic problem of the United States: the decline in industrial productivity, which has reduced the United States' ability to compete with other nations in the domestic and world markets. A major cause of this problem has been the rollback-related military buildup, which steals capital and technological development away from domestic industries. We called this phenomenon the looting of the United States.

The looting of the United States continues. MIT economist Lester Thurow warns that the 1980s military expansion will give Western Europe and Japan clear advantages in competing with U.S. industry.[3] A 1986 study by British economists shows that the more a nation spends on military research and development the less efficient that nation is in industrial performance.[4] According to Nobel laureate Lawrence Klein, a 10 percent increase in military expenditure can generate an extra $12 billion in trade imbalance. And the damage of the military buildup goes far beyond its direct effect on industrial productivity.

The military budget produced the huge federal budget deficit. As military spending rose, the deficit climbed from an average of $30 billion in the 1970s to the $200 billion range in the 1980s. As a result of this deficit, the total national debt—from all the unpaid portions of previous years' deficits combined—doubled from $1 trillion in 1981 to $2 trillion by 1986. At 10 percent interest, a $2 trillion debt costs $200 billion annually, thirteen times more than the federal government now spends on education, which is vitally needed to train the scientists, engineers, and skilled workers essential to a revitalized industrial base.[5]

According to Peter Peterson, Chairman of the Council on Foreign Relations and Secretary of Commerce under Nixon, the United States has barely begun to see the effects of the federal deficit. In an article entitled "When the Economic Valium Wears Off," Peterson warned that

> Foreigners keep sending their money here, patiently financing almost 60 percent of our budget deficits.... [Suppose] that our budget deficit remains at or above current levels. In that event, our Government's voracious appetite for credit—equal to a stunning 77 percent of net private savings last year—would increasingly have to be satisfied from domestic sources. We would face the specter from which the inflows of foreign capital have delivered us over the last several years—intensifying competition for funds,

rising interest rates, dwindling investment.... This would knock the wind out of housing, the stock and bond markets and growth prospects generally, placing borrowers, the banking system and Third World exporters in an ever-tighter squeeze.... [Reasonable assumptions predict that by 1991] deficits could climb above $300 billion, three times worse than the rosy estimates now emanating from Washington.[6]

Yet the problems caused by the military buildup will not easily go away. The Reagan military budget is a ten-year $2.7 trillion undertaking. Programs funded several years ago are only now going into the production phase, meaning that spending is forced to remain high. Just to keep currently funded programs in effect at the Fiscal Year (FY) 1987 level plus inflation will increase the military budget from $279.5 billion in FY87 to $331.8 billion in FY1991.[7]

Given the power of the military-industrial complex, a substantial portion of deficit reduction—if such reduction takes place—may come from social security and other domestic programs and from economic development. Even the basic economic building blocks of the nation needed for a healthy economy—roads, bridges, dams—are now being neglected in favor of the military. According to Pat Choate, senior policy analyst for TRW, Inc., and congressional advisor, "Much of America's infrastructure is on the verge of collapse." Almost 20 percent of the interstate highway system is crumbling, 72 percent of all transit buses must be replaced, and 20 percent of our dams need safety improvement. Nearly 45 percent of the nation's bridges are structurally deficient or obsolete; in New York and Missouri, where bridges collapsed in 1987, the deficiency figure reaches 64 percent and 70 percent respectively.[8] Choate estimated that $2.5 to $3 trillion dollars were needed during the 1980s just to maintain current levels of service; less than a third of this sum is being spent.

Long-term unemployment is another product of military spending. In the short run, in specific communities where military contracts reside, military spending creates jobs. But overall, the opposite is the case. The trade deficit—shown in Chapter Six to be due in no small part to military spending—means 25,000 lost jobs for each $1 billion reduction in U.S. exports. In addition, there is a reduction in jobs caused by budget shifts from domestic programs to military spending. One billion dollars spent on retail trade employs 65,000 people, $1 billion on education employs 62,000, and $1 billion on hospitals employs 48,000; but $1 billion for the MX Missile employs only 14,000.[9]

Each time funds are shifted from domestic to military spending, many minority people lose jobs. Military contractors tend to hire more highly-trained, white technocrats, while spending in health and education provides more jobs for minorities. The accomplishment of rollback itself is not the only reason why the Right seeks to polarize East-West relations. The anti-Soviet propaganda of rollback is also used to mobilize the U.S. population against a common enemy and in support of military spending. The anti-Soviet campaign is needed to explain why jobs and services need to be sacrificed in favor of a renewed arms race.

Finally, the priority of military spending is resulting in the destruction of U.S. education, the only hope for catching up in manufacturing productivity. Japan's eighth and ninth graders have mathematical and scientific skills equal to or better than over half of U.S. graduate and undergraduate students in business and economics.[10] Yet there is no education buildup, only a military buildup. This is truly the looting of the United State's future.

Rollback Shoots the United States in the Foot

For many reasons, rollback policy is counterproductive to the worldwide interests of the United States. Former Sen. Frank Church of Idaho, once chairman of the Senate Foreign Relations Committee, persuasively expressed the shortsightedness of rollback doctrine in a *Washington Post* article written shortly before his death:

> America's inability to come to terms with revolutionary change in the Third World...has created our biggest international problems in the postwar era. But the root of the problem is not, as many Americans persist in believing, the relentless spread of communism. Rather, it is our own difficulty in understanding that Third World revolutions are primarily nationalist, not communist. Nationalism, not capitalism or communism, is the dominant political force in the modern world. You might think that revolutionary nationalism and the desire for self-determination would be relatively easy for Americans—the first successful revolutionaries to win their independence—to understand. But instead we have been dumbfounded when other peoples have tried to pursue the goals of our own revolution two centuries ago....

Senator Church contrasted U.S. policy in Vietnam, a failed attempt to stop a revolutionary process, with current policy in China, which at no cost to the United States has brought great strength to the United States in Asia. He then continued:

> By our unrelenting hostility to Castro, we have invested him with heroic dimensions far greater than would be warranted by Cuba's intrinsic importance in the world. We are in the process of performing a similar service for the commandantes of Nicaragua.... We have left Cuba no alternative to increased reliance upon Russia, and we now seem determined to duplicate the same blunder with Nicaragua.... We should stop exaggerating the threat of Marxist revolution in Third World countries. We know now that there are many variants of Marxist governments and that we can live comfortably with some of them.
>
> [In Central America] the objective of U.S. policy should be to create the conditions in which the logic of geographic proximity, access to American capital and technology and cultural opportunity can begin to exert their inexorable long-term pull. Russia is distant, despotic and economically primitive. It cannot compete with the West in terms of the tools of modernization and the concept of freedom. But if we insist on painting the Cubas and Nicaraguas of this world—and there will be others—into a corner, we save the Russians from their own disabilities.[11]

Nicaragua provides an example of pushing a nation toward the Soviets and thereby polarizing an entire region. The Sandinista government has never shown any desire to become a Soviet satellite. According to a senior Western diplomat cited in the *Wall Street Journal* neither the Soviets nor the Cubans have any policy control in Nicaragua: "Nobody is running this thing except the Sandinistas."[12] No Soviet or Cuban military bases exist in Central America, and Nicaragua opposes such bases. The increased Soviet military and economic assistance to Nicaragua followed rather than preceded the hostile U.S. military and economic actions.

Vietnam is a nation that could have been moved away from the Soviet orbit. After the U.S. defeat in 1975 the Vietnamese wanted to restore normal relations with the United States in the hope of securing foreign investment and economic aid; Washington said no.

Senator Church was not alone in his call to get along with Third World revolutions. David Rockefeller has said that many places that call themselves Marxist aren't really so, and it doesn't matter as long as we can work with them.

One of the more absurd vignettes in the rollback scenario can be found in Angola, where Cuban troops protect the Chevron oil complex from military attack by U.S.-armed insurgents.[13] To no surprise, some U.S. business leaders have their doubts about rollback, a policy that can end up attacking their own facilities. Supposed anti-U.S. soldiers protecting U.S. capitalism is not just an Angolan aberration. In Nicaragua, Sandinista army patrols with anti-aircraft implacements protect an Exxon Corporation oil refinery from contra raids or U.S. air attacks.[14]

Just as the right wing succeeded in terminating U.S. trade with Nicaragua, the Right has also pressured the U.S. government to prohibit the Defense Department from buying oil pumped in Angola. Yet oil, $1 billion of which the United States bought from Angola in 1985, is the major way in which the United States can keep up relations and influence in Angola. Based on their oil exports, Angolans have an avowed interest in strengthening their trade and diplomatic relations with the West.[15]

The most counterproductive aspect of rollback is the right-wing position on no trade with the "evil empire," which hurts no one but U.S. business and U.S. workers. In 1980, 30 percent of Nicaraguan trade was with the United States; after the 1985 embargo, this trade dropped to zero. Nicaraguan trade with Western Europe rose from 18 percent in 1980 to 26 percent in 1984. And trade with the Soviet Union went from 1 percent of Nicaragua's total trade in 1980 to 20 percent in 1985.[16] Forty-eight hours after Reagan's economic embargo was announced, Nicaragua had found alternate markets for its critical exports, such as bananas, in Western Europe.

Looking at U.S.-Soviet trade, this situation is amplified a million-fold. The Right opposed the lifting of the Soviet grain boycott even though only U.S. farmers suffered from that boycott. The Right opposes any normalization of Soviet trade; the *Conservative Digest* quotes Aleksandr Solzhenitsyn regarding the USSR: "Let us stop selling to it and giving it loans," and the *Digest* comments, "That is sound advice which should be applied without delay to the entire Communist empire."[17] What the Right does not say is that the Soviet Union's size makes it a potential market that could help rescue the U.S. trade imbalance. Since Western Europe, Japan or industrializing Third World nations such as South Korea will gobble up any potential market the United States fails to penetrate, such right-wing policies act to assist these other economies at the expense of the United States.

Rollback, Lawlessness and International Isolation

Besides producing economic stagnation, rollback policy leads to political isolation, as the examples of Nicaragua and Cuba show. In 1986, the foreign ministers of the most important Latin American nations met with Secretary of State Shultz, trying to move the Reagan administration away from a military and toward a negotiated settlement in Central America. Also in 1986, the Contadora nations (Colombia, Mexico, Venezuela, and Panama) met with the foreign ministers of Brazil, Argentina, Peru, and Uruguay, and the eight made a joint statement opposing U.S. military aid to the contras and reaffirming the Contadora process that would end foreign interference in Central America. All the pro-U.S. Central American foreign ministers supported the declaration of the eight.[18] Among large Latin American nations, that left only right-wing Chile in the U.S. camp on the issue. The historic acceptance by the Central American governments of the 1987 Arias peace plan was one of the few occasions when the formerly subservient "banana republics" united against the colossus to the north. In a similar case, Cuba, blockaded and attacked by the United States for twenty-five years, now has many friends in Latin America and Africa and influence far in excess of its size and population.[19]

It is difficult for U.S. citizens to realize how people in other nations view the United States. If a country wishes to inhabit the bottom of the barrel in international prestige and influence, it will act so as to be perceived an international outlaw or (worse yet) an international terrorist. Through the eyes of much of the world, the United States—when it attempts to overthrow other sovereign governments—is seen in exactly this way. The 1973 CIA-engineered rollback in Chile was a major contributor to the view of the United States as an outlaw nation. U.S.-organized military aggression against a poor small Central American country is a daily reminder to the world that the American Revolution, rather than the Nicaraguan Revolution, has been betrayed. The Reagan administration itself virtually declared the United States to be an international outlaw by refusing to participate in the World Court case brought by Nicaragua against the United States. Imagine Ronald Reagan's glee had the Soviets, Libyans or Iranians acted in this manner. The very act of fleeing from the community of nations constituted for many observers a clear admission of guilt.

Nowhere is U.S. political isolation more evident than in the United Nations. Of 134 resolutions and decisions adopted by recorded or roll-call vote during the thirty-sixth session of the General Assembly (1981-82), the United States voted with the majority only twenty-two times. Of the 158 resolutions and decisions of the 1982-83 session, the United States was in the majority only twenty-four times. In the 1984-85 session, the ninety-nine nations of the non-aligned movement voted with the United States only 13 percent of the time, the lowest in history.[20] What was the right wing's reaction to this situation? If we can't win, let's leave.[21]

Rollback is bloody business. As we noted in Chapter Four, tens of thousands of civilians (some writers estimate 100,000) have been killed in Guatemala by the series of military dictatorships installed by the United States since 1954.[22] In Indonesia, between 500,000 and one million people were slaughtered in the rollback of 1965.[23] In Chile the U.S.-supported coup resulted in an estimated 30,000 murders by the Chilean military.[24] And in the Nicaraguan contra war, death toll figures of 40,000 have been reported.[25]

War tends to spread, as does lawlessness and terrorism. In 1987, an estimated 244,000 people were killed in twenty-two wars around the globe, "more wars than in any previous year in recorded history."[26] Thus far, no rollback operations have spread into global conflicts, though the potential exists for such a development. However, as noted in Chapter Five, nuclear threats have been used in rollback actions, and any regional conflict heightens the risk of nuclear confrontation. Only a cessation of the entire logic of force in international affairs will reduce the likelihood of eventual disaster.

Nuclear destruction is not the only cloud hanging over the planet. While the U.S. government ties itself in knots over tiny Nicaragua, the entire globe moves inexorably toward demographic-ecologic-economic havoc. The narrow right-wing preoccupation with the "evil empire" has taken the entire Western world off onto a tangent, ignoring the true world crisis for capitalism which lies in the ecologic and economic chaos looming ahead.

According to *The Global 2000 Report of the President of the United States,* as the world's population approaches the maximum carrying capacity of the earth, food prices will double. Increases in food production require oil and gas, which poor countries will be unable to afford. For the one-quarter of humankind that depends on wood for fuel, the demand for fuelwood will exceed supplies by 25 percent before the end of the century. Population growth will double the requirements for water in nearly half the world; yet those same regions will have erratic water supplies by the year 2000 as a result of extensive deforestation.

The spread of desert conditions and the deterioration of arable land will accelerate. A rise in carbon dioxide from the combustion of fossil fuels and the loss of forests will increase global temperatures, creating more drought. The resultant melting of the polar ice caps will raise the sea level, forcing abandonment of many coastal cities.[27]

The nuclear and ecological threats are related. Nuclear tests in 1960-61 may have punctured the stratosphere resulting in a 4 percent loss of ozone. Even right-wing Reagan administration Under Secretary of Defense for Policy Fred Iklé asserted that too many of such punctures could "destroy critical links of the intricate food chain of plants and animals, and thus shatter the ecological structure that permits man [sic] to remain alive on this planet."[28]

How about the Soviets?

To all the above arguments the Right might counter: "Reducing the military budget, learning to live with Third World revolutions, and worrying about carbon dioxide and ozone is all very nice, but doesn't it miss the point? If we cry Uncle and give in to the communists, we might as well be dead."

In fact, as we have been arguing, it is rollback policies that make the United States weaker, not stronger, both domestically and internationally. Besides, the Soviets are not doing so well themselves. As Chapter Seven demonstrated, the right wing and the military-industrial complex sell the myth of the Soviet threat in order to get more money for the military. What is the truth about the Soviet Union, both in its global influence and in its nuclear weaponry?

Soviet Influence in the World

The right wing bases its entire foreign policy on the Expanding Soviet Empire Theory (ExSET). In 1980 and again in 1986, the Center for Defense Information (CDI) published major studies of Soviet relations with every country in the world since 1945.[29] The data examined included treaty relationships, access to military facilities, stationing of troops, military advisors, arms transfers, economic aid, technicians, trade, United Nations voting patterns, high-level state visits, official statements, and opinions of experts. In a definitive manner, these studies disprove that the USSR is in fact an expanding empire.

According to the CDI,

> The percentage of Soviet-influenced countries in the world was 10 percent in 1945 in the aftermath of World War II, rose to nearly 15 percent in the late 1950s, declined to 9 percent in the mid-1960s, and finally rose back to over 12 percent in the mid-1970s. It has remained at 11 percent for the past 7 years...*Soviet world influence was at its height in the 1950s and there has been no significant positive Soviet geopolitical momentum for many years.*

Nearly half of the countries where the USSR has significant influence today are poverty-stricken nations at the bottom of the development ladder, countries with weak governments and little global importance. By and large, the Soviet Union has acquired needy friends which place substantial demands on the Soviets with little return. In looking at Soviet influence, one must take into account not only the number of nations involved, but the size and GNP of such nations. Concentrating on the larger nations:

> Soviet influence rose sharply in the late 1940s with the addition of China and again less dramatically in the late 1950s with the addition of Indonesia and Iraq. Soviet influence plummeted through the first half of the 1960s with the loss of China and Indonesia but then rose in the late 1960s and early 1970s with the addition of Egypt and India. The loss of Egypt and India in the 1970s has been only partially offset by successes in the former Portuguese colonies and elsewhere. In the late 1970s with the departure of India from the Soviet orbit there was a dramatic decline in the percentage of the world's population under Soviet influence...1958 was the high point of Soviet influence in the world. At that time Soviet-influenced countries had 31 percent of the world's population and 9 percent of the world's GNP, not including the Soviet Union. In 1979, the Soviets were influencing only 6 percent of the world's population and 5 percent of the world's GNP, exclusive of the Soviet Union.

Utilizing an index of world power developed by former CIA official Ray Cline, the pro-Soviet nations hold about 20 percent of world power compared with 70 percent for pro-Western nations and China; neutral nations wield 10 percent of the world's power. These figures did not change from 1974 to 1979, and may have swung even further to the Soviets' disadvantage.

The CDI found that "Soviet inability to hold the allegiance and support of important Third World countries over the longterm has been the major weakness of the Soviet Union in attempting to expand its influence." Even in the 1970s decade of détente that the right wing holds up as disastrous for the United States, "Soviet losses nearly equaled gains." From 1981-86, there was no change in Soviet world influence.

One might argue that Soviet failures were a result of U.S. actions. The CDI study concludes otherwise:

> *Third World governments, including those associated with the Soviet Union, jealously safeguard their sovereignty, with or without an American presence or the threat of U.S. intervention...* American actions have usually played no important role in the emergence of conflict between the Soviet Union and its clients. On the contrary, threatening American behavior has often helped solidify Soviet relations with affected countries. This has certainly been the case in Angola, Cuba, and Vietnam, for example. U.S. military intervention in the Third World has *not* helped to promote U.S. influence.

> Both the United States and the Soviet Union have faced enormous and growing obstacles to controlling events around the world.... A very important element of a possible informal 'code of conduct' for superpower behavior in the Third World is the willingness to live with failure. The Soviets in Egypt in 1972 and the Americans in Iran in 1979 could have used force to resist expulsion and did not. *Acceptance of the loss of influence without overreaction is necessary for both the United States and the USSR in the face of frequent setbacks.*

CDI's conclusions are echoed by many Soviet experts, including Marshall Shulman, Director of the W. Averell Harriman Institute for Advanced Study of the Soviet Union; Jerry Hough, Professor of Soviet Studies, Duke University; Elizabeth Valkenier, Department of Political Science, Columbia University; Stephen Kaplan, Brookings Institution; and statements by CIA analysts and by the U.S. Army War College.[30] CIA analysts frequently take a far less grim view of Soviet capabilities than does the Pentagon.[31] A major literature in Soviet scholarship exists arguing that the Soviets no longer hold the goal of world domination.[32]

Many scholars cite the Soviets' caution in projecting military power. According to Stephen Kaplan's exhaustive study, Soviet military power since World War II has been used with caution, prudence, and sensitivity.[33]

Afghanistan was the first use of Soviet combat troops outside Eastern Europe since World War II.[34] The oft-repeated statement that the Soviets possess conventional military superiority in Europe is contradicted by several studies, including by the Defense Department itself.[35]

According to Harvard Professor Joseph Nye, "while the United States has not prevented the Soviets from gaining some influence in the Third World, from a geopolitical point of view the Soviets have tended to win the small ones rather than the big ones."[36]

Even some very conservative and right-wing thinkers have separated themselves from the simplistic notion that "The Soviet Union underlies all the unrest that is going on." Edward Luttwak, an ExSET theorist, has to admit that the Soviet empire is a considerable drain on the USSR.[37] Alexander Haig, a hard-line conservative, finds the Soviets to be "adrift in a sea of troubles," and admits that since its banishment from Sadat's Egypt in 1972, the Soviet Union has been on the periphery of events in the Middle East.[38] Neoconservative Irving Kristol understands that the Soviets do not account for the problems of the Third World, and that the strong autonomous impulses in Third World movements sometimes work to the detriment of the USSR.[39]

The Nuclear Balance

Related to the myth of the Expanding Soviet Empire is the myth of Soviet Nuclear Superiority. This myth is also definitively false, as shown by Tom Gervasi in his 1986 book *The Myth of Soviet Military Supremacy*, using extensive data from such sources as the Department of Defense, Congressional testimony, and the prestigious London-based International Institute for Strategic Studies.

In the late 1970s the right-wing "Peddlers of Crisis" fabricated this myth to justify a renewed military buildup and to hide its espousal of nuclear supremacy. This mystification continued throughout the first Reagan administration.

A key figure in determining comparative nuclear strength is total strategic warheads. In December 1982 the United States led in strategic warheads 10,880 to 6,645. In other words, the United States could attack 4,235 more targets than could the USSR.[40]

During the 1982-84 period, the Reagan administration made every possible manipulation to hide the U.S.-USSR comparison of total strategic warheads. In 1982, the Department of Defense stopped publishing the count of U.S. vs. USSR total warheads in its *Annual Report*. The administration also excluded bomber warheads from the comparative data, a maneuver which made the U.S. advantage appear far less since the United States has far more bomber warheads.[41]

The administration then hid the fact that 1,216 Poseidon warheads were added to the U.S. strategic arsenal in the early 1980s. In May 1982, the administration released the figures of 7,450 U.S. strategic warheads rather than the 8,233 existing at the time. The 7,450 figure was compared with 7,400 for the USSR, even though the administration's own Department of Defense was simultaneously publishing the more accurate Soviet figure of 6,300.[42]

Early in 1984, Assistant Secretary of Defense for Atomic Affairs Richard Wagner implied to the House Appropriations Committee that the Soviets led in total warheads (strategic and tactical). Wagner reported that 34,000 nuclear weapons were in the Soviet stockpile compared with 26,000 for the United States; his figures were prominently published by the *Washington Post* and *New York Times*. The figures were simply wrong; only a month before Wagner's testimony, the Joint Chiefs of Staff in their *Fiscal Year 1985 Military Posture Statement* said that "the United States has more warheads." Detailed figures demonstrate that in 1984 the United States led in total warheads by 20,000—37,657 to 17,656. The conservative London-based International Institute for Strategic Studies stated in 1986 that "the data do not support the contention that U.S. *nuclear* forces are, taken as a whole, inferior to those of the USSR."[43]

Current Soviet Policy

The Soviets are not overrunning the Third World under an umbrella of nuclear domination. And it appears to be true—according to virtually all observers—that the new Gorbachev policy places primary emphasis on domestic economic development rather than international military power.

Sovietologist Jerry Hough argues that without a major technological revolution, the Soviet Union cannot maintain itself as a major world power, which is why Gorbachev has called for "a decisive revolution in the economy." This involves greater integration of the Soviet economy into the West, a development that both requires and promotes the reduction in world tensions.[44] Over the past fifteen years the Soviets have produced a sizeable and knowledgeable group of disarmament specialists who wield considerable clout, and the economic crisis has given this grouping increased credibility. Influential military strategists have joined with the disarmament experts to create a strong current of belief within the Politburo that nuclear weapons are all but unusable.[45]

An influential Eastern European critic of the USSR's overemphasis on military power, Rumanian Sociology Professor Silviu Brucan, also sees the economic crisis as the prime motor of current Soviet behavior. The Soviet Union achieved spectacular economic growth until 1961, after which industrial growth dived from 13.2 percent per year in 1951-55 down to 3.1 percent per year in 1981-82. Between 1955 and 1980, the absolute gap between Eastern and Western per capita gross national product almost doubled. If the USSR is to function as a modern society, much less play a significant role in the world, it must urgently rebuild its economic strength. However, Gorbachev's attempted shift from military buildup to economic restructuring can only take place in an international environment that the Soviets perceive as safe.[46]

Marshall Shulman, Director of Columbia University's W. Averell Harriman Institute for Advanced Study of the Soviet Union, also views that the Soviets "have started from the realization that their own economic priorities require them to get the level of military competition down somewhat, and that has compelled them to make a succession of proposals in the arms control field which go farther than anything they have ever done before."[47]

From the conservative viewpoint, Rebecca Strode of the National Institute for Public Policy, writing in the *Washington Quarterly* confirms that Soviet economic problems have forced major reductions in military spending.[48] The Center for Strategic and International Studies (CSIS) has concluded that in the Third World "Increasing caution seems to have crept into Soviet assessments, and there is a greater hesitation to aid a number of revolutionary movements largely because of the substantial financial burden involved." Gorbachev has a "preoccupation with pressing domestic problems."[49] According to Thane Gustafson, CSIS Director of Soviet Studies, Gorbachev's concern with economic reform is leading to pressure on the military-industrial ministries to pitch in and help out the civilian side; there will probably be a mood of caution in making new foreign policy commitments.[50]

Now let us return to the question "How About the Soviets?" From the above evidence, a new U.S. policy of reducing military budgets and learning to live with Third World revolutions has nothing to do with "crying Uncle." The level of nuclear weapons on both sides is so massive as to be virtually irrelevant as a factor in the great power equation. Neither the Soviets nor the United States are doing well in the Third World. And the Gorbachev leadership is focusing on averting a Soviet domestic disaster; economic survival as a great power rather than expansion appears to be the Soviet order of the day.

Similarly, economic survival rather than expansion should be the order of the day for the United States.

Freedom from the Bipolar Worldview

The right wing defines the entire world as bipolar: the wonderful West vs. the evil East. Similarly, the civilized North vs. the barbaric South (with the barbarians stirred up by the East). Working together with many traditional conservatives, the Right has succeeded in getting this distortion broadly accepted among the U.S. public. Many people have been convinced that the alternative to rollback is rollover.

In fact the world is not a bipolar East-West or North-South world; it is a multipolar, multidimensional world with many varieties of conflict, competition and potential cooperation. Many of the difficulties of the United States as a nation—those difficulties discussed earlier in this chapter—would be alleviated if the simplistic and widely accepted bipolar worldview were superseded by a realistic and thoughtful assessment of the complex world around us.

If we are seeking a rational and patriotic foreign policy, we must cease basing U.S. policy on East-West or North-South animosity. We must put an end to the bipolar worldview.

The first positive consequence of a non-bipolar worldview could be a substantial reduction in the military budget. Such a reduction would make possible many things. It would free us from the federal deficit. It would help shift capital and technology for use in modernizing our economy. It would make available funds to educate our citizens in managing and developing a society in the 21st century. And a substantial reduction in the military budget would reduce the size and thereby the influence of the military-industrial complex. As long as the military budget is large, the military-industrial complex is large, which gives it inordinate political influence to perpetuate the albatross of East-West hostility.

Can we really reduce the military budget without risking our security? Some very knowledgeable people say yes. According to Rear Adm. Gene LaRocque (U.S. Navy, retired), nearly 70 percent of the military budget

is to provide men and weapons to fight in foreign countries in support of our allies and friends and for offensive operations in Third World countries... Another big chunk of the defense budget is the 20 percent allocated for our offensive nuclear force of bombers, missiles, and submarines whose job it is to carry nuclear weapons to the Soviet Union.... *Actual defense of the United States costs about 10 percent of the military budget and is the least expensive function performed by the Pentagon....*[51]

Professor Earl Ravenal, a former Defense Department official and expert on international relations and the U.S. military, argues that the U.S. commitment to NATO accounts for about 50 percent of the military budget. Professor Ravenal has calculated a defense budget that would reduce U.S. forces in Europe to a level appropriate to the minimal risk of Soviet aggression there, cut down other overseas commitments to defend a more restricted perimeter that is truly based on U.S. security needs, and eliminate forces that implement an interventionist foreign policy. In 1983, such a budget would have been $110 billion less than the Reagan administration budget proposal.[52]

Related to military budget reduction, a nuclear test ban could be concluded, and the 1986 Reykjavík agenda—elimination of nuclear weapons—could be seriously reopened. A treaty proposed by the American Committee on East-West Accord—that the USSR and United States agree not to use military force in the Third World—could enter the politically relevant spectrum of views.[53] The restrictions in sales of high-tech products to communist countries—which does little more than give away lucrative export markets to the Japanese and Western Europeans—could be lifted, thus boosting U.S. exports. Under the new Soviet law allowing foreigners to hold up to 49 percent equity in Soviet industry, U.S. companies could invest in joint ventures with Soviet enterprises.[54]

Twenty years ago, who would have thought that the United States could be friends with China? We should begin to imagine the possibility of being friends with the Soviet Union.

An end to the bipolar worldview will allow the United States to concentrate on the real problems of economic relations between nations and the global threat of ecological chaos. The world is so interedependent that, in a sense, one can no longer distinguish domestic from foreign policy. U.S. jobs are dependent on the ability of Mexicans and Brazilians to buy U.S. products, which requires an equitable solution to the Third World debt. Joint U.S.-Soviet-European-Japanese efforts to improve Third World economies could raise living standards in poor countries, and subsequently help the more developed nations to sell more products; such an effort would require the terms of trade to be more favorable to poor nations who currently sell their goods at depressed prices. Concurrent with such a policy of global economic development must be an intensive program to save the world—ourselves included—from environmental ruin. A top priority might be reversing the "greenhouse" effect of rising global temperatures through the development of safe non-fossil fuels, coupled with massive reforestation efforts to lower carbon dioxide levels and reduce the scourge of drought. America should be the leader in the economic-ecologic reconstruction of the planet, not the leader in the arms race.

The People of the United States and Foreign Policy

Would the American people support such a far-reaching change in international worldview? Public opinion polls indicate that the answer is a resounding "Yes." But under certain conditions, that "Yes" could turn into a defiant "No."

For forty years, the U.S. public has nurtured two somewhat contradictory foreign policy beliefs: that the Soviet Union is a danger, and that the United States should avoid wars. It is important never to forget that almost all the foreign policy information received by the public comes from the established mass media. Only 15 percent of the public is relatively well-informed about foreign policy issues; the rest pays little or no attention. The swings back and forth in public opinion result more from well-publicized changes in government policy than from events in the external world. According to Ralph Levering's historical study of foreign policy opinion, 58 percent of those polled in May 1946, felt that Russia was trying to become the ruling power of the world. Then the Truman administration waged a major anti-Soviet campaign to persuade the public and Congress to accept the entire postwar containment strategy. By late 1948, the opinion was almost unanimous that the Soviet Union was an aggressive, expansion-minded nation.[55]

The Munich Syndrome had been sold to the U.S. public. But the Korean War raised questions in the public mind. Studies over the past sixty years show that the government can manipulate public foreign policy views except on one issue: war. In a war or foreign crisis, deep-seated patriotism comes into play and the majority initially backs the president.[56] But such support for U.S. military involvement generally wanes over time and—as U.S. personnel are killed—turns against the war. Korea and Vietnam are examples. After Korea, the percentage who believed that the United States could live peacefully with Russia went from 23 percent in 1955 to 66 percent in 1959. The public almost invariably approved sending military aid to handle trouble spots around the world, but opposed sending U.S. troops. In 1953, for example, 56 percent wanted to assist the French in Indochina, but only 12 percent wanted to send U.S. troops. In 1961, 44 percent supported military supplies to anti-Castro forces but 65 percent opposed the use of U.S. troops to aid in overthrowing Castro.

Through the 1960s, support for the Cold War declined; in 1962, 78 percent of male college students felt the United States should run any risk of war if needed to prevent the spread of communism, an opinion held by only 22 percent in 1972.[57] The Vietnam Syndrome was challenging the Munich Syndrome. By the late 1970s, the renewed media blitz of right-wing groups such as the Committee on the Present Danger had a major impact on renewing public Cold War fears. From 1976 to 1981, the percentage of the public favoring increased military spending grew from 22 percent to 51 percent, and in another poll to 71 percent. Interestingly, this peak was shortlived; by 1983, the percentage wanting a larger military budget plummeted to 14 percent. Over the period 1982-84, 80 percent opposed sending U.S. troops to El Salvador, and two-thirds of the public consistently disapproved of U.S. aid to the contras in Nicaragua. Though Oliver North's pro-contra performance at the Contragate hearings produced a rise in contra support, that increase was ephemeral; six weeks later contra support had dropped back to its previous level of one-third the population.[58]

In spite of the Reagan media barrage on the "evil empire," two-thirds of U.S. people in 1984 felt that the United States should let the Soviets have their system of government while we retain ours since "there's room in the world for both." Fifty-three percent thought the United States would be safer if we stopped trying to halt the spread of communism to other countries. Ninety-six percent believed that "picking a fight with the Soviet Union is too dangerous in a nuclear world." Seventy-five percent favored a bilateral nuclear freeze and 61 percent supported a unilateral six-month U.S. freeze to see if the Soviets would respond.[59] The public's attitude toward the Soviets is clarified by a 1986 Chicago Council on Foreign Relations/Gallup poll. Overwhelmingly, people supported greater cooperation with the USSR in arms control, cultural agreements and East-West trade. On the other hand, in preference ratings among twenty-four countries, the Soviet Union came out next to last, just above Iran.[60] Clearly the public roundly dislikes the Soviets but strongly desires to get along with them.

Bob Beschel, research fellow at the Harvard Center on Science and International Affairs, who specializes in U.S. perceptions of the Soviet Union, writes that the public vacillates between an image of the Soviets "as people just like us" and one that sees them as "evil, corrupt, and immoral." Even at the height of good relations, 20-25 percent are deeply anti-Soviet. Another 10-15 percent desire better relations. The remaining majority shift their views based on presidential leadership. As of 1984, the majority believed the USSR is aggressive, cheats on treaties, and gets the better of the United States in negotiations. However such anti-Sovietism does not run deep. The decisive mid-section of the population does not want to make friends with the Soviets but it is pragmatic: we need to get along with these guys even though we don't like it. People respond to the idea that "we can do business with Gorbachev and the Soviets." Doing business implies a certain wariness and selfishness paired with a recognition that mutual interests exist.[61]

The Chicago Council on Foreign Relations poll compared the attitudes of the public with the opinions of leaders in government, business, labor, the media, and academia. Only 30 percent of the public in 1986 agreed with the U.S. role in Vietnam; 57 percent of leaders agreed with the Vietnam war. Only 24 percent of the public favored both military and economic aid to anti-communist insurgents; 52 percent of leaders were in favor. Only 20 percent of the public felt that military aid to Central America will not escalate to direct U.S. military involvement; a far greater 52 percent of leaders took that position. Leaders are more interventionist and more supportive of the Reagan Doctrine than is the general public.[62] These data support the conclusions of Chapter Eight, that the foreign policy elite is relatively pro-interventionist. The public, on the other hand, is not.

While the public does not make foreign policy, it can set some limits. A strong anti-interventionist public places constraints on rollback policy, while an anti-Soviet public would remove such constraints. Given that the great majority of the public has no direct personal experience that provides information for foreign policy opinions, it is of great consequence how the public is informed by its leaders and the media. U.S. labor leaders have often told their members that communism is a worse enemy than the boss upstairs. Religious fundamentalists preach that communism is godless and must be struck down. But it doesn't have to be that way.

Why Global Rollback Remains a Threat

With proper leaders, the U.S. public could strongly support an end to bipolar foreign policy and a demilitarization of the planet. But under the conditions of an economic crisis, a sharp right turn could take place within the U.S. upper and middle classes. The United States faces simultaneous warnings of 1) a crisis in industrial productivity, 2) unprecedented trade and budget deficits, 3) high rates of individual and corporate indebtedness, and 4) U.S. banks holding hundreds of billions in debts to the Third World. If a serious 1930s-like crisis occurs, especially if coupled with a major foreign policy failure, such a rightward shift could verge on the extreme. Why?

No one likes to compare the United States with pre-Nazi Germany, and we do not believe that the United States will host a Nazi-type fascism. But the history of Germany does provide one example of what the upper and middle classes might do in the face of economic crisis and foreign policy defeat. These classes can move far right.

From 1928 to 1932, the German National Socialist (Nazi) Party's share of the vote skyrocketed from 2.6 percent to 37.3 percent. While many commentators have attributed the Nazis' success to its appeal to the lower middle class, Richard Hamilton recently published a major empirical study of actual votes cast. The facts unequivocally reveal that it was the upper middle class that most strongly voted for Hitler. Over half the Nazi votes were from communities of less than 25,000 population and were disproportionately Protestant. The Nazis were seen as patriotic, anti-communist, and religious. The people who voted Nazi were not so much people who had fallen economically, but people who feared falling and wanted to stay on top. It is noteworthy that in Italy also, support for Mussolini came from the upper middle class and from ex-military men.[63]

A key factor in the Nazi success was the activity of its organizers. Many were World War I soldiers who entered the "Free Corps," a remnant of the German army used to put down communist uprisings in 1920. When the Free Corps was dismissed, a number of its members became cadre for the Nazi Party.[64]

Hamilton concludes that it takes major catastrophes such as war or depression to change traditional political alignments in a nation. The political direction of the realignment depends on available leaders at the time; in late 1920s Germany, the Nazi party organizers were the agents of change.[65]

If a catastrophe takes place in the United States—whether war, depression or both—who will have the organizers ready to take advantage of the situation? Currently, the edge would go to the right wing, with its cadre trained—as described in Chapter Three—in the global rollback network: the Cold War CIA, the rollback actions of the Bay of Pigs and the Nicaraguan contra war, the Goldwater and Reagan presidential campaigns, the bureaucracies of the Reagan presidency, and the Heritage Foundation and other right-wing think tanks.

Will the upper and middle classes necessarily move to the right if economic crisis—possibly combined with foreign policy failure—is our fate? Not necessarily. A new Franklin Roosevelt could appear and attempt to resolve the crisis in a liberal direction. Or a new and smarter Joseph McCarthy could move in and parlay upper and middle class fears into a major anti-communist war of rollback.

Rollback policy has a considerable following in the United States, among business (especially the many businesses that profit in some way from the military), among public leaders—political, labor, and religious—and among portions of the general population. Rollback policy also appears to be developing a competent cadre—trained intellectuals, politicians, mid-level government operatives, and the shock troops of the global rollback network. If economic and social conditions in the United States deteriorate, we could still face the triumph of right-wing foreign policy.

Notes

Introduction

1. Marshall, J. et al. *The Iran-Contra Connection* (Boston: South End Press, 1987), pp. 3, 164, 170-74.
2. Butler, S. et al. *Mandate for Leadership II* (Washington, D.C.: The Heritage Foundation, 1984), pp. 377, 382, 471.
3. Tucker, R. "Fouling Up" *The National Interest,* Spring 1987, pp. 93-96.
4. *Washington Post National Weekly,* July 27, 1987.
5. Cockburn, L. *Out of Control* (New York: Atlantic Monthly Press, 1987), pp. 239-40.
6. Schurmann, F. *The Foreign Politics of Richard Nixon* (Berkeley: Institute of International Studies, 1987), p. 55.
7. *Taking the Stand: The Testimony of Lieutenant Colonel Oliver L. North* (New York: Pocket Books, 1987), p. xiv.
8. Layne, C. "The Real Conservative Agenda" *Foreign Policy,* Winter 1985-86, pp. 73-93.
9. Holsti, O. and Rosenau, J. *American Leadership in World Affairs* (Boston: Allen and Unwin, 1984), p. 109.
10. Johns, M. "Peace in Our Time" *Policy Review,* Summer 1987, pp. 69-71.

Chapter 1

1. "U.S. Military Interventions: 1789-1945" *Congressional Record,* June 23, 1969.
2. Schurmann, F. *The Logic of World Power* (New York: Pantheon Books, 1974), pp. 56-59.
3. *Ibid.,* pp. 48-65.
4. *Ibid.,* pp. 83-91.
5. Isaacson, W. and Thomas, E. *The Wise Men* (New York: Simon and Schuster, 1986); Shoup, L. and Minter, W. *Imperial Brain Trust* (New York: Monthly Review Press, 1977).
6. Etzold, T. and Gaddis, J. *Containment: Documents on American Policy and Strategy, 1945-1950* (New York: Columbia University Press, 1978), pp. 50-63.

7. Yergin, D. *Shattered Peace* (Boston: Houghton Mifflin Company, 1977), p. 198.

8. Schurmann, pp. 102-3.

9. Acheson, D. *Present at the Creation* (New York: W.W. Norton and Company, 1969), p. 356.

10. *Ibid.*, pp. 355-58.

11. Yergin, p. 282.

12. Schurmann, p. 96.

13. Freeland, R. *The Truman Doctrine and the Origins of McCarthyism* (New York: Alfred A. Knopf, 1972), p. 110.

14. Schurmann, p. 65.

15. Hammond, P. "NSC-68: Prologue to Rearmament" in Schilling, W. et al. *Strategy, Politics, and Defense Budgets* (New York: Columbia University Press, 1962).

16. Schurmann, pp. 49-53, 79-83.

17. Senator Joseph McCarthy's speech at Wheeling, West Virginia, later repeated in the U.S. Senate, February 20, 1950.

18. Spanier, J. *The Truman-MacArthur Controversy and the Korean War* (Cambridge: Belknap Press, 1959), pp. 57-59.

19. *Ibid.*, pp. 70-73.

20. Schurmann, p. 162.

21. Acheson, pp. 451-54.

22. *Ibid.*, p. 514; Spanier, p. 140.

23. Acheson, pp. 513-22; Spanier, Chapter 10.

24. Spanier, Chapters 11 and 12; Koen, R. *The China Lobby in American Politics* (New York: The Macmillan Company, 1960), p. 116.

25. Schurmann, p. 116.

26. Destler, I. et al. *Our Own Worst Enemy* (New York: Simon and Schuster, 1984), pp. 46-47.

27. Brown, S. *The Faces of Power* (New York: Columbia University Press, 1983), p. 108.

28. Twining, N. *Neither Liberty nor Safety* (New York: Holt, Rinehart and Winston, 1966), pp. 56-62.

29. Schilling, pp. 407-10.

30. Brown, p. 111.

31. Schurmann, pp. 163-64.

32. Barnet, R. *Roots of War* (New York: Penguin Books, 1972), p. 87.

33. Schurmann, pp. 149-51.

34. Etzold and Gaddis, pp. 33-34.

35. Mr. X, "The Sources of Soviet Conduct" *Foreign Affairs,* July 1947.

36. Brown, p. 89.

37. Etzold and Gaddis, pp. 125-28.

38. *Ibid.*, pp. 164-69.

39. *Ibid.*, pp. 173-203.

40. *Ibid.*, pp. 203-11.

41. *Ibid.*, pp. 211-23.

42. *Ibid.,* pp. 385-442.

43. Kolko, G. *Anatomy of a War* (New York: Pantheon Books, 1985), p. 74.

44. Brown, pp. 54-55.

45. Williams, W. A. *Empire as a Way of Life* (New York: Oxford University Press, 1980), p. 141.

46. Prados, J. *Presidents' Secret Wars* (New York: William Morrow and Company, 1986), p. 40-45.

47. Powers, T. *The Man Who Kept the Secrets* (New York: Alfred A. Knopf, 1979), p. 47.

48. Blum, W. *The CIA: A Forgotten History* (London: Zed Books, 1986), pp. 18-20; Prados, pp. 65-67; Schurmann, pp. 163-64, 411.

49. Prados, pp. 163-69.

50. Blum, pp. 67-76.

51. Powers, pp. 85-88; Prados, pp. 98-106.

52. Blum, pp. 174-81; Stockwell, J. *In Search of Enemies* (New York: W.W. Norton and Company, 1978), pp. 105, 236-37.

53. Powers, pp. 103-12, 121, 132-52; Blum, pp. 206-16; Prados, pp. 171-217.

54. Langguth, A. *Hidden Terrors* (New York: Pantheon Books, 1978), pp. 67-112; Blum, pp. 181-91.

55. Draper, T. *The Dominican Revolt* (New York: Commentary, 1968); Sklar, H. *Trilateralism* (Boston: South End Press, 1980), pp. 422-24; Blum, pp. 195-206.

56. Scott, P. "Exporting Military-Economic Development: America and the Overthrow of Sukarno, 1965-67" in Caldwell, M. *Ten Years' Military Terror in Indonesia* (Nottingham, England: Spokesman Books, 1975); Powers, pp. 88-91; Blum, pp. 108-13, 217-22.

57. Blum, pp. 243-250.

58. Schurmann, pp. 195, 438-41.

59. Hersh, S. *The Price of Power* (New York: Summit Books, 1983), Chapter 15; Blum, pp. 152-53, 156-60; Prados, pp. 298-303.

60. Hersh, pp. 273-75.

61. Hersh, Chapters 21 and 22; Blum, pp. 232-43; Powers, pp. 220-39; Prados, pp. 315-21.

62. Blum, pp. 299-304; Sklar, pp. 475-84.

63. Schurmann, pp. 179-80.

Chapter 2

1. Dugger, R. *On Reagan* (New York: McGraw-Hill Book Company, 1983), p. 353.

2. *Washington Post,* June 18, 1982.

3. Dugger, p. 353.

4. Aspaturian, V. "The Anatomy of the Soviet Empire: Vulnerabilities and Strengths" in Dunn, K. and Staudenmaier, W. *Military Strategy in Transition. Defense and Deterrence in the 1980s* (Boulder: Westview Press, 1984).

5. *Ibid.*

6. Butler, S. et al. *Mandate for Leadership II* (Washington D.C.: The Heritage Foundation, 1984), p. 285.

7. Pipes, R. *Survival is Not Enough* (New York: Simon and Schuster, 1984), pp. 40-45, 178.

8. Brzezinski, Z. *Game Plan: How to Conduct the U.S.-Soviet Contest* (Boston: The Atlantic Monthly Press, 1986), pp. 17, 21.

9. Aspaturian.

10. Pipes, pp. 45-50.

11. Pipes, pp. 51, 72.

12. Kristol, I. *Reflections of a Neoconservative* (New York: Basic Books, 1983), pp. 232-33.

13. Kirkpatrick, J. *Dictatorships and Double Standards* (New York: Simon and Schuster, 1982), p. 39.

14. Ledeen, M. *Grave New World* (New York: Oxford University Press, 1985), Chapter 5; Luttwak, E. *The Grand Strategy of the Soviet Union* (London: Weidenfeld and Nicolson, 1983); Gray, C. *The Geopolitics of the Nuclear Era* (New York: Crane, Russak and Company, 1977), p. 38.

15. Hollander, P. "The Two Faces of George Kennan" *Policy Review,* Summer 1984, pp. 28-34.

16. Tyroler, C. *Alerting America. The Papers of the Committee on the Present Danger* (Washington, D.C.: Pergamon-Brassey's International Defense Publishers, 1984), pp. 10-15.

17. Democratic Policy Commission, *New Choices in a Changing America* (Washington, D.C.: Democratic National Committee, 1986), pp. 59, 65.

18. Kristol, pp. 270-73.

19. Dugger, p. 352.

20. *Ibid.*, pp. 351-52.

21. Ronald Reagan in *Vital Speeches,* July 1, 1982.

22. Gebbie, M. and Smith, D. *Reagan for Beginners* (London: Writers and Readers Publishing Cooperative Ltd., 1984), p. 169.

23. Sanders, J. "Terminators" *Mother Jones,* August-September 1985.

24. Committee of Santa Fe, "A New Inter-American Policy for the Eighties" (Washington, D.C.: Council for Inter-American Security, 1980).

25. Butler, p. 227.

26. Dugger, p. 358.

27. Scheer, R. *With Enough Shovels* (New York: Vintage Books, 1983), pp. 7-8.

28. Butler, pp. 223, 305.

29. Brzezinski, Z. "The Future of Yalta" *Foreign Affairs,* Winter 1984-85, pp. 294-302.

30. Meyerson, A. "Ronald Reagan's Peace Offensive" *Policy Review,* Fall 1986, pp. 66-67.

31. Butler, p. 268.

32. Dugger, p. 360.

33. *Ibid.*

34. "The Defense Budget: A Conservative Debate" *Policy Review,* Summer 1985.

35. *Ibid.*

36. Hough, J. "Gorbachev's Strategy" *Foreign Affairs,* Fall 1985, pp. 33-55; Thompson, E.P. "Look Who's Really Behind Star Wars" *The Nation,* March 1, 1986.

37. Thompson, "Look Who's Really Behind Star Wars."

38. William Casey, *Vital Speeches,* January 15, 1984.

39. Brucan, S. "Economic Reform: The Strategic Implications" *World Policy Journal,* Summer 1985, pp. 467-80.

40. "Beyond Containment?: The Future of U.S.-Soviet Relations" *Policy Review,* Winter 1985.

41. *Ibid.*

42. Pipes, pp. 263-69.

43. *Ibid.,* pp. 74-76.

44. Lewis Tambs, former U.S. Ambassador to Costa Rica, *Vital Speeches,* December 15, 1980.

45. "Beyond Containment?: The Future of U.S.- Soviet Relations," *Policy Review,* Winter 1985, p. 27.

46. *Ibid.,* p. 28.

47. Dugger, p. 384.

48. *New York Times, August 25, 1987.*

49. Viguerie, R. "A World Without War—A World Without the Soviet Union" *Conservative Digest,* June 1984, pp. 46-47.

50. Butler, pp. 304, 307.

51. *New York Times,* November 28, 1984 and October 10, 1985.

52. *Wall Street Journal,* December 17, 1985.

53. Butler, p. 225.

54. Kirkpatrick, J. "U.S. Must Stand with World's Freedom Fighters," *Human Events,* February 22, 1986.

55. Kirkpatrick, *Dictatorships and Double Standards,* pp. 32, 49.

56. "Is SALT a Fair Deal?" in Tyroler, p. 160.

57. Rostow, E. "SALT II—A Soft Bargain, A Hard Sell" speech given on July 25, 1978.

Chapter 3

1. *Business Week,* December 29, 1986, p. 45; Maas, P. "Oliver North's Strange Recruits" *New York Times Magazine,* January 18, 1987.

2. *Washington Post,* December 10, 1984; Anderson, S. and Anderson J. *Inside the League* (New York: Dodd Mead and Company, 1986), pp. 150-52.

3. Marshall, J. et al. *The Iran-Contra Connection* (Boston: South End Press, 1987) pp. 25-27.

4. Ranelagh, J. *The Agency: The Rise and Decline of the CIA* (New York Touchstone Books, 1987), pp. 636, 811-12.

5. Saloma, J. *Ominous Politics* (New York: Hill and Wang, 1983), pp. 64-65.

6. Rice, B. "The Cold-War College" *The Nation,* October 4, 1971; *Wall Street Journal,* August 1, 1972; Relyea, H. "The American Security Council" *The Nation* January 24, 1972.

7. Gervasi, T. *The Myth of Soviet Military Supremacy* (New York: Harper and Row, 1986), p. 222; Anderson and Anderson, p. 174.

8. *New York Times,* February 4, July 2, and July 27, 1987.

9. Anderson and Anderson, pp. 46-47.

10. Waas, M. "Destructive Engagement: Apartheid's 'Target U.S.' Campaign" *The National Reporter,* Winter 1985.

11. *Time,* March 28, 1983; *Washington Post,* May 19, 1984; *San Francisco Chronicle,* December 5, 1986.

12. Anderson and Anderson, pp. 35-38; Conason, J. "Reagan and the War Crimes Lobby" *The Village Voice,* May 14, 1985.

13. Hervet, F. "Knights of Darkness: The Sovereign Military Order of Malta" *Covert Action Information Bulletin,* Winter 1986; Lee, M. "Their Will Be Done" *Mother Jones,* July 1983; Marshall et al., p. 69.

14. Anderson and Anderson, p. 47.

15. *Ibid.,* Chapters 14, 15, 16, 17.

16. *Ibid.,* Chapter 13; *New York Times,* September 15, 1985.

17. Anderson and Anderson, Chapter 9.

18. Hervet, "Knights of Darkness."

19. *Washington Post,* September 16, 1984; Hoon, S. and Langston, N. "Moon's Time of Trial" *Far Eastern Economic Review,* November 20, 1981; Anderson and Anderson, pp. 64-69, 123-30; Waas, "Destructive Engagement"; Mitsuo, K. "The Moonies Make a Comeback" *Japan Quarterly,* January-March 1985, pp. 46-50.

20. Clarkson, F. "Privatizing the War" *Covert Action Information Bulletin,* Fall 1984; Anderson and Anderson, p. 126.

21. Steinfels, P. *The Neoconservatives* (New York: Simon and Schuster, 1979) pp. 83-87.

22. Anderson and Anderson, pp. 55-56, 255.

23. Sanders, J. *Peddlers of Crisis* (Boston: South End Press, 1983), pp. 287-88; Gervasi, p. 221.

24. Anderson and Anderson, p. 75.

25. *Washington Post,* August 8, 1986.

26. Hinckle W. and Turner, W. *The Fish is Red* (New York: Harper and Row, 1981); *Wall Street Journal,* January 16, 1987; *New York Times,* November 15, 1976.

27. Marshall et al., p. 125.

28. Kwitny, J. *The Crimes of Patriots* (New York: W.W. Norton, 1987), p. 44.

29. Corson, W. *The Armies of Ignorance* (New York: The Dial Press/James Wade, 1977), pp. 320-23.

30. *New York Times,* June 18, 1986.

31. Schurmann, F. *The Logic of World Power* (New York: Pantheon Books, 1974), p. 413; Kwitny, J. "Money, Drugs and the Contras" *The Nation,* August 29, 1987; *Newsweek,* January 26, 1987.

32. Petras, J. "Speculators, Lumpen-Intellectuals, and the End of U.S. Hegemony" *Against the Current,* March-April 1987.

33. *Wall Street Journal,* April 18, 1980; Kwitny, *The Crimes of Patriots,* pp. 162-64.

34. Kwitny, pp. 115-19, 206-16.

35. *Ibid.,* pp. 43-52.

36. Marshall et al., p. 17; *Newsweek,* January 26, 1987.

37. Cockburn, L. *Out of Control* (New York: Atlantic Monthly Press, 1987), pp. 152-88.

38. *CENSA's Strategic Report,* June 1987 (Berkeley, CA: Center for the Study of the Americas).

39. Anderson and Anderson, p. 158.

40. *Ibid.,* p. 152.

41. *Washington Post,* September 17, 1984.

42. Wolf, L. "Accuracy in Media Rewrites the News and History" *Covert Action Information Bulletin,* Spring 1984.

43. O'Brien, M. "The Christian Underground" *Covert Action Information Bulletin,* Spring 1987.

44. Saloma, Chapter 3; *New York Times,* September 15, 1985.

45. Woodward, B. *Veil: The Secret Wars of the CIA 1981-1987* (New York: Simon and Schuster, 1987), pp. 25-26.

46. Prados, J. *Presidents' Secret Wars* (New York: William Morrow and Co., 1986), p. 113.

47. Kwitny, pp. 44-45.

48. Steinfels, pp. 83-87.

49. Prados, pp. 36-37; Anderson and Anderson, Chapters 2 and 3.

50. Anderson and Anderson, pp. 3-7, 40-45, 147.

51. Bachrack, *The Committee of One Million* (New York: Columbia University Press, 1976), p. 30.

52. Schurmann, pp. 161-72.

53. Marshall et al., p. 65.

54. Anderson and Anderson, pp. 47-48.

55. Schurmann, p. 178.

56. *Los Angeles Times,* December 18, 1983; Anderson and Anderson, pp. 107, 137, 214, 235.

57. Marshall et al., p. 33.

58. Anderson and Anderson, pp. 46-59.

59. *Ibid.,* pp. 60-63.

60. Marshall et al., p. 65.

61. Anderson and Anderson, pp. 52-54, 63-66.

62. Kwitny, pp. 46-47; *Ibid.*, pp. 45-47; Prados, pp. 73-76.
63. Marshall et al, p. 33.
64. *Christian Science Monitor*, May 29, 1970; Adams, N. and McCoy, A. *In Laos War and Revolution* (New York: Harper and Row, 1970), pp. 338-39.
65. Schurmann, p. 413.
66. Prados, p. 309.
67. Kwitny, pp. 50-51.
68. McCoy, A. *The Politics of Heroin in Southeast Asia* (New York: Harper and Row, 1972), pp. 55-58, 212-216.
69. *Ibid.*
70. Kwitny, pp. 110-42.
71. Kwitny, pp. 12-14, 27, 41-42, 186-87, 284.
72. Anderson and Anderson, pp. 136, 162-69.
73. Nairn, A. "Behind the Death Squads" *The Progressive,* May 1984; Anderson and Anderson, p. 176; Blum W. *The CIA: A Forgotten History* (London: Zed Books, 1986), p. 270.
74. Anderson and Anderson, pp. 163, 170-74.
75. Marshall et al., p. 53.
76. Simons, M. "Guatemala: The Coming Danger" *Foreign Policy,* Summer 1981 pp. 93-101.
77. Marshall et al., p. 31.
78. *Wall Street Journal,* April 18, 1980.
79. *New York Times,* November 15, 1976; *Wall Street Journal,* January 16, 1987
80. Hinckle and Turner, Chapter 6.
81. U.S. Senate, "Alleged Assassination Plots Involving Foreign Leaders," November 20, 1975 (Washington, D.C.: U.S. Government Printing Office, 1975)
82. *Los Angeles Times,* October 16, 1986.
83. Marshall et al., p. 45.
84. *Ibid.*, pp. 44, 47.
85. *New York Times,* November 15, 1976.
86. Anderson and Anderson, pp. 7, 142-43.
87. *Ibid.*, p. 143; Marshall et al., p. 24.
88. Anderson and Anderson, pp. 136-37.
89. *Ibid.*, pp. 147-48, 178; Lane, C. "'Mi Asesino,' the Freedom Fighter" *The New Republic,* April 15, 1985.
90. Anderson and Anderson, pp. 148, 178.
91. *Ibid.*, pp. 207-08.
92. *New York Times,* November 24, 1987.
93. Lane, "'Mi Asesino,' the Freedom fighter."
94. Anderson and Anderson, p. 148.
95. *Ibid,* pp. 146-47.
96. Black, G. "Delle Chiaie: from Bologna to Bolivia" *The Nation,* April 25 1987; Marshall et al., p. 24.
97. Blum, pp. 178-79.
98. *Ibid.*, p. 285.
99. Prados, p. 339.

100. Stockwell, J. *In Search of Enemies* (New York: W.W. Norton, 1978), Chapters 7 and 8.

101. *Ibid.*, p. 242.

102. Waas, "Destructive Engagement."

103. *Washington Post,* January 20 and 27, 1980.

104. Marshall et al., pp. 29, 41, 156.

105. *New York Times,* February 4, 1987.

106. Marshall et al., p. 194; *New York Times,* July 14, 1981.

Chapter 4

1. Committee of Santa Fe. "A New Inter-American Policy for the Eighties" (Washington, D.C.: Council for Inter-American Security, 1980).

2. Kirkpatrick, J. *Dictatorships and Double Standards* (New York: Simon and Schuster, 1982).

3. Butler, S. *Mandate for Leadership II* (Washington, D.C.: The Heritage Foundation, 1984), p. 268.

4. *Miami Herald,* June 5, 1983.

5. *Washington Post,* February 14, March 10 and 16, 1982 and May 8, 1983.

6. National Security Archive, *The Chronology* (New York: Warner Books, 1987), p. 7; *Newsweek,* October 10, 1983.

7. National Security Archive, pp. 1, 18.

8. *Washington Post,* May 8, 1983.

9. *Newsweek,* November 8, 1982.

10. *New York Times,* July 7, 1986.

11. National Security Archive, p. 29.

12. *New York Times,* June 11, 1984.

13. "'Say Uncle,' Says Reagan" *Time,* March 4, 1985; *New York Times,* February 24, 1985.

14. Karnow, S. *Vietnam. A History* (New York: Penguin Books, 1984).

15. Brown, S. *The Faces of Power* (New York: Columbia University Press, 1983), p. 298.

16. Holsti, O. and Rosenau, J. *American Leadership in World Affairs* (Boston: Allen and Unwin, 1984), Chapter 6.

17. *New York Times,* February 17 and March 2, 1985; Shultz, G. "New Realities and New Ways of Thinking" *Foreign Affairs,* Spring 1985, pp. 705-21.

18. Krauthammer, C. "The Reagan Doctrine" *Time,* April 1, 1985.

19. Kirkpatrick, J. *The Reagan Doctrine and U.S. Foreign Policy* (Washington, D.C.: The Heritage Foundation, 1985).

20. Ledeen, M. "How to Support the Democratic Revolution" *Commentary,* March 1985, pp. 43-46.

21. "Why did Conservatives Join the Anti-South Africa Brigade?" *Human Events,* December 29, 1984.

22. Bello, W. and Herman, E. "U.S.-Sponsored Elections in El Salvador and the Philippines" *World Policy Journal,* Summer 1984, pp. 851-69.

23. Democratic Policy Commission, *New Choices in a Changing America* (Washington, D.C.: Democratic National Committee, 1986), pp. 55-59.

24. "The Philippine Corollary," *The New Republic,* April 7, 1986.

25. *Ibid.*

26. Jacoby, T. "The Reagan Turnaround on Human Rights" *Foreign Affairs,* Summer 1986, pp. 1066-86.

27. *New York Times,* March 15, 1986.

28. "Liberals and Conservatives in the U.S. Are Seeking a Foreign Policy Consensus" *Wall Street Journal,* March 31, 1986.

29. Ledeen, "How to Support the Democratic Revolution."

30. Ledeen, M. "Fighting Back" *Commentary,* August 1985.

31. *New York Times,* March 11 and 19, 1987.

32. *New York Times,* January 9, 1986.

33. *New York Times,* May 21, 1987.

34. *San Francisco Chronicle,* June 19, 1987.

35. Neier, A. "The Contra Contradiction" *The New York Review of Books,* April 9, 1987.

36. *San Francisco Chronicle,* June 1 and July 29, 1987.

37. *New York Times,* June 22, 1987.

38. Stockwell, J. *In Search of Enemies* (New York: W.W. Norton, 1978), pp. 154, 177.

39. *New York Times,* July 31, 1986.

40. *New York Times,* May 19, July 14 and August 22, 1987; *San Francisco Examiner,* January 6 and 7, 1988.

41. DiLaura, A. "Preventing Terrorism: An Analysis of National Strategy" *SAIS Review,* Winter-Spring 1987, pp. 27-38.

42. Kirkpatrick, J. "The Teaching of Democratic Values" in *Dictatorships and Double Standards,* p. 238.

43. *New York Times,* November 15, 1984.

44. Frappier, J. et al. *Democracy in Nicaragua* (San Francisco: U.S. Out of Central America, 1985), p. 3.

45. *The Electoral Process in Nicaragua: Domestic and International Influences* (Latin American Studies Association, 1984), p. 1.

46. *Washington Post,* November 6, 1984.

47. Bello and Herman, "U.S.-Sponsored Elections in El Salvador and the Philippines."

48. Herman, E. and Brodhead F. *Demonstration Elections* (Boston: South End Press, 1984), pp. 127-28.

49. *Ibid.,* p. 129.

50. *Wall Street Journal,* May 10 and 11, 1984.

51. Herman and Brodhead, p. 120.

52. *Amnesty International Report 1985* (London: Amnesty International Publications, 1985), p. 171.

53. *Ibid.,* p. 143.

54. *Ibid.,* p. 152.

55. *Ibid.,* pp. 144-45.

56. Amnesty International, *Political Killings by Governments* (London: Amnesty International Publications, 1983), p. 27.

57. Interim Report of the British Parliamentary Human Rights Group, "Bitter and Cruel," November 1984; Bello and Herman; Nairn, A. "Behind the Death Squads" *The Progressive,* May 1984; Anderson, S. and Anderson J. *Inside the League* (New York: Dodd, Mead and Company, 1986), p. 165.

58. *New York Times,* May 13, 1987; *Pacific News Service,* July 6-10, 1987.

59. *New York Times,* April 19, 1987; *The Nation,* March 21, 1987, p. 350.

60. *New York Times,* July 1, November 16 and 30, 1987 and January 18 and 23, 1988; *San Francisco Examiner,* January 18, 1988.

61. Shultz, "New Realities and New Ways of Thinking."

62. *New York Times,* April 18 and July 9, 1987 and January 13, 1988.

63. Prados, J. *Presidents' Secret Wars* (New York: William Morrow and Company, 1986), pp. 366, 369.

64. Kwitny, J. *The Crimes of Patriots* (New York: W.W. Norton, 1987), pp. 15, 291.

65. *Ibid.,* pp. 101-03, 291, 310, 315.

66. Maas, P. "Oliver North's Strange Recruits" *New York Times Magazine,* January 18, 1987.

67. Kwitny, pp. 310-11, 335; Marshall, J. et al. *The Iran-Contra Connection* (Boston: South End Press, 1987), pp. 29, 41.

68. Marshall et al., pp. 28-29.

69. Kwitny, pp. 291-92.

70. Maas, P. *Manhunt* (New York: Random House, 1986), p. 26; Marshall et al., p. 41; Kwitny, pp. 310-11.

71. Kwitny, pp. 315, 379; *Los Angeles Times,* October 16, 1986; *New York Times,* December 10, 1986.

72. *New York Times,* October 12 and December 10, 1986.

73. Kwitny, J. "Money, Drugs and the Contras" *The Nation,* August 29, 1987.

74. *New York Times,* February 4, 1987; *Los Angeles Times,* December 7, 1986; Kwitny, *The Crimes of Patriots,* pp. 310-312.

75. *Los Angeles Times,* December 7, 1986; *Washington Post,* November 29, 1985; Perry, M. "The I.S.A. Behind the NSC" *The Nation,* January 17, 1987.

76. *Washington Post,* December 10, 1984; "Aid Commandos" *The Nation,* November 2, 1985; Marshall et al., p. 197.

77. *Washington Post,* November 29, 1985; Prados, pp. 63, 66, 371, 376.

78. Anderson and Anderson, p. 152; Bachrack, S. *The Committee of One Million* (New York: Columbia University Press, 1976), p. 274.

79. Blum, W. *The CIA: A Forgotten History* (London: Zed Books, 1986), pp. 144-45; Anderson and Anderson, p. 151; Marshall et al., p. 65.

80. *Washington Post,* December 10, 1984; "As Contra Debate Continues, Stateside Groups Offer Help" *Insight,* May 26, 1986.

81. Dickey, C. *With the Contras* (New York: Simon and Schuster, 1985), pp. 82-90.

82. *Ibid.*

83. *New York Times,* February 4 and July 2, 1987.

84. Marshall et al., p. 13.

85. Anderson and Anderson, pp. 107, 134-35; *Miami Herald,* May 13, 1987.

86. *New York Times,* August 20, 1987.

87. Bahbah, B. *Israel and Latin America: The Military Connection* (New York: St. Martin's Press, 1986), pp. 78-85; *Christian Science Monitor,* January 13, 1987; *Washington Post,* February 2 and July 15, 1987; *San Francisco Examiner,* December 4, 1986; *Israeli Foreign Affairs,* January 1987.

88. *Washington Post,* December 10, 1984.

89. *Washington Post,* May 3, 1985; *Miami Herald,* June 16, 1985.

90. *New York Times,* July 15, 1984; *Washington Times,* November 30, 1984.

91. *New York Times,* April 30, May 7, and August 1, 1987; *Washington Post,* March 7, 1987.

92. Waghelstein, J. "Post-Vietnam Counterinsurgency Doctrine" *Military Review,* May 1985.

93. Kelly, R. "Special Operations in the '80's" *Defense and Foreign Affairs,* August and September 1984.

94. Blaufarb, D. S. *The Counterinsurgency Era: U.S. Doctrine and Performance* (New York: Free Press, 1977).

95. U.S. Army. *Psychological Operations Techniques and Procedures,* Field Manual FM 33-5 (Washington, Department of the Army, 1966).

96. Center for Defense Information, *The Defense Monitor,* Volume 14, No. 2, 1985.

97. *New York Times,* July 19, 1986.

98. Center for Defense Information.

99. *New York Times,* November 26, 1986.

100. *New York Times,* September 6, 1986.

101. Center for Defense Information.

102. DiGiovanni, C. "U.S. Policy and the Marxist Threat to Central America" *The Heritage Foundation Backgrounder,* October 15, 1980.

103. *New York Times,* February 28, 1985.

104. *New York Times,* January 23 and March 19, 1985; *The Nation,* February 9, 1985.

105. *New York Times,* February 10, 1985.

106. *New York Times,* February 10 and March 27, 1985.

107. "A Conversation with Zbigniew Brzezinski" *The National Interest,* Fall 1986, pp. 28-35.

108. *New York Times,* March 19, 1985 and December 20, 1987.

109. *Wall Street Journal,* April 3, 1985.

110. *New York Times,* March 19, 1986.

111. Cockburn, L. *Out of Control* (New York: Atlantic Monthly Press, 1987), pp. 134-88; Kwitny, J. "Money, Drugs and the Contras"; *San Francisco Examiner,* March 16 and July 23, 1986.

112. Chomsky, N. *On Power and Ideology* (Boston: South End Press, 1987), p. 28.

113. Ramirez, S. "The Unfinished American Revolution and Nicaragua Today" in Dixon, M. and Jonas, S. *Nicaragua Under Siege* (San Francisco: Synthesis Publications, 1984).

114. Reding, A. "Nicaragua's New Constitution" *World Policy Journal,* Spring 1987, pp. 257-94.

115. Chomsky, p. 37.

116. *New York Times,* March 26, 1985.

117. Chomsky, N. "Libya in U.S. Demonology" *Covert Action Information Bulletin,* Summer 1986, pp. 15-24.

118. *New York Times,* April 3 and 28, October 3, 1986.

119. Chomsky, "Libya in U.S. Demonology."

120. Jack Anderson's column in *San Francisco Chronicle,* July 13, 1987.

121. *Ibid.*

122. *New York Times,* July 9, 1985.

123. Denton, J. "What Can Be Done to Fight Terrorism?" *Conservative Digest,* July 1986.

124. Herman, E. *The Real Terror Network* (Boston: South End Press, 1982), pp. 49-65.

125. *New York Times,* November 2, 1985; Sklar, H. *Reagan, Trilateralism and the Neoliberals* (Boston: South End Press, 1986), p. 62.

126. Bello, W. "Edging Toward the Quagmire: the United States and the Philippine Crisis" *World Policy Journal,* Winter 1985-86, pp. 29-58.

127. Bello, W. "Ferdinand, Cory and Uncle Sam" *The National Reporter,* Summer 1986.

128. Cline, R. "The Ballad of Cory and Johnny" *Conservative Digest,* February 1987, pp. 105-10.

129. *The Military Reform Debate* (West Point, N.Y.: U.S. Military Academy, 1982), p. 141; Record, J. *Revising U.S. Military Strategy: Tailoring Means to Ends* (Washington, D.C.: Pergamon Press, 1984).

130. Dunn, K. and Staudenmaier, W. *Military Strategy in Transition* (Boulder, Colorado: Westview Press, 1984), Chapter 9.

131. Thibault, G. *The Art and Practice of Military Strategy* (Washington, D.C.: National Defense University, 1984), Chapter 34.

132. Haffa, R. *The Half War: Planning U.S. Rapid Deployment Forces to Meet a Limited Contingency, 1960-1983* (Boulder, Colorado: Westview Press, 1984), p. 229; Dunn and Staudenmaier, Chapter 9.

133. U.S. Secretary of Defense. *Report to the Congress, FY 1986,* (Washington, D.C.: U.S. Government Printing Office, 1985), p. 16.

134. Dunn and Staudenmaier, Chapter 6.

135. *New York Times,* January 20, 1986.

136. Tonelson, A. "The Real National Interest" *Foreign Policy,* Winter 1985-86, pp. 49-72.

137. Dunn and Staudenmaier, Chapter 9.

138. Johns, M. "Peace in our Time" *Policy Review,* Summer, 1987, pp. 69-71.

139. Sanders, J. "Terminators" *Mother Jones,* August-September 1985.

140. "How to Free Nicaragua" *Conservative Digest,* April 1985.

141. Phillips, H. "Restore the Monroe Doctrine" *Conservative Digest,* August 1983.

142. *San Francisco Chronicle,* July 29, 1987.

143. Cline, "The Ballad of Cory and Johnny."

144. *San Francisco Chronicle,* July 1, 1987.

145. *New York Times,* November 11, 1987 and January 13, 1988.

146. Stilwell, R. "Averting Disaster in the Philippines" *Policy Review,* Winter 1988.

147. *San Francisco Examiner,* March 22, 1987.

148. *New York Times,* April 4, 1987.

149. Butler, p. 346.

150. *New York Times,* June 28, 1987.

151. Kennan, G. "Morality and Foreign Policy" *Foreign Affairs,* Winter 1985-86, pp. 205-18.

152. Record, J. "Jousting with Unreality" *International Security,* Winter 1983-84.

153. Kennan, "Morality and Foreign Policy."

Chapter 5

1. Kaku, M. and Axelrod, D. *To Win A Nuclear War: The Pentagon's Secret War Plans* (Boston: South End Press, 1987), pp. 49-55.

2. *Ibid.,* pp. 58-59.

3. *Ibid.,* pp. 1-2, 72-73.

4. *Ibid.,* p. 107.

5. *Ibid.,* pp. 100-1.

6. *Ibid.,* p. 126; Brown, S. *The Faces of Power* (New York: Columbia University Press, 1983), p. 71.

7. Kaku and Axelrod, p. 139.

8. Kaplan, F. *The Wizards of Armageddon* (New York: Simon and Schuster, 1983), p. 301.

9. Kaku and Axelrod, pp. 140-42.

10. *Ibid.,* p. 143.

11. *Ibid.,* pp. 138-146; Brown, pp. 174-78.

12. Kaplan, Chapters 13, 14, 25.

13. Kaku and Axelrod, p. 176.

14. *A Strategy for Peace Through Strength* (Boston, Virginia: American Security Council Foundation, 1984), pp. 148-49.

15. Gerson, J. *The Deadly Connection* (Philadelphia: New Society Publishers, 1986), p. 11.

16. *Ibid.,* pp. 11-13.

17. Kaku and Axelrod, Chapter 5.

18. U.S. Senate Concurrent Resolution 15 (1983) and House Concurrent Resolution 83 (1983).

19. Sanders, J. *Peddlers of Crisis* (Boston: South End Press, 1983), p. 256.

20. *Ibid.*, Chapters 5 and 6.

21. Tyroler, C. *Alerting America. The Papers of the Committee on the Present Danger* (Washington, D.C.: Pergamon-Brassey's International Defense Publishers, 1984).

22. Gervasi, T. *The Myth of Soviet Military Supremacy* (New York: Harper and Row, 1986), pp. 25, 91.

23. *Ibid.*, pp. 85-86, 91-95.

24. *Ibid.*, pp. 86, 92.

25. *Ibid.*, pp. 214-15.

26. *New York Times,* March 3, 1983.

27. Gray, C. and Payne, K. "Victory is Possible" *Foreign Policy,* Fall, 1980, pp. 48-57.

28. Scheer, R. *With Enough Shovels* (New York: Vintage Books, 1983), p. 29.

29. *Ibid.*, p. 8.

30. *Ibid.*, pp. 3, 12.

31. *Washington Post,* November 10, 1982.

32. Center for Defense Information, "Nuclear Warfighting Quotations by Reagan Administration Officials and Supporters," September 1983.

33. Iklé, F. "The Idol of Stability" *The National Interest,* Winter 1986-87, pp. 75-79.

34. Center for Defense Information.

35. Stober, D. "Teller Exaggerated 'Star Wars,' Scientists Say" *San Jose Mercury News,* February 4, 1988.

36. Sanders, p. 202.

37. Bowman, R. *Star Wars: Defense or Death Star?* (Institute for Space and Security Studies, 1985), pp. 38-41.

38. Thompson, E.P. "Let's Call It Quits: E.P. Thompson on the Cold War" *The Progressive,* December 1986.

39. English, R. "Offensive Star Wars" *The New Republic,* February 24, 1986.

40. Scheer, p. 295.

41. *New York Times,* March 7, 1985 and February 22, 1987; Perlman, D. "Star Wars on the Offensive," *This World (San Francisco Chronicle),* April 5, 1987.

42. Kaku and Axelrod, p. 15; *New York Times,* May 29, 1985.

43. Lehrman, L. and Fossedal, G. "How to Decide About Strategic Defense" *National Review,* January 31, 1986.

44. Bowman, p. 53.

45. *The Bombmakers,* NBC News, May 1987.

46. *New York Times,* February 11, 1985, August 28, 1988.

47. Kaku and Axelrod, p. 16.

48. Hiatt, F. "Getting Ready for World War IV" *Washington Post National Weekly,* August 25, 1986.

49. Halloran, R. "A Silent Battle Surfaces" *New York Times Magazine,* December 7, 1986.

50. Keller, B. "The Navy's Brash Leader" *New York Times Magazine,* December 15, 1985.

51. *New York Times,* March 30, 1987.

52. *New York Times,* October 3, 1984.

53. "Beyond Containment? The Future of U.S.-Soviet Relations" *Policy Review,* Winter 1985, p. 37.

54. Pipes, R. *Survival is Not Enough* (New York: Simon and Schuster, 1984), pp. 225-43.

55. Sanders, p. 149.

56. *Human Events,* January 5, 1985.

57. Bethell, T. "Why Arms Talks Must Fail" *National Review,* March 8, 1985; Crozier, B. "The Protracted Conflict" *National Review,* July 26, 1985; Glynn, P. "Why an American Arms Build-up is Morally Necessary" *Commentary,* February 1984.

58. *Wall Street Journal,* July 10, 1984.

59. *San Francisco Chronicle,* February 11, 1987; *New York Times,* May 30 and November 29, 1986.

60. *New York Times,* February 22 and March 13, 1987.

61. *New York Times,* October 25, 1986.

62. *New York Times,* October 10, 1986.

63. *New York Times,* October 16, 1986.

64. Smith, H. "The Right Against Reagan" *New York Times Magazine,* January 17, 1988.

65. *New York Times,* October 25, 1986.

66. *New York Times,* October 24, 1986 and January 28, 1987; *A Strategy for Peace Through Strength,* p. 152.

67. Heatherly, C., ed. *Mandate for Leadership* (Washington, D.C.: The Heritage Foundation, 1981), pp. 94-95.

68. Butler, S. et al. *Mandate for Leadership II* (Washington, D.C.: The Heritage Foundation, 1984), pp. 244, 292.

69. *New York Times,* July 13, 1986.

70. *New York Times,* July 7, 1987.

71. *New York Times,* July 9, 1987; *Washington Post National Weekly,* April 13, 1987.

72. Talbot, S. *Deadly Gambits* (New York: Vintage Books, 1985), p. 263.

73. *New York Times,* December 9, 1987.

74. Iklé, F. "Nuclear Strategy: Can there be a Happy Ending?" *Foreign Affairs,* Spring 1985, pp. 810-26.

75. Waller, D. et al. "SDI: Prospects and Challenges" Staff Report submitted to Senators Proxmire, Johnston and Chiles, March 17, 1986, p. 61.

76. Fletcher, J. "The Technologies for Ballistic Missile Defense" *Issues in Science and Technology,* Fall 1984, pp. 25-26.

77. Chomsky, N. *On Power and Ideology,* (Boston: South End Press, 1987), p. 98.

78. The Union of Concerned Scientists, *Empty Promise* (Boston: Beacon Press, 1986), p. 187.

79. Iklé, "Nuclear Strategy: Can there be a Happy Ending?"

80. *Los Angeles Times,* April 13, 1987.

81. Parnas, "Science and Technology of Directed Energy Weapons" Report to the American Physical Society Study Group, April 1987; *New York Times,* April 24, 1987; *San Francisco Chronicle,* August 12, 1987.

82. *New York Times,* January 31, 1988.

83. *New York Times,* September 25, 1985.

84. Bowman, pp. 9-11, 62-63.

85. *Business Week,* March 2 and May 25, 1987; *New York Times,* February 6 and February 7, April 9, 1987.

86. Smith, H. "The Right Against Reagan."

87. *Ibid.*

88. *New York Times,* December 15 and 16, 1987.

89. *New York Times,* January 3, 1988.

90. *New York Times,* January 20 and 28, 1988.

91. *New York Times,* December 6, 1987.

92. *New York Times,* January 20, 1988.

93. Report of the Commission on Integrated Long-Term Strategy. *Discriminate Deterrence* (Washington, D.C.: U.S. Government Printing Office, 1988).

94. *New York Times,* May 5 and August 1, 1987.

Chapter 6

1. Halliday, F. *The Making of the Second Cold War* (London: Verso Editions, 1983), pp. 55-72; Komer, R. "What 'Decade of Neglect?'" *International Security,* Fall 1985, pp. 70-83.

2. Ferguson, T. and Rogers, J. *Right Turn* (New York: Hill and Wang, 1986), p. 95.

3. Center for Defense Information, "Soviet Geopolitical Momentum: Myth or Menace?" *The Defense Monitor,* Vol. XV, No. 5, 1986.

4. Frank, A.G. *Crisis: In the World Economy* (New York: Holms and Meier Publishers, 1980), p. 3.

5. Castells, M. *The Economic Crisis and American Society* (Princeton: Princeton University Press), pp. 115, 134.

6. *Ibid.,* p. 90.

7. Frank, A.G. *Reflections on the World Economic Crisis* (New York: Monthly Review Press, 1981), p. 67.

8. World Bank, *World Development Report, 1980.*

9. Frank, p. 33; Bluestone, B. and Harrison, B. *The Deindustrialization of America* (New York: Basic Books, 1982), pp. 147-48.

10. *Business Week,* October 12, 1974 and October 16, 1978.

11. Frank, *Crisis: In the World Economy,* p. 20.

12. Altman, E. and Sametz, A. *Financial Crises, Institutions and Markets in a Fragile Environment* (New York: John Wiley and Sons, 1977), p. vii.

13. Frank, A.G. "Defuse the Debt Bomb? When Apparent Solutions Become Real Problems" *World Policy Journal,* Summer, 1984.

14. Moffitt, M. *The World's Money* (New York: Simon and Schuster, 1983), p. 400.

15. Moffitt, pp. 401-02.

16. *New York Times,* December 24, 1986.

17. Moffitt, p. 404.

18. *New York Times,* July 21, 1986.

19. *San Francisco Chronicle,* November 24, 1986.

20. Frank, A.G., "Defuse the Debt Bomb?"

21. *South, The Third World Magazine,* August 1984.

22. *New York Times,* March 19, 1985.

23. *New York Times,* December 26, 1986.

24. *New York Times,* June 8, 1986.

25. *New York Times,* January 13, 1985.

26. Brown, S. *The Faces of Power* (New York: Columbia University Press, 1983), p. 420.

27. Falk, R. "Lifting The Curse of Bipartisanship" *World Policy Journal,* Fall 1983, pp. 127-57.

28. Halliday, p. 180.

29. *Business Week,* November 19, 1984, December 29, 1986, February 9 and November 16, 1987; *Washington Post National Weekly,* January 11-17, 1988.

30. Moffitt, p. 400.

31. Faux, J. "The Democrats and the Post-Reagan Economy" *World Policy Journal,* Spring 1986, pp. 183-218; *Business Week,* February 2, 1987.

32. Brenner, R. "How America Lost the Edge: The Roots of U.S. Economic Decline" *Against the Current,* March-April 1986.

33. *Business Week,* February 2, 1987.

34. Edsall, T. *The New Politics of Inequality* (New York: W.W. Norton, 1984), p. 208.

35. *Business Week,* February 2, 1987.

36. *New York Times,* April 28, 1986.

37. Castells, p. 102.

38. *New York Times,* October 9, 1986.

39. *San Francisco Chronicle,* December 18, 1984.

40. *Business Week,* July 15, 1985.

41. Cypher, J. "The Basic Economics of 'Rearming America'" *Monthly Review,* November 1981, pp. 11-27.

42. *Washington Post National Weekly,* January 12, 1987.

43. *Business Week,* February 9, 1987; *New York Times,* October 14, 1986.

44. *New York Times,* November 30, 1986.

45. DuBoff, R. "Unemployment in the United States: An Historical Summary" *Monthly Review,* November 1977, pp. 10-24; Thayer, F. "Avoiding a Crash:

Public Investment, Private Regulation" *World Policy Journal,* Summer 1985, pp. 415-49.

46. *New York Times,* July 13, 1986.

47. Nossiter, B. "Reagan's Road to Stabilization" *The Nation,* January 10, 1987.

48. *Washington Post National Weekly,* January 19, 1987.

49. *Washington Post National Weekly,* November 10, 1986; *Dollars and Sense,* November 1987, p. 22.

50. *Dollars and Sense,* December 1986.

51. *New York Times,* November 14, 1986.

52. *New York Times,* February 7, 1987.

53. *Newsweek,* January 12, 1987.

54. *Washington Post National Weekly,* January 12, 1987.

55. *New York Times,* January 15, 1987.

56. Davis, M. *Prisoners of the American Dream* (London: Verso Editions, 1986), pp. 304-05.

57. *Business Week,* February 9, 1987; *New York Times,* July 29, 1986.

58. Nossiter, "Reagan's Road to Stabilization"; *New York Times,* December 26, 1986.

59. *Washington Post National Weekly,* December 15, 1986.

60. *Business Week,* February 9, 1987.

61. *New York Times,* December 24, 1986.

62. *New York Times,* July 29, 1986; *Business Week,* August 31 and December 7, 1987.

63. *New York Times,* October 8, 1986; *Business Week,* February 2 and November 16, 1987.

64. *Business Week,* February 2, 1987.

65. *Business Week,* November 16, 1987.

66. *New York Times,* October 25, 1987.

67. Schurmann, F. *The Logic of World Power* (New York: Pantheon Books, 1974), p. 145.

68. Barnet, R. *Roots of War* (New York: Penguin Books, 1972), p. 4.

69. Moffitt, Chapter 1.

70. *Ibid.,* Chapter 3.

71. Solomon, R. "'The Elephant in the Boat?': The United States and the World Economy" *Foreign Affairs,* Spring 1982, pp. 573-92.

72. Bluestone and Harrison, p.42.

73. Moffitt, p. 53.

74. Bluestone and Harrison, p. 42.

75. *Ibid.,* pp. 44-45.

76. *Ibid.,* p. 6.

77. *Ibid.,* p. 26.

78. Castells, p. 105.

79. *Congressional Record,* April 24, 1985, p. E 1681.

80. Moffitt, Chapter 3.

81. *Ibid.,* pp. 83-84.

82. Dellums, R. *Defense Sense* (Cambridge: Ballinger Publishing Co., 1983), p. 163.

83. McFadden, D. and Wake, J. *The Freeze Economy* (Nuclear Weapons Freeze Campaign, 1983).

84. DeGrasse, R. *Military Expansion, Economic Decline* (Armonk, N.Y.: M.E. Sharpe, Inc., 1983), p. 70.

85. Sidel, V. "Buying Death with Taxes: Impact of Arms Race on Health Care" in Adams, R. and Cullen, S. *The Final Epidemic* (Chicago: University of Chicago Press, 1981), pp. 38-39.

86. Sivard, R.L. *World Military and Social Expenditures 1982* (Leesburg, Virginia: World Priorities, 1982), p. 15.

Chapter 7

1. Burnham, W.D. *The American Party Systems* (Oxford University Press, 1967), pp. 203-04.

2. Sale, K. *Power Shift* (New York: Vintage Books, 1976); Phillips, K. *The Emerging Republican Majority* (New Rochelle, N.Y.: Arlington House, 1970); Klare, M. "The Traders and the Prussians" *Seven Days,* March 28, 1977; Schurmann, F. *The Logic of World Power* (New York: Pantheon Books, 1974); Sanders, J. *Peddlers of Crisis* (Boston: South End Press, 1983); Sklar, H. *Trilateralism* (Boston: South End Press, 1980).

3. Domhoff, W. *Fat Cats and Democrats* (Englewood Cliffs, N.J.: Prentice-Hall, 1972), p. 158.

4. Shoup, L. and Minter, W. *Imperial Brain Trust* (New York: Monthly Review Press, 1977), p. 117; Ferguson, T. and Rogers, J. *Right Turn* (New York: Hill and Wang, 1986), pp. 46-57.

5. Sale, p. 100.

6. Ferguson and Rogers, pp. 68-74.

7. *Ibid.,* p. 94; Sklar, p. 448-50.

8. Sklar, p. 570.

9. *Ibid.,* pp. 563-65.

10. Ferguson and Rogers, p. 78.

11. *Ibid.,* pp. 89-92.

12. *Ibid.,* pp. 98-99.

13. *Ibid.,* pp. 103-05.

14. Sanders, pp. 204-10; Ferguson and Rogers, p. 99.

15. Ferguson and Rogers, p. 99.

16. Halliday, F. *The Making of the Second Cold War* (London: Verso, 1983), pp. 224-33.

17. Sanders, pp. 184-86.

18. *Wall Street Journal,* April 30, 1980.

19. For list of Trilateral members, Sklar, p. 99.

20. Ferguson and Rogers, p. 95-96.

21. *Ibid.,* p. 111-13.

22. Sklar, pp. 560-62.

23. Ferguson and Rogers, pp. 114-16.

24. *Ibid.,* pp. 119-27.

25. *Ibid.,* pp. 147, 153.

26. *New York Times,* May 4, 1984.

27. DeGrasse, R. *Military Expansion, Economic Decline* (Armonk, N.Y.: M.E. Sharpe, Inc., 1983), p. 8.

28. Pascall, G. *The Trillion Dollar Budget* (Seattle: University of Washington Press, 1985), p. 160.

29. DeGrasse, p. 11; Gross, B. *Friendly Fascism* (Boston: South End Press, 1980), p. 192.

30. Pierre, A. *The Global Politics of Arms Sales* (Princeton: Princeton University Press, 1982), p. 26; Klare, M. *American Arms Supermarket* (Austin: University of Texas Press, 1984), p. 13.

31. Klare, *American Arms Supermarket,* pp. 33-34.

32. *Fortune,* April 30, 1984; Pascall, p. 164.

33. *Business Week,* December 29, 1986.

34. Cypher, J. "The Basic Economics of 'Rearming America'" *Monthly Review,* November 1981, pp. 11-27.

35. U.S. Department of Defense, *100 Companies Receiving the Largest Dollar Volume of Prime Contract Awards, Fiscal Year 1985* (Washington, D.C.: U.S. Government Printing Office, 1985).

36. Davis, M. *Prisoners of the American Dream* (London: Verso, 1986), pp. 242-43.

37. Thompson, E.P. "Look Who's Really Behind Star Wars" *The Nation,* March 1, 1986; *New York Times,* May 12, 1985.

38. *New York Times,* July 3, 1986.

39. U.S. Department of Defense, *100 Companies...*

40. *New York Times,* April 9, 1985.

41. Adams, G. *The Politics of Defense Contracting: The Iron Triangle* (New Brunswick, N.J.: Transaction Books, 1984), pp. 227-444.

42. Tirman, J. *The Militarization of High Technology* (Cambridge, Mass.: Ballinger Publishing Co., 1984), pp. 128-31.

43. Adams, pp. 289, 316, 346.

44. U.S. Department of Defense, *100 Companies...*

45. Adams, pp. 227-444.

46. DeGrasse, p. 7; Tirman, pp. 23-24.

47. Adams, pp. 185-95.

48. Sabato, L. *PAC Power* (New York: W.W. Norton, 1985), p. 19.

49. *New York Times,* August 28, 1987.

50. *New York Times,* April 9, 1985.

51. Adams, G. and Weiss, L. "Military Spending Boosts the Deficit" *Bulletin of the Atomic Scientists,* April 1985, pp. 26-27.

52. Ferguson and Rogers, p. 124-26.

53. Adams, G. and Gold, D. "Recasting the Military Spending Debate" *Bulletin of the Atomic Scientists,* October 1986, pp. 26-32.

54. Weisner, J. "A Militarized Society" *Bulletin of the Atomic Scientists,* August 1985, pp. 102-05.

55. *Washington Post,* November 19, 1985.

56. Sklar, p. 288.

57. Wolfe, A. *The Rise and Fall of the Soviet Threat* (Boston: South End Press, 1984), pp. 16-39.

58. Gervasi, T. *The Myth of Soviet Military Superiority* (New York: Harper and Row, 1987), p. 218.

59. Kaplan, F. *The Wizards of Armageddon* (New York: Simon and Schuster, 1983), pp. 125-31.

60. Sanders, pp. 197-203, 222-28.

61. Wolfe, pp. 97-107.

62. *Khrushchev Remembers* (Boston: Little Brown, 1971), pp. 519-20.

63. *New York Times,* February 3, 1987.

64. *Business Week,* November 16, 1987.

65. *New York Times,* November 9, 1987.

66. *New York Times,* December 5, 1987.

67. Sklar, pp. 533-52.

Chapter 8

1. Domhoff, W. *Who Rules America Now?* (New York: Simon and Schuster, 1983), pp. 82-98, 136-46; Domhoff, W. *Fat Cats and Democrats* (Englewood Cliffs, N.J.: Prentice-Hall, 1972), p. 148.

2. Sanders, J. *Peddlers of Crisis* (Boston: South End Press, 1983).

3. Steinfels, P. *The Neoconservatives* (New York: Simon and Schuster, 1979), pp. 83-87.

4. D'Souza, D. "Marty Come Lately" *Policy Review,* Fall, 1985.

5. *In These Times,* August 6-19, 1986.

6. Krauthammer, C. "Divided Superpower" *The New Republic,* December 22, 1986.

7. Krauthammer, C. "The Poverty of Realism" *The New Republic,* February 17, 1986.

8. Tucker, R. *The Purposes of American Power* (New York: Praeger Publishers, 1981); Layne, C. "The Real Conservative Agenda" *Foreign Policy,* Winter 1985-86, pp. 73-93; Tonelson, A. "The Real National Interest" *Foreign Policy,* Winter 1985-86, pp. 49-72.

9. Kennan, G. "Morality and Foreign Policy" *Foreign Affairs,* Winter 1985-86, pp. 205-18.

10. Saloma, J. *Ominous Politics* (New York: Hill and Wang, 1983), pp. 8-12.

11. *Ibid.,* pp.14-19.

12. Bethell, T. "Liberalism, Stanford-Style" *Commentary,* January 1984.

13. *Washington Post National Weekly,* May 26, 1986.

14. Saloma, p. 31.

15. *Washington Post National Weekly,* May 26, 1986.

16. Domhoff, *Who Rules America Now?,* pp. 85-88.

17. Destler, I. et al. *Our Own Worst Enemy* (New York: Simon and Schuster, 1984), pp. 106-10, 121-26; Petras, J. "Speculators, Lumpen-Intellectuals, and the End of U.S. Hegemony" *Against the Current,* March-April 1987.

18. Domhoff, p. 88.

19. Brinkley, A. "Peering into Think Tanks" *The New Republic,* September 16 and 23, 1986.

20. Sanders, pp. 149-50.

21. Democratic Policy Commission, *New Choices in a Changing America* (Washington, D.C.: Democratic National Committee, 1986), pp. 55-59.

22. Edsall, T. *The New Politics of Inequality* (New York: W.W. Norton, 1984).

23. *Washington Post National Weekly,* August 25, 1986.

24. Ferguson, T. and Rogers J. *Right Turn* (New York: Hill and Wang, 1986), p. 143.

25. *Ibid.,* p. 202.

26. *Ibid.,* pp. 138-43.

27. Adams, G. *The Politics of Defense Contracting. The Iron Triangle* (New Brunswick, N.J.: Transaction Books, 1984), pp. 111-14.

28. *Washington Post National Weekly,* April 7, 1986.

29. Adams, G. and Gold, D. "Recasting the Military Spending Debate" *Bulletin of the Atomic Scientists,* October 1986.

30. *Washington Post National Weekly,* May 26, 1986.

31. Ferguson and Rogers, p. 143.

32. Edsall, pp. 31-33.

33. *Washington Post National Weekly,* January 19, 1987.

34. Davis, M. *Prisoners of the American Dream* (London: Verso, 1986), p. 293.

35. *In These Times,* August 6-19, 1986.

36. *Washington Post National Weekly,* April 14, 1986.

37. *Ibid.*

38. Ferguson and Rogers, p. 152.

39. Hart, G. *America Can Win* (Bethesda, Md.: Adler and Adler, 1986); *Washington Post National Weekly,* April 14, 1986.

40. *New York Times,* June 13, 1986.

41. Democratic Policy Commission, *New Choices in a Changing America.*

42. *New York Times,* June 13, 1986.

43. Sanders, J. and Schwenninger, S. "The Democrats and a New Grand Strategy, Part II" *World Policy Journal,* Winter 1986-87, pp. 1-50.

44. *New York Times,* June 13, 1986.

45. *New York Times,* March 18, 1986.

46. *Washington Post National Weekly,* May 26, 1986.

47. *Business Week,* June 13, 1988; Kondrake, M. "Carter Redux?" *The New Republic,* May 23, 1988; *Washington Post National Weekly,* May 2-8, 1988.

48. *Washington Post National Weekly,* June 30, 1986.

49. Scheer, R. *With Enough Shovels* (New York: Vintage Books, 1983), pp. 29-30, 53-54; William Buckley's column in the *San Francisco Examiner,* May 26, 1988; *New York Times,* April 28 and June 2, 1988.

50. Edsall, T. "The Political Impasse" *New York Review of Books,* March 26, 1987.

51. *New York Times,* November 8, 1986.

52. *New York Times,* October 24, 1986; Edsall, "The Political Impasse."

53. Edsall, "The Political Impasse."

54. Davis, p. 224.

55. Ferguson and Rogers, p. 34; *New York Times,* August 31 and November 6, 1986.

56. Schurmann, F. *The Logic of World Power* (New York: Pantheon Books, 1974), p. 183.

57. Schurmann, F. *The Foreign Politics of Richard Nixon* (Berkeley: Institute of International Studies, 1987), pp. 13-15, 55, 156-62.

58. Heatherly, C., Ed. *Mandate for Leadership* (Washington, D.C.: The Heritage Foundation, 1981), p. 596.

59. Holwill, R. *The First Year* (Washington, D.C.: The Heritage Foundation, 1982), pp. 1, 190.

60. Kristol, I. *Reflections of a Neoconservative* (New York: Basic Books, 1983), p. 230.

61. Butler, S. et al. *Mandate for Leadership II* (Washington, D.C.: The Heritage Foundation, 1984), pp. 449-51, 464.

62. *Ibid.,* p. 449.

63. Barnet, R. *Roots of War* (New York: Penguin Books, 1972), pp. 27-33.

64. Etzold, T. *The Conduct of American Foreign Relations* (New York: New Viewpoints, 1977), pp. 73-77.

65. Heatherly, p. 948.

66. Butler, p. 377.

67. *Washington Post National Weekly,* May 25, 1987.

68. Blumenthal, S. *The Rise of the Counter-Establishment* (New York: Times Books, 1986), p. 65.

69. *Ibid.,* pp. 287, 291.

70. *Ibid.,* p. 315.

71. Losche, P. and Schulze, P. "Konservatismus bis zur Jahrtausendwende?" (Manuscript, November 1986).

72. Sklar, H. *Reagan, Trilateralism and the Neoliberals* (Boston: South End Press, 1986), pp. 12-13.

73. *San Francisco Chronicle,* July 17, 1987.

74. Hughes, T. "The Twilight of Internationalism" *Foreign Policy,* Winter 1985-86, pp. 25-48.

Chapter 9

1. *Business Week,* November 16, 1987.

2. *New York Times,* June 11, 1987.

3. "A Regal Battle to Reign" *Insight,* August 10, 1987.

4. *Washington Post National Weekly,* December 15, 1986.

5. *The Tower Commission Report* (New York: Random House, 1987), p. 98.

6. Phillips, K. *Post-Conservative America* (New York: Vintage Books, 1983), pp. 208-12.

7. Edsall, T. "And Now, the Political Consequences" *Dissent,* Spring 1987.

8. Freiberger, Paul, "The Business of Glasnost" *San Francisco Examiner and Chronicle,* December 13, 1987.

9. *New York Times,* December 11, 1987.

10. *New York Times,* January 20, 1988.

11. Moro, D. "The National Rebirth of Russia. A U.S. Strategy for Lifting the Soviet Siege" *Policy Review,* Winter 1988.

12. *New York Times,* January 10, 1988.

13. Evans, M.S. "Toward a New Conservative Agenda" *Human Events,* January 16, 1988.

14. *New York Times,* December 12, 1987.

15. *New York Times,* January 5, 1988.

16. *Human Events,* January 23, 1988, p. 21.

17. *New York Times,* December 11, 1987.

18. *New York Times,* November 18, 1987.

19. *New York Times,* October 25, 1987.

20. *New York Times,* November 24, 1987.

21. *New York Times,* December 4, 1987.

22. *New York Times,* June 2, 1988.

23. Annunziata, L. "Democrats and the Arias Plan" *The Nation,* April 18, 1987.

24. *New York Times,* August 8, 1987.

25. *New York Times,* November 18, December 18, 21, and 23, 1987.

26. *New York Times,* December 18 and 20, 1987.

27. *New York Times,* December 10, 1987 and January 3, 1988.

28. *New York Times,* December 18, 1987.

29. *New York Times,* January 19, 1988.

30. *New York Times,* January 13, 1988.

31. *San Francisco Examiner,* February 4, 1988.

32. Purcell, S. "The Choice in Central America" *Foreign Affairs,* Fall 1987, pp. 109-28.

33. *New York Times,* May 12, 1988.

34. *San Francisco Examiner,* February 5, 1988.

35. Falk, R. "Lifting the Curse of Bipartisanship" *World Policy Journal,* Fall 1983, pp. 127-57.

36. Blumenthal, S. "Dateline Washington, D.C.: The Conservative Crackup" *Foreign Policy,* Winter 1987-88, pp. 166-88.

37. Hyland, W. "Reagan-Gorbachev III" *Foreign Affairs,* Fall 1987, pp. 7-21.
38. Kalb, M. "Where Consensus Fails" *New York Times Magazine,* October 27, 1985.
39. Tucker, R. "The Purposes of American Power" *Foreign Affairs,* Winter 1980-81; Sklar, H. *Reagan, Trilateralism, and the Neoliberals* (Boston: South End Press, 1986) p. 22.
40. *New York Times,* January 11, 1988; *San Francisco Chronicle,* January 17, 1988.
41. *New York Times,* September 27, 1987.
42. *New York Times,* September 27, 1987; *Washington Post National Weekly,* December 21, 1987.
43. *Business Week,* January 11, 1988.
44. Kennedy, P. *The Rise and Fall of the Great Powers* (New York: Random House, 1988); Kennedy, P. "The (Relative) Decline of America" *The Atlantic Monthly,* August 1987.

Chapter 10

1. Gerson, J. *The Deadly Connection* (Philadelphia: New Society Publishers, 1986).
2. Somerville, J. "Patriotism and War" in Cassel, C. et al. *Nuclear Weapons and Nuclear War* (New York: Praeger, 1984).
3. Council on Economic Priorities, *Newsletter,* May 1981; *Washington Post,* April 25, 1981.
4. *New York Times,* November 11, 1986.
5. *U.S. Budget in Brief, Fiscal Year 1985* (Washington, D.C.: U.S. Government Printing Office, 1985); *U.S. News and World Report,* February 13, 1984; *Business Week,* March 26, 1984; "The Federal Deficit: The Real Issues" *Monthly Review,* April 1984.
6. *New York Times,* May 6, 1986.
7. *Washington Post National Weekly,* January 26, 1987.
8. *U.S. News and World Report,* September 27, 1982 and July 11, 1983.
9. Dellums, R. *Defense Sense* (Cambridge: Ballinger Publishing Co., 1983), p. 185.
10. Tsurumi, Y. "The Challenges of the Pacific Age" *World Policy Journal,* Fall, 1984.
11. Church, F. "We Must Learn to Live with Revolutions" *Washington Post,* March 11, 1984.
12. *Wall Street Journal,* April 3, 1985.
13. Brooke, J. "Cuba's Strange Mission in Angola" *New York Times Magazine,* February 1, 1987.
14. *Wall Street Journal,* November 14, 1986.
15. Brooke, "Cuba's Strange Mission in Angola."

16. *New York Times,* May 2, 1985.

17. Lee, R. "How America is Being Taken in Trade" *Conservative Digest,* June 1986.

18. *Wall Street Journal,* March 6, 1986; *New York Times,* February 11, 1986.

19. *New York Times,* May 5, 1985.

20. *New York Times,* September 17, 1985.

21. *Conservative Digest,* July 1986, p. 3.

22. Amnesty International, *Political Killings by Governments* (London: Amnesty International Publications, 1983), p. 27; Jonas, S. et al. *Guatemala: Tyranny on Trial* (San Francisco: Synthesis Publications, 1984), p. viii.

23. Blum, W. *The CIA: A Forgotten History* (London: Zed Books, 1986), pp. 217-21.

24. Report of the Economic and Social Council, Commission on Human Rights, United Nations, February 4, 1976.

25. *San Francisco Examiner,* January 10, 1988.

26. *San Francisco Examiner and Chronicle,* February 7, 1988.

27. *The Global 2000 Report to the President of the U.S.* (New York: Pergamon Press, 1983), pp. 1-3, 36-37.

28. Cousins, N. "Who Owns the Ozone?" in Falk, R. et al. *Toward a Just World Order* (Boulder, CO: Westview Press, 1982).

29. Center for Defense Information, "Soviet Geopolitical Momentum: Myth or Menace?" *The Defense Monitor,* Vol. IX, No. 1, January 1980 and Vol. XV, No. 5, 1986.

30. Valkenier, E. *The Soviet Union and the Third World* (New York: Praeger, 1983); Hough, J. *The Struggle for the Third World* (Washington, D.C.: The Brookings Institution, 1986); Kaplan, S. *The Diplomacy of Power* (Washington, D.C.: The Brookings Institution, 1981); CIA and War College statements cited in Center for Defense Information, 1986.

31. *New York Times,* July 16, 1986.

32. Valkenier, E. "East-West Economic Competition in the Third World" in Shulman, M. *East-West Tensions in the Third World* (New York: W.W. Norton, 1986); Hough, p. 268.

33. Kaplan, pp. 667-81.

34. Brown, S. *The Faces of Power* (New York: Columbia University Press, 1983), p. 559.

35. *New York Times,* November 9, 1986.

36. Nye, J. *The Making of America's Soviet Policy* (New Haven: Yale University Press, 1984), p. 327.

37. Luttwak, E. *The Grand Strategy of the Soviet Union* (London: Weidenfeld and Nicolson, 1983), p. 111.

38. Haig, A. *Caveat: Realism, Reagan, and Foreign Policy* (New York: Macmillan, 1984), pp. 319, 354.

39. Kristol, I. *Reflections of a Neoconservative* (New York: Basic Books, 1983), p. 232.

40. Gervasi, T. *The Myth of Soviet Military Supremacy* (New York: Harper and Row, 1986), pp. 25, 92-95.

41. *Ibid.,* pp. 82, 96-97.

42. *Ibid.,* p. 99; *New York Times,* May 2 and May 10, 1982.

43. *Ibid.,* pp. 99-106, 118, 416-28.

44. Hough, J. "Gorbachev's Strategy" *Foreign Affairs,* Fall, 1985.

45. Hough, "Soviet Decision-Making on Defense" *Bulletin of the Atomic Scientists,* August 1985.

46. Brucan, S. "East-Bloc Economic Reform: the Strategic Implications" *World Policy Journal,* Summer, 1985.

47. *New York Times,* September 7, 1986.

48. Strode, R. "The Soviet Armed Forces: Adaptation to Resource Scarcity" *Washington Quarterly,* Spring 1986.

49. Bugajski, J. "The Soviet Union and the Third World" *The Washington Quarterly,* Fall, 1986.

50. Gustafson, T. "Will Soviet Foreign Policy Change Under Gorbachev?" *The Washington Quarterly,* Fall 1986.

51. Dellums, pp. 113-14.

52. *Ibid.,* pp. 137-46.

53. *New York Times,* September 15 1985.

54. *New York Times,* January 18, 1987; *Business Week,* April 20, 1987.

55. Levering, R. *The Public and American Foreign Policy, 1918-1978* (New York: William Morrow and Co., 1978), pp. 23, 29, 97.

56. *Ibid.,* pp. 29, 111-19, 151.

57. *Ibid.,* pp. 138-39.

58. Ferguson, T. and Rogers, J. *Right Turn* (New York: Hill and Wang, 1986), pp. 19-24; *San Francisco Chronicle,* August 21, 1987.

59. Yankelovich, D. and Doble, J. "The Public Mood: Nuclear Weapons and the USSR" *Foreign Affairs,* Fall 1984, pp. 33-46; Ferguson and Rogers, pp. 23-4.

60. Reilly, J. "America's State of Mind" *Foreign Policy,* Spring 1987.

61. Perkovich, G. "Beyond the Cold War" *Nuclear Times,* January/February 1987.

62. Reilly, "America's State of Mind."

63. Hamilton, R. *Who Voted for Hitler?* (Princeton: Princeton University Press, 1982), pp. 37-42, 82, 122, 218-19, 376-77, 455.

64. *Ibid.,* p. 343.

65. *Ibid.,* pp. 439-41.

Index

Abshire, David 166, 167
Acheson, Dean 2, 13, 15
Accuracy in Media 62, 63, 68, 76
Aderholt, Harry 71, 98
Afghanistan 43, 48, 56, 79, 82, 83, 100, 200, 227
Air America 61, 70-72
Albania 25, 66
Allende, Salvador 32, 85, 158
American Enterprise Institute 55, 183, 187
American Legislative Exchange Council 198
American Security Council 42, 55, 56, 58, 59, 63, 68, 73, 76, 78, 99, 120, 122, 135, 140, 164, 173
Amnesty International 31, 94
Angola 43, 48, 56, 72, 77-78, 82, 83, 90, 100, 192, 205, 222
Anti-Ballistic Missile (ABM) Treaty 134, 139, 140, 141, 142
Anti-Bolshevik Nations (ABN) 57, 66
Aquino, Corazon 95, 109, 112-113
Arbenz, Jacobo 26, 73
Arena Party 57, 76
Argentina 73, 76-77, 95, 99
Arias, Oscar 208-209, 223
Arms control 133-142
Arms Control Association 169
Asia-firsters 12-13, 110
Asian People's Anti-Communist League (APACL) 56, 57, 59, 66, 68-70
Aspaturian, Vernon 37-39, 49, 110
Aspin, Les 188
Assassinations 27, 74, 75, 97
Atlanticists 67, 110, 140
Austerity capitalism 150, 151

B-1 Bomber 172, 173
Baldridge, Malcolm 191

Barbie, Klaus 66, 77
Bay of Pigs 27, 60, 74, 97
Belgian Congo (Zaire) 27, 60, 74, 77
Bermudez, Enrique 89
Blackwell, Morton 198
Blumenthal, Sidney 197, 199, 212
Boland Amendment 1
Bolivia 60, 74
Bolshevik Revolution 24
Bosch, Juan 29
Brazil 28, 73
Bretton Woods 148, 155, 162
Brock, William 191
Brookings Institution 172, 182, 184, 208
Brzezinski, Zbigniew 2, 39, 43, 104, 134, 142, 184, 199, 200, 205, 208, 214
Buckley, William 43
Bundy, McGeorge 200
Bureaucracy, foreign policy 194-199
Burma 25, 61, 70
Bush, George 124, 166, 191, 192
Business Council 172
Business Roundtable 168

Cadres, right-wing 53, 97-99, 197-199, 216, 237
Calero, Adolfo 2, 7, 89
Cambodia 31, 43, 82, 83
Carlucci, Frank 98, 176
Carter, Jimmy 31, 34, 99, 163-164
Casey, William 2, 5, 45, 57, 64, 83, 100, 106, 113
Castle Bank & Trust 61
Castro, Fidel 27, 74, 75, 112
CAUSA (Confederation of Associations for the Unity of the Societies of America) 58, 59, 100, 113, 127
Center for Defense Information (CDI) 225-227

Center for Strategic and International Studies (CSIS) 40, 55, 59, 63, 79, 167, 183, 184, 230
Central Intelligence Agency (CIA) 2, 5-7, 20, 25-34, 54-55, 59, 61, 62, 63, 65-79, 83-84, 89-90, 93, 96-99, 158, 180, 192, 197
Cerezo,Vinicio 94
Chamberlain, Neville 8, 111, 207
Chamorro, Edgar 89
Chase Manhattan Bank 163, 183
Chiang Kai-Shek 16, 17, 18, 25-26, 56, 67, 68-69, 76
Chile 15, 32-33, 58, 73, 75, 77, 158, 223, 224
China 14-15, 16, 20, 25-26, 67-70, 118
China Lobby 59, 67, 99
Chrysler Corporation 149, 170
Church, Frank 201-202
Civil Air Transport 26, 27, 30, 61, 70, 73, 98, 99
Cline, Ray 59, 64, 69, 109, 113, 167, 184, 220
Clines, Thomas 54, 64, 71-72, 74, 79, 97, 98
Coalition for a Democratic Majority 60, 180, 183, 187, 188, 190, 211
Coalition for Peace through Strength 55, 58, 122, 124, 173
Colby, William 71-72
Command, Control, Communications and Intelligence (C3I) 126, 132
Commission on Integrated Long-Term Strategy 141-142, 214
Committee for Economic Development 152
Committee for the Free World 47
Committee of One Million 67-68
Committee of Santa Fe 42, 46, 59, 82, 100
Committee on East-West Accord 165
Committee on the Present Danger (CPD) 40, 47, 50, 55, 59, 63, 68, 79, 117, 122, 124, 126, 133, 134, 143, 165, 168, 172, 174, 176, 180, 183, 192, 207, 211
Conservative Caucus 62, 73, 99, 100, 112, 140, 207

Conservative Digest 62, 108, 112
Contadora 223
Containment 3-4, 14-24, 34-35, 120
Contragate (Iran-Contra scandal) 1-9, 53, 75, 79, 88, 97, 115, 199, 203-206
Contras, Afghan 49, 61
Contras, Chinese 25-26, 27, 60, 67-70
Contras, Cuban 33, 60, 72, 74, 75, 77,
Contras, Nicaraguan 49, 57, 59, 60, 61, 63, 75, 77, 79, 83, 89-90, 98, 99, 103-106, 107-108, 208-210
Coors, Joseph 164, 183
Corsican underworld 65
Council for Inter-American Security (CIS) 59, 100, 210
Council for National Policy 63
Council on Foreign Relations 13, 67, 121, 122, 162, 165, 169, 172, 176, 179, 182, 184, 209, 213
Counterforce 119-120
Cranston, Alan 166, 172
Cruz, Arturo 89
Cuba 15, 21, 27, 43, 71, 72, 74-75, 83, 107
Cuban Missile Crisis 119, 121, 217

d'Aubuisson, Roberto 69, 76, 87, 93
Death squads 28, 57, 69, 72-77, 86, 94
Decter, Midge 47
delle Chiaie, Stefano 77
Democracy 49, 83-96, 115, 130, 216
Democratic Business Council 187
Democratic Leadership Council 187, 188, 190
Democratic Party 20, 34, 40, 85, 87, 88, 164, 185-191, 193, 215-216
Democratic Policy Commission 40, 87
Détente 144, 163, 206
Dole, Robert 91, 192, 200
Dominican Republic 29, 73, 85
Drug smuggling 60-62, 63, 66, 70-72, 98, 99, 105
Duarte, Jose Napoleon 76, 84, 87, 93, 94
Dukakis, Michael 190
Dulles, Allen 25, 27
Dulles, John Foster 18, 19, 21, 30, 118

Eagleburger, Lawrence 205
East-West trade 21, 46-47, 206-207, 215, 222
"Eastern Establishment" 12, 13, 16, 17, 161, 162, 163
Eastern Europe 18-19, 22-23, 25, 42-43, 47, 57, 66-67
EATSCO 79, 97
Economic crisis, U.S. 148-159, 218-220
Economic crisis, world 144-148
Economic warfare (economic des-tabilization) 44-48, 103-106
Edsall, Thomas 186, 192, 206
Eisenhower, Dwight 19, 20, 21, 27, 34, 65, 118, 121, 175
El Salvador 58, 69, 73, 76-77, 84, 87, 92-94
Elections, Central America 91-93
Escalation dominance 50-51, 120-121
Ethiopia 43, 82
Europe-firsters 12-13, 15
"Evil empire" 3, 37, 48, 140
Expanding Soviet Empire Theory (ExSET) 37-41, 49, 59, 82, 110, 166, 184, 206, 216, 225-227

Falk, Richard 165, 210
Falwell, Jerry 63, 200
Federal budget deficit 138, 152, 218-219
Feulner, Edwin 198
First strike 119, 121, 126, 127, 131, 132
Fisher, John 42, 56, 58
Ford, Gerald 174, 197
Ford Motor Company 156, 170
Freedom of the press 93-94

Gaither Commission 174
General Dynamics 171, 172
General Electric 55, 156, 171
General Motors 170
Geneva summit 136
Gephardt, Richard 187
GIDO (guns-in, drugs-out) 62, 70-71, 98
Global rollback network (Rollnet) 2, 9, 53-79, 81-82, 96-101, 197, 216
Goodyear Tire and Rubber 170

Gorbachev, Mikhail 47, 134, 135, 136, 140, 141, 176, 206-208, 213, 229-230
Goulart, Joao 28
Graham, Daniel 55, 56, 58, 59, 63, 73, 99, 122, 127, 174
Gray, Colin 40, 124
Greece 15, 31
Greenhouse effect 233
Grenada 73, 83, 111, 121
Grumman 171
Guatemala 15, 26, 35, 72-74, 77, 85, 93, 94, 95, 98, 121, 159, 224
Guatemalan National Liberation Move-ment (MLN) 57, 73

Haig, Alexander 191, 196, 228
Haiti 87
Hakim, Albert 97, 98
Hart, Gary 188, 189, 199
Helliwell, Paul 61, 64, 70, 74
Helms, Jesse 76, 86, 140, 165, 195, 200
Helms, Richard 32-33
Heritage Foundation 38, 40-42, 47-48, 49, 59, 63, 73, 82, 91, 102, 103, 106, 111, 113, 117, 126, 130, 135, 183, 195, 196, 198, 207
Hitler, Adolph 8, 14, 57, 207, 236
Hoover Institution 55, 59, 126, 135, 141, 183
Horizontal escalation 109-110
Hough, Jerry 45, 208, 227, 229
Hughes, Thomas 200
Human Events 86, 112, 134
Hungary 19
Hunt, E. Howard 26, 66, 73

Iklé, Fred 59, 98, 102, 124, 136, 184, 214, 225
Indonesia 29-30, 224
Inter-American Dialogue 169, 200
International arms sales 1, 61, 63, 170
Internationalism 12-13, 161
Iran 26, 43, 78-79, 82, 83, 100, 107
Irvine, Reed 62, 76,
Isolationism 11-13, 16
Israel 56, 78, 100

Jackson, Henry 180, 185
Jamaica 33-34, 73
Johnson, Lyndon 29, 34

Kemp, Jack 44, 86, 200
Kennan, George 2, 13, 20, 21, 114, 115, 181
Kennedy, Edward 199
Kennedy, John 27, 28, 29, 30, 34, 74, 118, 121
Kennedy, Robert 27
Keynesian economics 145, 150
Khomeini, Ayatollah 107, 113, 114
Khrushchev, Nikita 119, 175
Kirk, Paul 187
Kirkland, Lane 166, 184
Kirkpatrick Doctrine 49, 83
Kirkpatrick, Jeane 5, 40, 46, 49, 59, 82-86, 87, 88, 91, 112, 134, 167, 184, 200
Kissinger, Henry 2, 32, 136, 140, 142, 166, 167, 184, 185, 200, 213, 214
Knights of Malta 57, 58
Korean Central Intelligence Agency 58, 69, 99
Korean War 15, 17-18, 19, 24, 51, 67, 118, 121, 233
Krauthammer, Charles 181-182
Kristol, Irving 39, 40-41, 48-49, 59, 180, 196, 228

Lansdale, Edward 63, 71
Laos 31, 43, 61, 70, 71, 74, 82, 83, 98
Latin American Anti-Communist Confederation (CAL) 57, 76, 77
Leadership Institute 198
Ledeen, Michael 40, 78, 86, 88, 113, 184
Lehman, John 59, 112, 132
Letelier, Orlando 75, 77
Libya 43, 79, 82, 83, 97, 106-108, 111, 114, 173
Liebman, Marvin 67, 68
Linowitz, Sol 166, 169, 200
Lockheed 171
"Low intensity" conflict 50, 81, 98, 100, 101-109, 214
Luce, Clare Booth 59
Luciano, Lucky 60, 66

Lumumba, Patrice 27, 77
Luttwak, Edward 40, 44, 111-112

Mafia 27, 60, 65, 74, 75, 77
MacArthur, Douglas 17-18, 24, 99
MacLaury, Bruce 185
Manley, Michael 33
Marshall Plan 12, 15, 66, 155
Marcos, Ferdinand 72, 82, 84, 112, 108-109
McDonnell Douglass 171
McFarlane, Robert 4
McNamara, Robert 2, 119, 169, 200
McCarthy, Joseph 5, 17, 20, 68
Messing, Andy 62, 99
Military-industrial complex 55-56, 63, 67, 78, 82, 119, 130, 138, 169-175, 177, 216
Military spending 145, 157, 169-176, 218-220, 231-232
Monroe Doctrine 11
Moon, Sun Myung 58, 69
Moonie Empire 58, 59, 63, 68-70, 112, 140
Mossadegh, Mohammed 26
Mozambique 77-78, 90-91, 100, 192
Mozambique National Resistance (Renamo) 90-91
Munich Syndrome 8, 14, 20, 111, 233, 234
Mutual Assured Destruction (MAD) 119, 120, 129-130, 139
MX Missile 130, 131

National Conservative Political Action Committee 62
National Defense Council 98
National Security Council 5, 64, 92
Nationalism 11-13, 16
Nazis 31, 57-58, 66, 74, 86, 236
Neoconservatives 135, 180-182, 185
Neoliberals 182
Nicaragua 7, 41, 82-84, 89-93, 94, 103-106, 107-108, 159, 164, 189, 190, 200, 204-205, 208-210, 221, 222, 224
Nicaraguan Democratic Force (FDN) 89
Nitze, Paul 2, 4, 50, 134, 174

Nixon, Richard 7, 32, 34, 51, 119, 121, 136, 163, 195, 197
Noriega, Manuel 158
North, Oliver 2, 5, 6, 7, 54, 63, 79, 89, 93, 98, 101, 113, 205
NSC-68 16, 23-24, 174, 185
Nuclear superiority 45, 50, 117-133, 135-137, 228-229
Nuclear war-fighting 119, 120, 124, 125, 132, 133
Nugan Hand Bank 61, 72, 78, 97. 98
Nunn, Sam 187, 188, 190

Office of Strategic Services (OSS) 61, 64, 70
Olin, John M. Foundation 183
O'Neill, Thomas 188, 199
Operation Mongoose 27
Organization of American States (OAS) 158
Ortega, Daniel 92

P-2 Masonic Lodge 57, 75, 77
Packard, David 55, 59
Patria y Libertad 33, 75
Pentagon 31, 98, 102, 109, 117, 118
Perle, Richard 59, 134, 141, 184, 185
Petersen, Peter 176, 218
Philippines 87-88, 93, 95, 112, 108-109, 157, 159
Phillips, Howard 62, 99, 112, 140, 207
Phillips, Kevin 205
Pinochet, Augusto 33, 82, 75, 86
Pipes, Richard 38-40, 46, 49, 59, 124, 133, 135
Political Warfare Cadres Academy 69, 73, 76
Poindexter, John 6, 113
Posada, Luis 75, 97
Prodemca 59
Productivity, economic 148, 149, 157
Profits, corporate 149
Profits, military 149
Prosperity capitalism 144, 145
Psychological Operations (psyops) 102, 105, 106-107

Qaddafi, Muammar 79, 97, 106-107

Rand Corporation 119, 121, 174
Reagan Doctrine 48-50, 65, 78, 81-115, 159, 180, 181, 189, 194, 208, 235
Reagan, Ronald 5, 7, 37, 39, 41, 42-43, 47, 74, 75, 79, 84, 96, 106, 111, 114, 124, 126, 130, 134, 135, 167, 168, 169, 175, 176, 191, 194, 198, 203-204
Republican Party 5, 20, 34, 85, 88, 122, 164, 191-193, 215-216
Reykjavík Summit 134, 135, 136
Right wing (Right) 1-9, 53-79, 96-101, 164-168, 183, 184, 195-199, 203-212
Robb, Charles 187, 190
Robertson, Pat 63
Rockefeller, David 163, 165, 221
Rockefeller Foundation 169, 200
Rockefeller, Nelson 191
Rockwell Corporation 172
Rodriguez, Felix 71, 74, 97
Rollback 3-4, 14, 16-24, 192, 195, 217-225, 237
    economic 43, 46-48, 127
    economic-military 43-45
    global 4, 41, 63, 82, 120, 127, 192, 211
    selective 4, 24-35, 211-212
    Third World insurgency 43, 48-50, 81-115, 192, 199
Rosenthal, A.M. 208
Rostow, Eugene 50-51, 59, 122, 185, 207

SALT I Treaty 134
SALT II Treaty 79, 134, 140, 142
Sandoval Alarcon, Mario 73, 76, 99
Sapoa accord 209
Saudi Arabia 56, 58, 61, 78, 98, 100
Savimbi, Jonas 83, 78, 90
Scaife, Richard Mellon 63, 184
Schlafly, Phyllis 62
Schlesinger, James 119, 184, 213
Schurmann, Franz 11, 12, 34, 69-71, 194, 195
Scowcroft, Brent 136
Scowcroft Commission 143

Sea Supply Corporation 70, 74
Secord, Richard 2, 6, 54, 71, 78-79, 97, 98, 100, 113
Shackley, Theodore 27, 54, 71-72, 74, 79, 97, 98
Shah of Iran 72, 78-79, 82, 83, 98, 99, 100
Shultz, George 2, 5, 6, 42, 95, 112, 113, 139, 192, 200
Singlaub, John 2, 54, 55, 58, 62-63, 64, 68, 71, 73, 76, 99, 100, 103, 113
Solarz, Stephen 189, 199
Soldier of Fortune 98, 100 (IT
Somoza, Anastasio 49, 73, 84, 97, 159
South Africa 56, 58, 77-78, 84, 86, 90, 100, 159
Southern Air Transport 61, 62, 98
South Korea 56, 58, 69, 100, 157
Soviet Union 13, 14, 20-24, 37-48, 84, 107, 110, 133-142, 206-208, 222, 225-231, 234-235
Special Operations Forces (SOF) 99, 101-103, 108
State Department 5, 6, 16, 17, 18, 67, 194-198
Stilwell, Richard 64, 70, 99, 113
Stock market, 1987 crash 141, 153, 154, 176, 204
Strategic Defense Initiative (Star Wars) 44-45, 56, 120, 126-130, 133, 135-142, 170, 171, 188, 192, 215
Strauss, Robert 188

Taiwan 25, 26, 58, 59, 68, 100, 157, 167
Tambs, Lewis 46
Team B Report 174, 192
Teller, Edward 45, 56, 126, 127
Terrorism 60, 75, 91, 107-108
Thailand 31
Third World 39-40, 48-50, 81-115, 215, 216
Third World debt 147
Third World revolutions 143, 144, 164, 166, 220
Tibet 26
Trade deficit 156

Traditional conservatives 1-9, 53, 122, 139, 141, 162-169, 175, 176, 177, 191
Trafficante, Santos 71, 74
Trilateral Commission 21, 163, 169, 172, 174, 176, 183, 185, 187, 191, 206, 211
Truman Doctrine 15, 67, 85, 162
Truman, Harry 16, 17, 18, 19, 22-24, 64, 85, 118
Tucker, Robert 6, 87, 114, 181, 213

Unemployment 150, 151, 219
Unification Church 62, 69, 99, 127
United Fruit Company 26, 35
United Nations 17, 18, 37, 223-224
U.S. Atlantic Council 165
U.S. Council for World Freedom 57-58

Vance, Cyrus 165, 166, 199, 200
Vietnam 31, 60, 61, 70, 74, 82, 85, 221
Vietnam Syndrome 8-9, 86-87, 234
Vietnam War 7, 31-32, 51, 85, 99, 102
Viguerie, Richard 48, 62, 68
von Marbod, Erich 72

Warnke, Paul 123, 165, 166
Washington summit 139-140
Washington Times 58, 62, 96
Watergate 7, 74, 75
Wattenberg, Ben 183
Weinberger, Caspar 4, 42, 102, 110, 112, 114, 124-125, 141, 166, 200, 207
Western Europe 15-16, 65-66, 140, 158
Weyrich, Paul 76, 183
Wilson, Edwin 72, 79, 97, 98
World Anti-Communist League (WACL) 2, 57-58, 59, 62, 66-67, 68, 73, 75, 76, 77, 86, 98-100, 112, 127
"Worldwide democratic revolution" 81, 86, 88, 91
Wright, Jim 209

Young Americans for Freedom 68, 73
Young, Andrew 165, 199